Prof Geo. S. Morris

with the cordial respects

of Jno Miller.

Princeton N.J. Oct 18th '75.

# METAPHYSICS;

OR, THE

# SCIENCE OF PERCEPTION.

BY

JOHN MILLER,

PRINCETON, N. J.

---

NEW YORK:
DODD & MEAD, PUBLISHERS,
751 BROADWAY.

TO THE MEMORY

OF

MY FATHER.

# CONTENTS.

CHAPTER XX.



CHAPTER XXI.



CHAPTER XXII.



CHAPTER XXIII.



CHAPTER XXIV.



CHAPTER XXV.



CHAPTER XXVI.



CHAPTER XXVII.



CHAPTER XXVIII.



CHAPTER XXIX.



CHAPTER XXX.

CHAPTER XXXI.



CHAPTER XXXII.



CHAPTER XXXIII.



CHAPTER XXXIV.



CHAPTER XXXV.



CHAPTER XXXVI.



CHAPTER XXXVII.



CHAPTER XXXVIII.



CHAPTER XXXIX.



CHAPTER XL.



CHAPTER XLI.

CHAPTER XLII.



CHAPTER XLIII.



CHAPTER XLIV.



---

## BOOK II.

### LOGIC; OR, THE SCIENCE OF PERCEPTION AS KNOWLEDGE.

CHAPTER I.



CHAPTER II.



CHAPTER III.



CHAPTER IV.



CHAPTER V.



CHAPTER VI.

## CHAPTER VII.



## CHAPTER VIII.



## CHAPTER IX.



## CHAPTER X.



## CHAPTER XI.



## CHAPTER XII.



## CHAPTER XIII.



## CHAPTER XIV.



## CHAPTER XV.



## CHAPTER XVI.



## CHAPTER XVII.

## BOOK III.

### ONTOLOGY; OR, THE SCIENCE OF PERCEPTION AS THE KNOWLEDGE OF BEING.

CHAPTER XXI.



CHAPTER XXII.



CHAPTER XXIII.



CHAPTER XXIV.



CHAPTER XXV.



CHAPTER XXVI.



CHAPTER XXVII.



CHAPTER XXVIII.



CHAPTER XXIX.



CHAPTER XXX.



CHAPTER XXXI.

CHAPTER XXXII.



CHAPTER XXXIII.



CHAPTER XXXIV.



CHAPTER XXXV.



CHAPTER XXXVI.



CHAPTER XXXVII.



CHAPTER XXXVIII.



CHAPTER XXXIX.



CHAPTER XL.



CHAPTER XLI.



CHAPTER XLII.



CHAPTER XLIII.

CHAPTER XLIV.



CHAPTER XLV.



CHAPTER XLVI.



CHAPTER XLVII.



CHAPTER XLVIII.



---

# BOOK IV.

## PATHICS; OR, THE SCIENCE OF PERCEPTION AS EMOTION.

INTRODUCTORY CHAPTERS.

CHAPTER I.



CHAPTER II.



CHAPTER III.



CHAPTER IV.

## PART I.

### EUDEMONICS; OR, THE SCIENCE OF PERCEPTION AS AN EMOTION OF PLEASURE OR OF PAIN.

#### CHAPTER I.



#### CHAPTER II.



#### CHAPTER III.



## PART II.

### ÆSTHETICS; OR, THE SCIENCE OF PERCEPTION AS AN EMOTION OF TASTE.

#### CHAPTER I.



#### CHAPTER II.



#### CHAPTER III.



## PART III.

### ETHICS; OR, THE SCIENCE OF PERCEPTION AS AN EMOTION OF CONSCIENCE.

INTRODUCTORY CHAPTERS.

#### CHAPTER I.

CHAPTER II.



CHAPTER III.



CHAPTER IV.



DIVISION I.

THE MORAL QUALITY.

CHAPTER I.



CHAPTER II.



CHAPTER III.



CHAPTER IV.



DIVISION II.

THE MORAL DUTIES.

CHAPTER I.



CHAPTER II.



CHAPTER III.

## CHAPTER XVI.



## CHAPTER XVII.



## CHAPTER XVIII.



## CHAPTER XIX.



## CHAPTER XX.



## CHAPTER XXI.



## CHAPTER XXII.



## CHAPTER XXIII.



## CHAPTER XXIV.



## CHAPTER XXV.



## CHAPTER XXVI.



## CHAPTER XXVII.

CHAPTER XXVIII.



CHAPTER XXIX.



CHAPTER XXX.



CHAPTER XXXI.



CHAPTER XXXII.



CHAPTER XXXIII.



CHAPTER XXXIV.



CHAPTER XXXV.



CHAPTER XXXVI.



CHAPTER XXXVII.



CHAPTER XXXVIII.



CHAPTER XXXIX.

CHAPTER XL



CHAPTER XLI.



CHAPTER XLII.



DIVISION III.

THE MORAL CHARACTER.

CHAPTER I.



CHAPTER II.



CHAPTER III.



CHAPTER IV.



CHAPTER V.



CHAPTER VI.



CHAPTER VII.

## BOOK V.

### THEOLOGY; OR, THE SCIENCE OF PERCEPTION AS KNOWLEDGE OF THE BEING OF A GOD.

## CHAPTER X.



## CHAPTER XI.



## CHAPTER XII.



## CHAPTER XIII.

# METAPHYSICS;

OR, THE

# SCIENCE OF PERCEPTION.

---

IT is a doctrine of this book that there are no simple ideas. It has been a usual doctrine that simple ideas cannot be defined. It is the doctrine of this book that no ideas can be defined; that definition is a mere approach to a boundary; and hence the endless lists; no thought ever having attracted much discussion without great vagrancy in defining it; that vagrancy being greatly increased as thought wanders off from the concrete; abstract thought, and, above all, speculative thought, being endlessly at sea, and hard to fix by any understood limits.

Metaphysics, therefore, has been endlessly defined; and, therefore, we will be more pardoned for saying, that it has never been defined at all.

Metaphysics, in fact, is no certain thing; and indeed, how can it be, till men have adjusted a certain Metaphysics? It may be compared to islands of floating logs. They have no place; nor indeed any final shape. They are driven by the winds. Name such islands, and to-morrow they may be one or ten. It would puzzle you to define a horse, and yet there is some fixity about that mammal. But Metaphysics has not yet taken shape; and, therefore, defining it is like measuring Prometheus for a coat. As consciousness becomes more searched, and its shapes more settled, Metaphysics will become more fixed; and then different men will be thinking of the same thing; for how possibly can you define an object, if, like substance, or like cause, or like atoms, or intuitive belief, the men you speak to each treat that object differently, and half of them deny the very existence of the thing for which you carve the definition?

So let us open a door, and, as into the woman's department of an insane asylum, plunge into the clamor:—

Aristotle defined Metaphysics as "the art of arts and science of sciences"; Pythagoras, as "the knowledge of things existent as existent"; Plato, as "the greatest music"; "the Physicians, as "the medicine of of souls." Leibnitz defined it as "the science of sufficient reasons"; Hobbes, as "the science of effects by their causes"; Descartes, as "the science of things, evidently deduced from first principles"; Wolff, as "the science of things possible inasmuch as they are possible"; Condillac, as "the science of truths sensible and abstract"; Fichte, as "the science of the original form of the ego or mental self"; Schelling, as "the science of the absolute"; Hegel, as "the identity of identity and non-identity;" and Hamilton, as "the science of effects as dependent on their causes."*

Babel evidently must date from Peleg: and if men must divide their views, and claim the luxury of invent-

* Hamilton's Lect., pp. 35, 37, 41.

ing systems, how possibly can there be one definition? The islands must float and form; and if at length some bold promontory arrest the whole of them, matters will be different. They will grow to the main land of knowledge. They will get the soil and the fruit, and even the flowers, of some particular spot; and though, even then, they will not be unchangeably defined, they will be settled into one, and take fewer speeches to tell their boundary.

If Perception, for reasons hereafter to be given, is the only thing in the conscious current, we should like to choose its part of the shore for anchoring Metaphysics. We have become persuaded of five aphorisms:—First, under Pyschology,—that there is nothing consciously in the mind but Perception; second, under Logic,—that there is nothing intuitively known but Perception; third, under Ontology,—that unless being is Perception it is not intuitively known; fourth, under Pathics,—that Emotion is numerically the same as Perception; and fifth, under Theology,—that unless God is Perception He is not intuitively known. These make Perception the total consciousness; and, reserving our account of what Perception is till we come to treat it, we will view Metaphysics as the "Science of Perception."

This will be our name, therefore.

And we will arrange for five Books;—the First, Pyschology, or the Science of Perception As Such; the Second, Logic, or Perception put to use; not statical, as in Psychology, but dynamical, moving forward into what we call knowledge; Logic, therefore, or the Science of Perception as Knowledge; third, Ontology, or the Science of Perception as the Knowledge of Being; fourth, Pathics, or the Science of Perception as Emotion; and fifth, Theology, or the Science of Perception as Knowledge of the Being of a God.

If this exhausts the subject we are right in defining Metaphysics as the "Science of Perception."

# BOOK I.

# PSYCHOLOGY;

OR, THE

# SCIENCE OF PERCEPTION AS SUCH.

---

## CHAPTER I.

### THE CONSCIOUS CURRENT.

A CURRENT to which the term conscious belongs, is incessantly passing through every mind in its waking moments. All that we know of mind, and all that we know of matter, and all that we know of anything, is comprised in all that may be known of this current. If this is not admitted at once, it will be claimed as demonstrated in this discussion, the object of which will be, by the means of observation as in chemical or geological science, to mark all that is, and all that is not, consciously present in this diverse, but continual current of our consciousness.

## CHAPTER II.

### A CERTAIN PHENOMENON OF THE CONSCIOUS CURRENT.

LOOKING into the current by aid of consciousness, we see one phenomenon, and that an unceasing one. It is that which has employed the metaphor of seeing, and sometimes of the other senses, to describe it. The words, apprehension, cognition, perception, discerning, and the like, are of course not synonymous, as no words are; but they are all instances of this phenomenon. They all serve immediately to mark it. For though they are ambiguous to the last degree, each one having at least three meanings; cognition, for example, meaning a mental power, or a mental act, or a mental object; yet, without staying now to discriminate the list, any or all of them will help us to our point, which is, that everywhere in the conscious current there is a phenomenon like that of vision, of which vision is itself an instance, which consists in beholding, apprehending, perceiving, whatever you choose to call it, and which consists in something common to all these, and which consists of what the mind is aware of when it thinks of itself as standing by a window, and seeing interminable objects. They may be inward or outward, present or absent, imagined or remembered, just as the mind considers or determines that they came or were originated, but they all have one mark,—that they are sights in some way, or perceivings, and the train of them is incessant: they never slumber, but are ever passing in continuous procession before the mind.

An impatient challenger will say:—Why spoil nice distinctions? A metaphysical system is to be begun by taking neat discriminations that the world has labored upon, and throwing them all together like types out of a case. And my only answer is, that I am a positive* philosopher; that I am an empiricist;* that I begin at the beginning; that I know nothing about sensation at the start, or self or external matter, (I mean, logically I do not); that I *find* the types all out of the case, and am to sort them by what I see; and

* In the better sense of these words.

as I have a volume to print of absolute realities, it is important for me to know that it is to be eternally set up out of these metal pieces and nothing else; and, after I have determined that, I can turn them up, and look at the letters, and, if you please, distribute them, if only you have once confessed that you have nothing else, and that they contain the whole language of our possible consciousness.

## CHAPTER III.

### A NAME FOR THAT CERTAIN PHENOMENON.

THE name for the mental seeing of which we have been speaking shall be Perception.

The reasons for this are three:—

First, that as far as this system shall appear to have any truth it will wrest away the word from false uses to which moderns have applied it. Sensation has been held to mean the conscious phenomena of the mind under the direct impressions of sense, and Perception those additional phenomena in which the mind cognizes by a different power the being and relations of external things.

We deny any such distinction; and believing, therefore, that Sensation includes all, we keep Perception for another use.

Second, that use is ancient. It is popular; and can be found in any dictionary. To frame another was a wresting from an understood to an artificial use; as when Sir William Hamilton speaks of our being *conscious* of external matter. Such things rarely prosper. The lines that have been ploughed by the intercourse of ages will in the end assert themselves again. It is better, if a man wants a term, to frame a new one. Then, if his discovery holds, it will be kept distinct, without the danger of warping back under the efforts to get home again of an old and differently understood expression.

Thirdly, the term is convenient. Apprehension, or cognition, or feeling, or sight, all have more specific uses. Idea would have been a good term; but it has no verb to answer to it. Moreover, it has not the three senses of Perception which are all convenient. So impossible is it always to give notice, that it is convenient to have a term which the intelligent reader will understand himself when it undergoes the change. Usage has so triplified all these words for the sake of the convenience. And virtue, as first a quality, second a feeling, and third a character; and taste, as first a sense, second a flavor, and third a sensation; and truth, as first a truth, second the truth, and third my truth, or truthfulness,—are all like the term which we have chosen, which we forewarn the reader thus early he will have to discriminate when we employ it without warning in any of three entirely distinct meanings; as for example first, as the power to perceive, second, as an act of perceiving, and third, as the object perceived; a shifting not easily misunderstood, and more likely to guard the discourse from an improper sense than if a different word were invented for each of the changes we have thus prefigured.

Perception, therefore, or having ideas or discernments of whatever sort, is a grand phenomenon of the conscious current.

## CHAPTER IV.

### PERCEPTION THE ONLY PHENOMENON OF THE CONSCIOUS CURRENT.

IT is the great task of this treatise to show that Perception is the only phenomenon of the conscious current.

To do this we must, of course, appeal to Consciousness.

And in doing that we will in this chapter ask the more immediate questions of that very near and very familiar informant.

Let the reader, therefore, charge himself with the inquiry whether, in the first place, perceptions are ever absent from the mental current. Do they not merge into each other? Are they not continuous? Is it not so, now as I raise the question? Was it not so always, as far as he can trace it in his memory? If Perception is perpetual, then this current exists *in* the mental current; and if anything else exists, it lies round it, or makes another current; and if that be so, let us know distinctly what that other current is. Can we conceive of consciousness without that stare of perpetual vision, like the Sphinx looking off into the desert? And as one hour is but an epitome of a life-time, let a man try to any amount he pleases, and see if the stream is not a perpetual stream of ideas, a watching of an everlasting procession, a gaze never for one moment pretermitted, and having in it wife and family and world and time and hope, and whatever belongs to this successive and never for one moment to be arrested personal experience.

Now, out of the principle already brought forward of respect for language, I do not for one moment doubt that there is such a thing as Will and Knowledge and Emotion, and that these are in the current. I do not for one moment blind my mind to the fact that people will laugh at such a starting forth upon an argument, possessed of a perfect consciousness that they will and feel as well as perceive, and that they do so in the current; nor dare I forget that men will cast off impatiently the thought that everybody in a city, for example, or on a crowded battle-field, does nothing more mentally than perceive, and thereby produce all the changes that are concerned in each enterprise of men.

A fair way, however, of defending such a view is in detail. We have chosen a phenomenon. We have given it a name. We have identified it as in the current. We have asked whether it be not always in the current; and whether it be not itself a current; whatever companions or coexistences it may have along with it under the introspections of the mind. We have not denied a sense to Will, and to Emotion, and to Knowledge, and to Consciousness, or to any other of the accredited words in the vocabulary of man. But then we do not deny the meaning of *house*, or the meaning of *structure*, or the meaning of *shelter*, or the meaning of *walls and roof;* and yet we should be sorry to suppose that, totally distinct as these meanings were, it necessarily came to be the case that the thing intended to be described might not in the end turn up as in its substance the same.

Now let us take these diverse phenomena. We will encounter three of them in the next chapter. We will show that Consciousness, Emotion and Cognition are but Perception in its three aspects. We will then go on to each of them, and show, by a consideration of each, the whole psychological nature of what we call Perception. There will intervene the Laws of Perception. We will then go on to Will, and show, what no man will be ready to suppose, that Will is not a Faculty, because not even a simple operation of the mind, but a highly complex operation, in part of perceptions of cause and of power, which are the last to be acquired. A little infant scarce has a will, when its simpler visions are of the very brightest kind. We will show that Will, not philologically, but *in esse*, means Perception, just as house means building, and that Kant's favorite analysis into Cognition, Emotion and Conation will stand very well a philological test, but will utterly break down as dividing actual perceptions.

We will then treat of Abstraction and Comparison, and other miscellaneous acts, reducing them by the same analysis; hoping to make clear as the conclusion of this First Book—and the foundation of those that are to follow it, this philosophical dogma:—That there is nothing consciously in the mind but different Perceptions.

## CHAPTER V.

### THREE ASPECTS OF PERCEPTION.

THERE are three aspects of Perception,—Consciousness, Emotion, and Cognition.

## CHAPTER VI.

### CONSCIOUSNESS.

LET no one suppose when we speak of Consciousness as an aspect of Perception that we mean an instance of it. If Consciousness were a mere instance of

Perception, it would answer well enough to the statement that there was nothing else than Perception in the current of the mind; but it would bring at once the cavil as to an over-generalization. 'True enough,' it would be said; 'there is a cognizing feature in Consciousness. The element of sight or vision or mental discerning is seen in it; but sight of a blue cloud, and sight of a joyful sense, and sight of a mental volition, are so intrinsically different, that the generalization is harmful. We have simplified too much. And it will be a gain in analyzing to unloose that clasp again, and separate these forms of perceiving into different faculties and acts.'

Vital, therefore, to our scheme, is the analysis which makes Consciousness not an instance but an aspect of Perception, that is to say, a mere word for describing one fact about Perception. It belongs to every perception. It belongs only to Perception. It is but a name for Perception, as *dwelling* is the name for a house; not that Perception means Consciousness, for they imply different traits of the same mental act; but it means Consciousness just as much as color means light; and we know that nothing can be received by the eye (unless it be darkness) except light, and, moreover, nothing, just as obviously, but the one simple thing color.

I know we are conscious of volition, and conscious of emotion, and if these acts, I mean volition and emotion, were not perceptions, I would be willing to admit that Consciousness in this case was a special and distinguishable instance. But recollect, we intend to prove that these *are* perceptions. It is but an instance of Perception being conscious of itself. And as it is impossible to conceive of a perception being unconscious; as an unconscious perception would be an absurdity, like a sight that was not a sight, or a perceiving that did not perceive,—I think I am back at my thesis that Perception and Consciousness are one; not one significantly, for color and light are not one, but one in the act meant; that is Perception is called Perception because of one aspect of the act, and Consciousness just simply because of another.

If a friendly hand steps in to help us to a thought, viz., Consciousness rather refers to self, and Perception to not-self, we discard the discrimination. Perception also refers to self. That is, the word has been mixed with ideas about a perceiving power or agent. It takes an agent to perceive, just as much as it takes an agent to be conscious. And one word no more implies a thinking agent than the other. Both start the ghost of self equally and the ghost of other things. There is no difference between Consciousness and Perception except a very great one, that while they are descriptive of the one act, one is descriptive of the perceiving in itself, and the other of an awareness of itself inseparable from the very nature of perceiving.

## CHAPTER VII.

### ALL CONSCIOUSNESS PERCEPTION.

Consciousness is not a vague sense like warmth stealing over the system. It is not a dull guard like a duenna watching her charge, and sleeping sometimes, just keeping an eye to Perception busy at its work; but it is minute like Perception itself. You take an ether and pour it on type. Let it be of the rarest sort. And let it harden like adamant, and without shrinking in a grain; and it will not take the print of what it rests upon with such inimitable edge as Consciousness of the Perception that it unveils. Consciousness *is* Perception.

Let me be conscious, for example, of a sensation of color. I am not conscious of a vague expanse, but I am conscious of everything revealed in the sensation. If it be the color of the blue sky, I am conscious of just how much is perceived: the shape of the clouds, and their edge, and their angles, and their surface, their difference of hue, and their difference of place, and their difference of figure, the moon and stars, or a comet, or a nebular mass, if these are the things that we are conscious that we perceive. And if they raise any emotion, we are conscious of the length and course and degree of the emotion. If they move the will, we are conscious of it, and exactly what will and how much. We are conscious of just as much as we perceive, and we are conscious of it just as clearly. And consciousness gets all that perception gets, and will report it to us in the way of metaphysical research. And there is no part of consciousness that is sensational, or that we merely *feel* in contradistinction to a detailed intelligence reporting everything that belongs to the perception photographically to the mind.

## CHAPTER VIII.

### ALL PERCEPTION CONSCIOUSNESS.

On the other hand all Perception is Consciousness.

Not only is all Consciousness Perception, that is, every conscious gaze a perceiving, and all of it a perceiving of that that we are conscious of, but all Perception is conscious. And if all Perception is conscious, that is, every part of it;—if when I perceive a triangle all is conscious—the perception of the sides conscious, and the angles and the interlying space; if when I perceive a strain of music all is conscious, the changes, and the tone, and the time, and the note; to the last tittle of the perceptive thought that I have of any part of it, I think you cannot refuse the verdict that the whole of Perception is Consciousness. For if there be not the smallest part of the whole perceptive phenomenon that is not conscious, and that of the same realities, the perception and the consciousness may be different indeed in what they are intended to denote, but not in what they are intended to cover as phenomena of mind.

And therefore, intending as we do to reject Perception in its modern sense, and "Intuitive Beliefs" as utterly absurd; intending to reject the Hamiltonian idea of a Regulative Faculty, and all that German creed about a *vernunft* and a *verstand* and their intrinsic difference; intending to deny Brown's teachings about Cause and Effect, and all the different ideas about Substance that have been asserted hitherto, we are glad to have such a fund in Perception and Consciousness itself. Outness and Substance and Ego and God and Matter and Cause and Power and Will and Muscle and Motion, when they have fairly given up to us all that we perceive, that is all of which we are conscious, by the help too of memory and certain *continuous* features of our thought, will be found to have given us a stock in trade on which we may boldly start without any help of these Kantian or Cartesian ideas.

## CHAPTER IX.

### EMOTION.

EMOTION is that feeling of Pleasure or Pain *that is found in every Perception.*

This itself will be regarded as a new doctrine.

But take the slenderest touch upon the person; take the most cursory thought; take the perception that two and twelve make fourteen; take anything—I think it will be hard to find any act so entirely indifferent as not to give any pain or any pleasure, or perhaps one or two forms of pleasure of a microscopic sort along with it to the mind.

We will show hereafter that pain and pleasure are what keep thoughts in the current, and that if these sink into a condition of indifference they fail of their place and yield to others that are elbowing into the mind. (See B. I., Chap. XXV.).

What is this pain or pleasure?

Some may say:—Too wide a generalization again!

The pain of an aching tooth, or the pain of a halting line in poetry—what possibly have they together?

Now I confess that our theory in this respect must rise or fall with our theory of Perception.

If Perception be too widely generalized, and, above all, if we do not bring Volition particularly to be an instance under it, then I admit that Emotion will be confused. But if Perception be the only conscious phenomenon, Emotion cannot be more diverse than that. And, in fact, that will be the very rule of the diversity. Emotions will have the same diversities as Perceptions. If an aching tooth and a halting rhyme give different forms of pain, so are they different objects of Perception.

We must watch the proof.

If Perception proves good enough as a fasciculum for all our thoughts, Emotion will answer for all our Pains and Pleasures.

## CHAPTER X.

### ALL EMOTION PERCEPTION.

BUT now Emotion *is* Perception.

I put my hand upon the stove;—what do I perceive? I perceive heat. What more do I experience? I experience pleasure. Now is the heat first, and the pleasure afterward? Is the heat one feeling, and the pleasure another? Is not the pleasure the feeling of heat? And if you come to understand yourself perfectly, is not the confusion that hangs about the thing, only and entirely this, that philologically both terms are needed; that philologically they are entirely different; but that out of this philologic discrepance two feelings do not emerge, but only one, called pleasure, as discrepant from pain, and called heat,* as discrepant from other perceptions or emotions of sense, all of which are either pains or pleasures.

If I have an emotion, therefore, I have a perception; and the emotion and perception are the same.

If I have an emotion of pleasure at seeing a wire bridge, or in reading a line of Homer, of course there is something in the bridge or in the poetry that gives the emotion. It is not the paint or the cold iron in the one, or the printer's ink or the shape of the letters in the other. It is something that can be distinguished in

* Heat as a mere word, is rather objective than a feeling. Sense of heat would be a truer expression. Heat is the attributed something, evidences of which are otherwise visible, that produces the sense or leads to the emotion.

our contemplation. Now be it the curve of the bridge, or be it the smoothness of the line, certain it is that the pleasure-imparting feature must be perceived. It is in perceiving the curve or the rhyme that the pleasure is received. And consciousness will bear out unquestionably this assertion—that while perceiving the curve and perceiving the pleasure are different acts (see chapter on Abstraction), perceiving the curve and perceiving what gives the pleasure are not different acts. Perceiving the curve and perceiving the pleasure are different acts, just as perceiving a tune and perceiving the sweetness of a tune are different acts. This last is an abstraction from the other. But perceiving the curve and perceiving the beauty of the curve are not different acts, for the beauty cannot be abstracted. It is not a separate perception. It is only a convenient term for the power of the curve to give the pleasure.* And, therefore, the perception of the beauty, and the perception of the curve are one, and the emotion is a fact of the perceiving, a thing that belongs to it, an aspect of the perceiving act, a thing that can be separated from it as color can be from light, but a thing that cannot be sep-

* I am not speaking now of beauty in a sort of reflected sense. These dualties work the mystery. It is too early to grapple with this other sense. I am speaking of beauty as the trait of the curve that gives pleasure. I say, that is not to be separated from the curve itself. There is a meaning of beauty that makes it a sort of painting of the pleasure upon the curve outwardly; much as though the curve were blue, and the blueness, though a sense, were imagined as painted upon it. It will be very necessary to go into these things. Beauty does not happen to be a name of the feeling (and therefore we have to say, *sense* of beauty); but meaning generally the empirical trait that produces the feeling, it also makes objective the pleasure itself; that is, it sometimes means the emotional sense, as though it were actually painted on the curved line. These niceties, though they are mere dictionary facts, still have to be gone into to keep the subject clear. We will advert to them again on a better occasion.

arated from it in any sense of one not being a mere feature of the other.

## CHAPTER XI.

### ALL PERCEPTION EMOTION.

If I come in from the cold, and hold my hand to the fire, all my Perception must be Emotion in that particular case. My perception of a genial heat, and my perception of a genial pleasure, are identically the same, except, with reference to the old and never-to-be-forgotten fact that heat and pleasure are significantly different. Philologically they are diverse and usefully discriminated; pleasure indicating that aspect of the heat in which it is opposite to pain, and heat that aspect of pleasure in which it is of a distinct perceptive kind.

If I lie upon my bed at night, and hear a strain of harmony, the consciousness must be the same; all the harmony being pleasure, and all the pleasure being harmony; care only being taken, as in the other case, to preserve happily discriminated the philologic force of both expressions.

Now, if Perception and Emotion be the same in these simple acts, why may they not be in all experience?

My Perception of a bridge is ten thousand things. My Perception each moment is a crush of contending experiences. If I could analyze each one into parts, and bring down my thought to the simplest alphabet of seeings, is it not obvious that the point could never come where the heat or the harmony or the scent, confessedly emotional throughout, should cease to be so, and where colder thoughts supervene that are not entirely pervaded with the character of Emotion?

Is not the obvious theory that comes out when we bring the thing in this way under the edge of each man's conscious consideration, that he has no unemotional ideas; that feeling is as inseparable from thought as light from color; that a man feels a truth if he ever sees it, and sees a truth only when he feels it; and that that feeling is so co-constitutional with the sight, that all the emotion perceives and all the perception feels equipollently and alike all that is the object of the one or of the other?

## CHAPTER XII.

### COGNITION.

Cognition is that aspect of Perception that gives it its name; that is, its perceptive or apprehensive aspect.

Knowledge, as we shall see hereafter, is a word of two meanings. It means Conscious or Unconscious Knowledge. Unconscious Knowledge is nothing more than the power to know when the occasion arrives; as when I know Greek, or know my own interest. It is merely potential knowledge; and is in fact nothing more than the perceptive capacity, however it may be fed. The matters so knowable are called knowledge in the objective sense.

Conscious Knowledge is all that belongs to the present inquiry, as when I say, 'I know blueness, for I have the sensation now;' or, 'I know rightness,' or, if you please, 'I know the beautiful, for I am looking at benevolence or looking at a lily this very moment.'

It is true that Conscious Knowledge is to be

divided * into Intuitive and Empirical, and Empirical into three sorts or species easily distinguished; each and all of which, if conscious, are in the current, and if in the current are mere perceptions; unless some one can still show us something consciously cognitive that is not perceptive, that is, not a difference in sense only between Perception and Cognition (which would be easy, as no words are absolute synonyms), but a difference numerically between a perceiving viewed as emotional or conscious, and a cognizing viewed as informing us at the time of this or that perceivable reality.

## CHAPTER XIII.

### ALL COGNITION PERCEPTION.

IF Cognition included Unconscious Knowledge, of course Perception, which is a conscious act, would have nothing to do with so much of Cognition as included the unconscious part. But it has been already intimated that Unconscious or Potential Knowledge is not knowledge at all in a sense pertinent to our inquiry. It is an extending of the word Knowledge to take in another and ulterior fact as to what the mind might could or would cognize in certain circumstances. All Cognition is Perception; but it must be distinctly understood as conscious Cognition at the time. This word Knowledge will continue to give us difficulty, till, under the head of Logic, we discriminate its use, and dissect off that sense which answers to Perception, and that wider sense which means only what could be perceived if the proper occasion could be given. In this last sense, of course, it is not true that all Cognition is Perception.

* See Logic.

Again, if there be any such things as Intuitive Beliefs, Cognition is not Perception. The doctrine of Intuitive Beliefs pretends a knowledge of many things, and pretends to give it firmly and beyond a cavil, and, when I come to understand the ground, it is not that I perceive them, or perceive the proof of them, but that I have an inborn conviction or Intuitive Belief of what I am said to know.

I cannot stop for this doctrine, because it belongs to another place.* I can only challenge it. I frankly admit that it is very prevalent. It is the most catholic error of modern times. If it were true, all my theory would be at an end. If it be false, I can easily trust to your consciousness to admit that Cognition, unhelped-out by any mysterious principle of belief, must fit itself distinctly to what is left, and must be a perceiving act in every case of a conscious cognition.

## CHAPTER XIV.

### ALL PERCEPTION COGNITION.

WHETHER all Cognition be a Perception, which may be doubted, if Substance or Causation are cognizable by being believed without being perceived, still it would remain true that all Perception is Cognition.

One can prove this by imagining the opposite. Can we perceive anything without knowing it? and is there any part of the perceived thing, or of the perceiving itself, that we do not perceive and therefore know? The whole of Perception, therefore, is knowledge.

* See Logic.

## CHAPTER XV.

### NO SIMPLE PERCEPTIONS.

I WISH here to interject a chapter setting forth the fact that there are no simple perceptions. It will bear upon Definition and the use of words. I do not mean only that there are no simple perceptions that occur in thinking, or that there are none found in nature. I mean far more than that: I mean that we cannot conceive of a simple perception. By no abstraction of thought can we have what by a change of term may be called a simple idea. A note of music might seem near it, but can we separate that from time, and from the change from silence to the audible note? Color does not answer so well, for it is inseparable both from space and figure.

All thought is complex, therefore; and perception is a complex act; and the simplest is the beginning of complex knowledge.

## CHAPTER XVI.

### WORDS.

IF there are no simple perceptions, it follows of course that there are no simple words. If we cannot conceive of simple ideas, and yet could call them by names, it would follow that we could call by names things that we cannot conceive.

Words are the names of perceptions, using perception in all of its three meanings. They are not more numerous than perceptions; for though consciousness, emotion, and cognition are but three aspects of the one perception, yet perception can bend an eye upon each of these three aspects, and they become, alike, perceptions in turn. Color, light, and beauty may be each peculiarities of the same illumination, but I can bend a perception upon each, and have a perception of each peculiarity.

## CHAPTER XVII.

### DEFINITION.

If there are no simple ideas, the common maxim that a simple idea cannot be defined is, of course, a philosophical nullity.

The doctrine has been that a simple idea cannot be defined, but that a complex one can be; and that the province of definition, as a consequence, is the treatment of complex ideas.

The reason that a simple idea cannot be defined, has been thought to be that it cannot be made simpler; and that, therefore, consciousness must be called in, as in the instance of yellow color, for example, without definition, to witness the meaning of the idea.

Now it is a fundamental article of our metaphysical belief that this is what consciousness has to do in every case; that there are no absolute definitions; that what has been asserted usually of simple ideas is totally untrue of them, for the all-prevailing consideration that no such ideas are possible; but that what has been asserted of simple ideas is true of all ideas, and very much for the reasons that have been employed to establish that impossible proposition.

Definition, which means the fixing of a *boundary*, is a thing that has never been reached in any conceivable instance. We hold that it only approximates an idea, so that it can be perceived in consciousness. We do not deny the word, or discard it at all; we reverence all language; but we hold that definition marks the boundaries of thought about as well as a pointer dog a flock of partridges. It is a matter of hints, exceedingly successful if the mind can lay hold of the thing intended. And the proof that it is nothing more is to be found in the fact, first of all, that men are never agreed in definition, and second, that no absolute definition can be quoted in all the literature of mankind.

It appears, therefore, that there are no simple ideas; that there are, therefore, no simple words; that words from the necessity of the case are very imperfectly defined; and that definition is but a hint thrown into our consciousness. The noblest definition is preponderantly undefined. Take the most exact that are ever given. They have no boundary. Take the most simple. They are complex enough to be incorrect. Labor to the very last, and you will devise a thing that shades out into something else. "God is a Spirit, infinite, eternal and unchangeable, in his being, wisdom, power, holiness, justice, goodness, and truth": a famous definition no doubt, yet, in fact, what does it define? What is a spirit? How is God a Spirit? * Are not all spirits of which we have a bounded comprehension our spirits? And are not our spirits totally different, and scarcely analogous in the most distant respects, to the Almighty?

* We doubt much whether the passage, Jo. iv. 23, means as definitely "God is a Spirit," as it is translated. Christ is speaking of worshipping "in spirit," and then adds by way of confirmation, "Spirit is God." That is, we are to worship with our higher lights and feelings, and those are gifts. "The Lord is that Spirit." If we live, it is not we that live, but Christ that liveth in us.

Definition, therefore, like thought itself, is rather a hint than a direct translation of the reality.

## CHAPTER XVIII.

### THE LAWS OF PERCEPTION.

If consciousness, though a separate idea, is not so separate an act as to forbid the thought that there is nothing consciously in the mind but Perception, the Laws of Perception can give us no trouble as separate consciousnesses, or indeed by any separate claim whatever. The Laws of Perception are the mere order of being perceived that is found by observation in the perceptions themselves.

I am conscious that perception is incessant; but when I say I am conscious of that law, I do not mean that I am conscious of the law at all as I am conscious of the perception; I do not mean that there are two things in the current, perceptions and laws of perception, which I see jostling each other as coördinate phenomena. I only mean, I see perceptions. And I am conscious of the law that they are incessant, only as another way of saying that I am conscious of perceptions always; which is really, that I am conscious of perception, and just conscious of it all the time.

Now I do not aver that my being conscious of perception always is in such a sense no different phenomenon from perception as to be involved in perception. On the contrary it is an inexplicable law. There is no reason in the act why it should be always our act, i. e. why it should continue unceasingly. Yet though not involved as consciousness for example is in the very act of perception, in such a sense as that perception might not occur without it, yet it is involved in the act of perception in such a sense as that it is no separate object of consciousness, and is in fact the mere peculiarity of perception that it is seen to be consciously incessant.

The Laws of Perception are six:—that it is Incessant; that it follows the Strongest Emotion; that it is Fading; that it affects the body in its nervous, muscular, and sanguineous systems; that it is Continuous; and that it is Recurring. These six are fundamental and inexplicable. We can give no cause, though we can see the final cause. We cannot reduce these six to anything more simple in the mind; yet we can plainly see why the six should be so ordered, and how the power, wisdom, and goodness of God can be clearly manifested by the results of these comprehensive Laws of our Perception

## CHAPTER XIX.

### LAW I:—PERCEPTION AS INCESSANT.

PERCEPTION, in our waking moments, is absolutely unceasing.

To suppose this in the conscious nature of perception is an absurdity. We are conscious of perception. We have found that it is unceasing. But that we are conscious that it is in its nature unceasing is an absurdity in terms.

That the mind is essentially active means only that we observe it to be. That the mind cannot close its eye is false. It does so to all but a few passing impressions. That the mind cannot be conceived of as at rest is utterly an error. It probably is so in sleep, and if not, is always conceived of as being. And if it is said, It cannot be conceived of when we are awake, that is a truism, and only means that the mind is observed to be awake, and its perceptions incessant.

## CHAPTER XX.

### PERCEPTION AS TRANSIENT.

In mentioning six laws of perception we have intended laws that are primary, and which are all the laws that are witnessed in the conscious current. Yet these laws combine into others which are of course not primary, which are convenient to mention, and which have much to do as merciful provisions of thought. Such a law is the law of Perception as Transient.

Perception as Incessant would be very grievous if there were no provision to shift and change it. An eternal looking at one thing like the Sphinx in the desert would be intellectual death. There must be a scene-shifter. Such an effect has this law of Transience. It is not a primordial law, but flows from two others, the second and third as above enumerated. If we could wait, it would emerge when those come to be considered (Chaps. XXV. and XXVI.), but we need it now. Several laws that we shall notice are not primary, were not mentioned in our list, but are convenient consequences to mark thus early in our discussion.

## CHAPTER XXI.

### PERCEPTION AS LIMITED.

It will be seen hereafter that Recurrence, which is one of the laws of Perception, throws within its reach, if I may use a material expression, great stores of objects. It will be seen still further on, that Sensation is another great store-house of possible perception. And indeed each moment in the body presses upon the scene an amount of objects that would make millions and millions of our present amount of consciousness. Perception selects, therefore; or to express it in another shape, there is a law of Perception as Limited. We cannot state the limit, or say how large a picture may come upon our conscious vision. We cannot even state how small a one may; for, as we have already shown, a simple perception is never even conceived of by the mind. It is exceedingly far from being the case that the mind has but one idea in it at a time if by idea be meant one simple conception, just as a printer takes up one simple type. But if by idea be meant more what the names implies, IDEA, the thing seen, the thing actually perceived, then we are moving in a circle; the mind's having but one idea means only that it has what it has, one mind-full or one perception; and the truth in consciousness is, that though these minds-full are very different, yet they are limited; or in other words the mind does not go off discursing over whole horizons, or all stores both of sense and memory, but measures out for itself dainty portions; a law that we will find not primordial but depending upon others that we will mention; but then a noble trait, making all the difference between wide and discursive nothingnesses, and a series of pictures of convenient form and connected management in our vision.

## CHAPTER XXII.

### PERCEPTION AS A CONSCIOUS CURRENT.

Perception, therefore, being Incessant, and then being also Transient, and then, still more than that, being also Limited, we have as a consequence, or rather as the expression of these three laws in one, the phenomenon with which we set out, viz. the phenomenon of a Conscious Current; in which we found, first very modestly, that there were perceptions, secondly, that there were always perceptions, third, only perceptions, and now that the Conscious Current itself is but the effect of three laws (two of which are to be traced to others), namely, the laws that we have already considered, that is to say, the Incessant, Transient, and Limited nature of the one phenomenon of mental perception.

## CHAPTER XXIII.

### PERCEPTIONS AS ASSOCIATED IN ORDER.

It is found by experience that perceptions are associated in order. They do not follow each other in utter confusion, but by method. When they are ideas of sense, of which we shall speak hereafter, we do not see the corner of a house mixed up with the summit of a mountain, or the hind legs of a cow with a rock that may be in sight beyond her; but we perceive the cow or the house as a collected whole, and are blind to the rock and the mountain. We are conscious of sights that mean something, and let stray adjuncts fall out of our knowledge at the time.

In the regions of the past the law is similar; it is

one of eclectic pictures or grouping. Memory does not bring to us indigested heaps, but curt topics. And in the current, thought follows thought not wildly but in form. The order of perception is the most beautiful order in the universe. Now how is this?

It is not an order which the first conscious experience detects, and which becomes an ultimate phenomenon. We find a cause for it. And though cause is a new idea, which we have not yet the facilities to explain, yet we must use the word like many another, in anticipation of its detected sense.

Perception is not in ranks of beautiful and connected pictures as a mere statical fact with no material at all to go further and explain it, but it is suggested as well as associated. We arrive at the conclusion that perception occasions perception, and occasions connected and apt perception; in other words that the beauty of their order is not a final and inexplicable fact in our perceptive consciousness, creating, therefore, a distinct and original law, but that we may state further in two particulars :—First, that there is a cause at work which produces the order, and second, that the operation of the cause springs from the laws already stated of the perceptions of the mind.

I had thought of having two chapters, one headed Perceptions as Associated, and the other, Perceptions as Suggested; the one referring to the mere order of perceptions, and the other to the power of perceptions to produce that order, the one by suggesting another; but as neither law is original, and both have been sufficiently premised, I go on rather to the laws which are original, considering, however, as we go by, that prolific source of metaphysical debate, the Laws of Association, as they have been attempted to be methodized in the catalogues of different times.

## CHAPTER XXIV.

### THE LAWS OF ASSOCIATION.

By the Laws of Association are intended the laws of a law. And it is exceedingly important to find out what that law is before we attempt to arrange the laws that regulate it.

Now that law is in fact two. We have already seen that there is a law of perceptions as having order, and another as producing order, the one phantasmical simply, the other causal. By the one I say, I have seen my thoughts, and they occur to me in beautiful order; by the other I say, I have seen my thoughts, and they produce order, that is, one suggests another, and the rule of the suggestion proves to be a regular and beautiful series in the mind.

Now the laws of the one law are the laws of the order; what it consists in; whether contiguity, or resemblance, or causation. And the laws of the other law are the laws of suggestion, viz. what it is in one thought that produces another, and what the laws of relation are between one thought and another which can be supposed to be connected with the rising of one upon the occasion of the other in the mind.

These two sets of laws, however, need not be so very discriminatingly enumerated, and that for two reasons, first, that men have never agreed upon them, and, second, that where they have in part agreed, the lists of the first have been largely made up of the same things as are found in the lists of the other. Contiguity, for example! Where men have talked of the mere order of perceptions, they have talked of contiguity as one of the forms of order. And where they have talked of absolute suggestion, they have talked of contiguity as one of the suggesting laws.

We intend to dispense with all these categories; and intending that, we merely glance at them. We admit, of course, that contiguity suggests ideas; and if a man is *like* his neighbor, the idea of one is apt to suggest the idea of the other: and resemblance, therefore, and relation, and, let me say, *order* of any possible description, is apt to suggest anything else in the order. And, therefore, the very wideness of the range might move our suspicions. Any possible form of relation, I don't care what it is, be it cause or sequence or contrast,—any possible connected thing,—is basis for suggestion. And it may well excite the doubt whether anything that must be so loose-twisted when we come to the detail, can be the promising clue to lead us to account for the beautiful series of our perceptions.

We are satisfied, therefore, with the remark, that Contiguity or Resemblance, sometimes both, sometimes neither, sometimes other things, have been enumerated by different philosophers, sometimes as the rule, sometimes as the cause, of the associated order of perceptions; that the entire difference of opinion as to what do and what do not constitute the catalogue, awakens the reasonable fear that catalogue-making of this wide and particular kind is not the practicable analysis; that a study of these oft repeated attempts would seem to show that ORDER of any kind is the rule of the current; that any conceivable species of relation or connection or contrast—whatsoever in fact makes thought interesting or vivid or progressive,—tends to enter; and therefore, that while contiguity and resemblance and all these are doubtless laws of the current, it is expedient to go beneath these mere instances of order, and find what more original law occasions and includes all these multifarious characteristics of the train suggested or associated.

## CHAPTER XXV.

### LAW II:—LAW OF THE STRONGEST EMOTION.

THE law of perception as Transient, the law of perception as Limited, the law of perception as in a Current, and the law of perception as in an Orderly Current, that is, as associated and suggested, have all been said not to be original, and must all depend, if that be the case, upon some other characteristics of perception, that could occasion and include them.

Now one characteristic of perception is the advantage that those perceptions have to get a place in the current that can rouse our emotions. If I am sitting in an open landscape listlessly gazing into space, it is a familiar fact that plenty of things may happen that sensation never reaches. The roar of a mill may be utterly unknown to me. Sense is an eclectic instrument. It takes what interests it. The eye of the heaven may directly look at me and I see absolutely nothing. For to suppose that I hear all the myriad sounds that are about me, and see all the sights, is contradicting my sense. My sense reports that I have some limited perceptions, and beyond them have no perceptive consciousness.

But now let a voice call. It may not be half as loud as the thunder of the mill; yet I hear it instantly.

Sense and memory are two latent stores, and I take out of them my limited perceptions. There are shoals of perceptions in the past, and how they come back to me is a thing hereafter to be considered. But they do not come back to me in shoals. Just as in a splendid landscape I get report of things that strike me and nothing else, so in the field of memory the bird or the flower or the patch of cloud or the waterfall may not emerge to consciousness, but something I care for, something I feel when it is perceived, and, therefore, something that will keep my thought moving in the path of fresh emotion, rather than scouring over desert wastes that have no life and no amusement in their history.

I derive, therefore, a law that I will call the Law of the Strongest Emotion; and I will define it to be that law by which those perceptions that are within reach of the mind, either from sense or memory, tend to come up into it, which, other things being equal, will be at the time the most pain or the most pleasure.

Now Contiguity and Resemblance and all those other laws fall under this; for the most orderly thoughts are of course the most pleasant thoughts. Thought becomes practical. A cow is a more pleasant thing to look at than the tail of a cow associated with the branch of a tree and part of a mill-race. We are pleased with whole pictures. Thought becomes profitable when of an orderly kind; and, therefore, additionally pleasant. And from this kind law, that emotional perceptions shall emerge, Providence educes the whole theory of our associations, namely, that nearness and likeness or relation or order of any sort shall characterize the current, for the one satisfactory and perfect principle that what moves us shall characterize it, and order of whatever sort is more calculated for perceptive emotion than a chaos of jumbled sights without law and without meaning in its character.

Here we catch a glimpse of the secret too of suggestion, as well as of association, in perception. A perception being already in the mind makes order with another within our reach, and not with still another. A song I hear interests me in connection with a friend, but not in some indifferent relation. I see a knife. It was such a knife amputated my arm. The knife and scene together will make a painful picture, and therefore, it suggests the scene. Thought does not cause thought in the ordinary significance of causation. But perceptions, which are in a continuous flux, tend to have rising with them others that will make moving pictures, whether of pain or pleasure, from the one simple principle that perceptions have the advantage to come next that are perceptions of the deepest emotion.

## CHAPTER XXVI.

### LAW III:—PERCEPTION AS FADING.

We are not quite ready to generalize the whole till we bring in another principle; that is, the Law of Perception as Fading. This does not flow from the last; because, why should not the perception we have remain the strongest? Why, when I have seen a meteor, and it continues the most extraordinary spectacle of the hour, do I not continue thinking of it, and that by the force of the same law, the law of the strongest emotion?

We need another law, therefore. If the law of the strongest emotion held its rule without being restricted by another, we should think of one thing all the time. We should fall into one great gulf of thought, and stay in it. We need a dynamic principle, to change and shift, that thought may move on into knowledge. And we have this by the grace of the Almighty, who has ordered another great principle of thought, namely, that it shall fade away. I put my hand upon my cheek, and presently I cease to feel it. This fact is partly bodily and partly mental. But the mental fact is true in all perception. It is our third great law, the law of Perception as Fading. It is an inexplicable law. I cannot trace it to the rest. But by it perception has hardly been originated before it begins to fade, and the law of a stronger emotion comes in, to push out the faded one, and to bring in something new, so as to cater for the thought in more and more varied subjects of contemplation.

You understand now the reason of the fact that Perception as Transient is not an original law. It is transient because it fades, and the new thought pushes it out. You see also why Perception as Limited is not an original law. It is limited by the stronger emotion. Perception is pared down to the capacity of the vision, and fades off all the selvage of the picture, till we are left with that which will make the maximum impression on the mind. Moreover the other laws, of Perception in a Current, and Perception in an Orderly Current, all come into their place. For Perception as Fading, and Perception as most likely to appear when most emotional, and Perception as most emotional other things being equal when most in order, contain all these other laws, and account for all the beauty of the train in its associated order and suggestions.

## CHAPTER XXVII.

### THE LAW OF THE STRONGEST EMOTION THE ONLY LAW OF MENTAL ASSOCIATION.

I do not mean by this of course, that the Law of Perception as Incessant and the Law of Perception as Fading are not necessary to the Law of Association. We have shown that they are, and in what exact way they are: in fact, all the laws of perception are necessary each one to every other; but I mean that what are usually called laws of association, and which are in fact laws of a law, are all actual laws no doubt; that is, causality and nearness and likeness and contrast are all facts that beget suggestion; but so are any related peculiarities. The list might be categorically endless. And the primal law is that which we have noted, viz., that there rises into consciousness when the last perception fades, the one that we will feel the most, the other things that must be equal being the ease of the sensible impression, or the ease of the recollecting act, both of these things, however, having the obvious effect of making it more emotional.

If there is any other primordial law, the way will be for its advocate to bring it forward. And till then the strongest argument against it seems to be that no other one is needed, and indeed that no other one seems really possible, so completely does this one perform the work of every possible suggestion.

## CHAPTER XXVIII.

### KANT'S THREE GREAT CLASSES OF THE PHENOMENA OF THE MIND.

Having disposed of Consciousness, Emotion, and Cognition, and shown that they were but aspects of

Perception, and, as acts, numerically not different, it is time to take the most difficult opponent of our simplifying scheme, viz., Volition.

Kant early in the promulging of his system divided the mental phenomena into three—the Cognitive, the Emotional, and the Conative. The Cognitive is near akin to what we have entitled Perception. The Emotional, according to Kant, is a separate phenomenon, and is the feeling of Pleasure or Pain. The Conative, to use a word employed by Sir William Hamilton, is the Will in its phenomenal *nisus* or *conatus;* a thing, of course, which, we freely admit, is plainly to be apprehended in the current.

It is better always to employ the words of a school in arranging its own defence.

"The phenomena of which we are conscious," says* Sir William Hamilton, expounding the analysis of Kant, "are seen to divide themselves into three great classes. In the first place, there are the phenomena of Knowledge; in the second place, there are the phenomena of Feeling, or the phenomena of Pleasure and Pain; and in the third place, there are the phenomena of Will and Desire.

"Let me illustrate this by an example. I see a picture. Now, first of all, I am conscious of perceiving a certain complement of colors and figures,—I recognize what the object is. This is the phenomenon of Cognition or Knowledge. But this is not the only phenomenon of which I may be here conscious. I may experience certain affections in the contemplation of this object. If the picture be a masterpiece, the gratification will be unalloyed; but if it be an unequal production, I shall be conscious perhaps of enjoyment, but

* Lectures on Metaphysics. Boston Edition, pp. 127, 129.

of enjoyment alloyed with dissatisfaction. This is the phenomenon of Feeling, or of Pleasure and Pain. But these two phenomena do not yet exhaust all of which I may be conscious on the occasion. I may desire to see the picture long, to see it often, to make it my own, and perhaps I may will, resolve and determine so to do. This is the complex phenomenon of Will and Desire. * * * *

"This division of the phenomena of mind into the three great classes of the Cognitive faculties, the feelings or capacities of Pleasure and Pain, and the Exertive or Conative powers, I do not propose as original. It was first promulgated by Kant; and the felicity of the distribution was so apparent, that it has now been long all but universally adopted in Germany by the philosophers of every school; and, what is curious, the only philosopher of any eminence by whom it has been assailed; indeed, the only philosopher of any reputation by whom it has been, in that country, rejected,—is* not an opponent of the Kantian philosophy, but one of its most zealous champions. To the psychologists of this country it is apparently wholly unknown. They still adhere to the old scholastic division into Powers of the Understanding and Powers of the Will; or, as it is otherwise expressed, into Intellectual and Active Powers."

Now we have already attempted to show that two of these phenomena, Cognition and Emotion, are the same in different aspects not, (as we guarded before) the same, as words, in respect of their significance, for one is significant of perception in its cognitive or apprehensive aspect, and the other of preception as pleasure or pain. And to show that this is but naming the

* Krug.

same act, to abstract from it its different aspects, I took the simplest perceptions, like the perception of heat, or like the perception of a single note, or like a glance at the beautiful azure, and I said that the feeling of the thing and the seeing of the thing were numerically the same. Tell me only that part of the complex perception that I am pleased to have, and I can state three things about my being pleased in having it :—First, that I do not have the perception first and the pleasure afterward; second, that I do not have the perception as one thing (i. e. the sight or the sound or the taste or the scent) and the pleasure as another thing. The perceiving is the pleasure. And, thirdly, taking perception in its third sense, i. e. as the perceived thing, I do not have the perception in the one case to be the blue, and in the other case the beauty of the blue, in the one case the scent, and in the other case the fragrance of the scent, in one case the sound, and in the other case the melody of the sound, but the phenomenon is consciously one; the blue and the beanty; the scent and the fragrance; the sound and the melody; not philologically I know, but metaphysically and in respect of the thing perceived,—are incontestably, because consciously, the very same.

When Hamilton employs the picture, he confuses us by the immensity that we perceive. Such a thing is a forest. But let him take out the thing that gives the pleasure; not the paint; not the frame; not the thread ribbing up the canvas; not the mill; not the woman; not the horse; not the pond, with the ducks; not the thing that wakens the comfortable home sense, or the amatory boy sense, or the horse-fancier or duck-fancier or even picture-fancier emotions; nay, let him cast out from the piece all the pleasure-giving *powers* that it may have, apart from what he is having at the time; and that perception, at the time, that he is having of some limited part or beautiful whole of the picture is itself the pleasure bearer, itself the happy thing. That he sees the picture, and sees the beauty of the picture; that he sees the pleasure that it gives, and feels it; that he perceives the beauty that he feels, and feels the beauty that he perceives,—are not expressions I know of the same meaning; as none are that are ever verbally different; but they are expressions about the same act; and are all satisfied by the statement that perceptions are either pains or pleasures.

But I must go on to what chiefly concerns us now, the third class, or Conative phenomena of mind, or, as Hamilton calls them, the phenomena of Desire and Will.

## CHAPTER XXIX.

### VOLITION.

VOLITION is the act of the mind, and Will the faculty in which it is supposed to originate. This distinction is not well kept up; but, as we are speaking of the conscious current, we will choose Volition as the conscious act, rather than Will which is the imagined faculty.

Now what is Volition?

Let it be said in reply that it is one of the most complex words of which we have any knowledge.

Lest we spoil however the clearness of our analysis by making it prematurely, let us interpose at this point certain facts about the will that no other writer has noticed, as we are trusting much to them to conciliate regard to what may be supposed beforehand to be very improbable assertions.

We propose in the end to teach that Will is no faculty at all, or, to follow our rule of reverence for all language, is a most complex assemblage of faculties, made up of powers to perceive, and to influence by perception, as we shall presently consider: that Volition, as apart from the body, is no act other than perception; and the truths we would interpose as conciliating favor for what we are thus to teach, are discoveries that narrow in astonishingly the province of Volition.

## CHAPTER XXX.

### VOLITION HAS BUT TWO PROVINCES.

VOLITION has but two provinces; in the body, to move the muscles, and in the mind, to create attention.

A man can will to move the voluntary muscles, so called, and he can will to hold an idea. Besides these neither hell nor heaven have any accountable volitions.

## CHAPTER XXXI.

### LAW IV:—PERCEPTION AS IT AFFECTS THE BODY IN ITS NERVOUS, MUSCULAR, AND SANGUINEOUS SYSTEMS.

IN a way that cannot be explained, and that certainly never will be explained except in the mere recitation of the phenomena, certain perceptions of the mind produce certain changes of the body. We perceive both; that is, we are conscious of the perceptions, and we consciously perceive the changes. When I perceive certain shameful things, I blush. I can be conscious of the perception. I can feel the blushing. I can see it in another. And if I am a physiologist, I can trace the physiological effects to any extent while I keep within the body. I can do more than that. I can perceive that there is a cause. Without anticipating too soon certain logical and ontological facts, I will assume as admitted for the present, that I can infer causation. I can conclude upon a causal nexus; and that, as uniting the shameful thought and the irruption of the blush upon my neck and countenance.

But really what that is that leaps across the gulf, and really the causal nisus that makes the shame affect the sanguineous system, we hope no thinker would ever be absurd enough even to conjecture.

The like are a round of mental perceptions, all of which have certain influences upon different parts of the body.

Now, when we come to consider, the parts are three,—the Muscular, the Nervous, and the Sanguineous parts.

Possibly we ought to say four; and that the Glandular parts are also affected.

Possibly we ought to say two; for the Sanguineous parts, as in the instance of blushing, are affected through the muscles. Possibly the paleness of anger, or the flush of anger, or the hair standing erect through fear, or the sinking of the heart, or the sweat pouring out through our agony, might all be traceable to the muscles. The nervous system is involved, of course, because it acts upon the muscles. But as the muscles can pump the veins, and of course act and react upon the flux and reflux from the heart, it would pose a physiologist to say what the mind does or does not act upon in these expressions of the body.

And, indeed, it makes no difference. What we are asking for are the conscious phenomena of the current.

And we see that on certain perceptions of wrong, or on certain perceptions of shame, or on certain perceptions of risk, or of reasons for joy, the heart and indeed other viscera are moved, causally this work hereafter will show, but exactly for what cause, no mortal, and perhaps no angel, need ever consider.

Metaphysically and not physiologically, therefore, our question is a narrow one; and we have answered it by saying that all that takes place in the mind before a blush or before a cold sweat breaks out upon us, or a mortal paleness, or a joyful flush, is a perception of the rousing or terrifying object, with its inter-entering pain or pleasure.

Let no one say, No! There is more. There is the flush, or the sinking. That I admit. But these are the physical sensations. Let no one be confused as to the perception that occasions the blush by those other perceptions which are the sensations of the blush itself.

So now in respect to Volition; it is a phenomenon of mind producing a phenomenon of body. (I speak thus of the First Province of this *Bestrebungs Vermögen* as the Germans call it.) The phenomenon of mind is the thing we are asking after. The phenomenon of body tends sadly to confuse it. The phenomenon of mind is something we must be actually conscious of. The phenomenon of body unfortunately we are also conscious of as far as concerns the nisus and the changes in our sensations. The metaphysical problem is to get these things thoroughly separated; to get the struggle that the body makes, and the weariness and the pain and the actual effort, so far as they are consciously sensational, and in fact the sequence that we consciously advise ourselves of; that is, the sense-attempt following or rather instant upon the phenomenon of the mind,—separate, and that in the distinctest way, from this last itself.

I have a perception and I blush. I have this perception in the very birth, if I may speak so, of the conscious sensation on my cheek.

So I have a mental something, and I move. And I have that mental something at the very birth of that conscious sense that is awakened in the muscle. The two are together, and it is hard to separate them.

But certainly it is practicable to put apart that mental phenomenon which is not of sense, and that muscular swell and push which is not of mind; which is merely reported of; which is throughout a sense perception; not occasioned in any visible way; and only intruding upon Will because it is so intimately mixed with that mental act anterior to its motions.*

## CHAPTER XXXII.

### MUSCULAR VOLITION.

LET us recall our mind to the idea that one of the provinces of Volition is to move a certain tissue of the body called muscles.

* We are reminded that we might state as a seventh law of perception, its power to be operated on through the avenues of sense. This is plainly as much primordial as what we have just been discussing, viz., its power to operate upon the nerves and muscles. In fact physiology lays both mechanisms bare. One set of nerves travels to the muscles, and one set of nerves travels from the sense and carries its *notitiæ* to the brain and mind. Doubtless the law that it is aroused by sense is a primordial law of perceptive consciousness: so primordial, however, that it hides under its very prominence, and can hardly be divorced from the idea of the very nature of perception. We can imagine perception divested of all its other laws, but hardly that it could have been awakened without there having been sensation.

It is interesting to know that there are certain muscles of the body that the will cannot move, but which shame can, so that they pump up the blood to certain conspicuous and tale-telling parts, viz., the human countenance. The muscles that the will moves are known. The muscles that shame moves, or anger or dread or joy or brooding melancholy, might doubtless be also known. And possibly there are some muscles that are not moved at all except by physical causes not influenced by the mind.

1. Now if there are some muscles influenced by the mind, not influenced by the mere perceptions of the mind as in shame or fear, they are of the nature of a rare exception, and this is a *prima facie* reason against the idea of Volition being anything more than Perception.

2. Again, the overbearing thought that our new generalization is preposterous, for that Volition is an imperial act, and Perception a tranquil vision; that Volition has moved the world, and that Perception merely marks and notices; and that the mere apothegm, Volition is Perception, is enough to stamp the thinker as hopelessly at variance with his species,—all this first-blush and very strong preoccupation against us, we must meet by begging people to consider how much which is foreign to the point is wrapped up in the very word Volition.

3. For, thirdly, it takes in what belongs to sensation. It takes in the nisus, which we have no more right to intermix than the flushed sense in the phenomenon of blushing. It takes in the immediate sequence, which like redness is an observed fact. It takes it in, however, and makes much of it, and it has had much to do in confusing the mind. It takes it in in the manufacture of *choice* and *decision*, and in

most of these imperial titles of the will; for what is the idea at the bottom of all these, but the sequence that has been observed in the body, of muscular motion upon the want or will of the mind?

Let palsy come, and it is a fine metaphysical illuminator.

Let a man be shut down to his mere mental act, and he finds, when the sequence ceases, as, for example, in a paralyzed arm,—that all that was imperial ceases, and he is left only with perception; perception of want, perception of pain, perception of pleasure, *Desire*, as these complicated perceptions have been called; and there being no more sequence, decision ceases, which he finds only to be a complex act made up of immediate desires and expectations.

Moreover the nisus disappears; and that helps to clear him. He wills and wishes, but makes no attempt; or, to be more analytically accurate in the consciousness, he makes one part of what he meant by the attempt, but not the other part. He makes the mental, but not the physical attempt. That is, he makes so much of the attempt as was in the perception. He comes to the perception that this was the right time to act. He sees and feels that now he wants to act and by all previous usage must and would act and had always overwhelmingly expected and imperiously felt sure to act; but soon perceives that so much of the thing as consisted in an attempted nisus was physical, and has departed from him;—that it miserably confounds the will; that in look it is sensation; that sensation is mental but not a part of the volition; or that if it is a part, it is a part *ex usu loquendi*, and hence of this man's or that man's idea of volition as he may get it mixed with the more pure phenomenon.

4. Moreover the philological peculiarities are significant. All nations originate will in wishing. All thought about it is traced back to the same seminal expression.

The *boulomai* of the Greeks, the *volo* of the Latins, the *vouloir* of the French, the *quérer* of the Spaniards, the *chaphatz* of the Hebrews, and like terms in other dialects and tongues even more so than in our own, all teach the lesson, that though willing and wishing are not the same, Will taking in more of the adjuncts of a complex and more extended signification, yet that seminally they are the same phenomenon, and that wishing is nothing more than complex perceptions of a good, inter-entering into which is the complexity of their pains and pleasures.

5. If anybody is conscious of anything more than I have described in Volition, let him state distinctly what that consciousness is.

6. And, in the last place, in order to be perfectly fair, let me state, more than I have yet done, the whole of the phenomena that are seen in Muscular Volition.

Let us suppose, in order to clear the facts, that it were possible for a man to cultivate the habit of blushing. I am not sure that it might not be actually possible, so that a man might be able to blush at pleasure. Now how would he do it? Not by moving the muscles of the blood-vessels, as he does those of the arm, but by the other province of will, viz., attention. He might learn, like many a play-actor of a high power, to attend or not to attend, that is, to perceive or not to perceive deeply and with high emotion the object of shame; and, so, to blush or not to blush. Actors in private life learn to keep back a blush. And turning pale or turning livid are said to be powers of wonderful tragedians.

Now when we come to treat of that second province (Attention) these things will be better understood. But for the present, what would be the difference phenomenally between blushing and moving the arm?

One difference would be that in blushing we would not have the same consciousness of a muscular nisus. In moving the arm we would have a sensation. In moving the veins we would do it mediately, and would have no sensation other than the flush of the blushing. The loss of the nisus, therefore, would impair the phenomenon of will. And yet the sequence would remain, and, therefore, much of the imperial act.

Now what is the inference? A man blushes at pleasure, and a man moves at pleasure. Where is the difference? The blushing is operated by nerve and muscle, and the moving by nerve and muscle. The blushing is an immediate sequence, and the moving an immediate sequence, and both caused by something in the current. There is a nisus in one case, and no nisus in the other, and a plain deficiency in this other of the usual character of Volition. There is a directness in the one case, and an indirectness (on account of the interposition of shame), in the other; and yet both are acts of will, and both act upon the nerves, and both act upon the muscles, and both are followed by sensations, and both may become imperial on account of unvarying sequence. Now what is the conclusion? Why that perception, raising the blush in one case, may raise the motion in the other; that both act upon the muscles. If mere shame may move in that, why not desire in this? Volition is mixed up with the sense, as indeed shame is. To a palsied man it alters with the disease. In its muscular province it runs into its results; and the nisus and the sequence which are mere sensational perceptions; which are not part of the will, but helpless consequences,—have need to be dissected out of it before we can arrive at the anterior phenomenon as it is to be seen in the current.

So, what is Muscular Volition?

First, it is Perception of that complex sort which we shall explain (see Ethics, Introd. Chap. III.) under the name of Desire. But let me be understood. A desire to move my arm would be too gross a statement. A desire to move my arm would be too consciously vague to be the truth in Muscular Volition. From childhood up I have learned the movements of the arm. From random scuffles in my mother's lap I have learned what I can do, and what are the sensations in doing it, like a girl strumming her guitar.

Through facts of causality which I am to explain in our ontological discussion I reach perceptions of cause and a trust to analogical recurrences. My arm, therefore, is too gross a statement. I have learned each muscle of my arm; not anatomically, but in its practical capacities. My desire, therefore, is for the recurrence of a specific well understood motion.

Now along with this, I have, in the second place, instantaneous with the wish, a perception that it will be gratified, founded, as we shall afterwards explain, upon uniform experience.

Instantaneous with this, thirdly, I have sensation: the charm actually operates:

Characteristic of this sensation, fourthly, the nisus, which belongs to no other form. It wearies and struggles and exhausts like no other emotion of sense. And being simultaneous with the desire, I feel my way along it, and shape it, and alter it, by the experiences of my perceptive volitions.

Now I do not say there is no difficulty in all this. There is a puzzle as to how a man can march when he is not awake. There is a puzzle as to how the lungs can move sometimes when we desire, and sometimes when we have no desire in the matter. There is a puzzle as to how the fingers move with the velocity of thought over the key-board of an instrument. But it only convinces me more that it is by the velocity of thought; that the girl beating on the keys is as quick as her perceptive consciousness; that at each touch there is perception and emotion; and that the complexity of the facts is less difficult in our scheme than in any other.

Add now to all this, that the best philosophers have always spoken confusedly on the subject of the Will; that Hamilton calls it * that "complex phenomenon of Will and Desire": that he has claimed to fix the succinct division, into Cognition, Emotion, and Conation; and then called the last, Will and Desire; Desire unquestionably being quite inseparable from Emotion; and then that all men and all languages mix Will and Wish indistinguishably and by the very necessities of spoken thought constantly together; moreover that the other province of Volition, viz., Attention, is about to be proved to be nothing more than an instance under the Law of the Strongest Emotion,—and I think that the first improbabilities of our scheme ought not unduly to depress it, and that there is a higher improbability by far (if we accomplish that last mentioned generalization) in the idea of a primal faculty of the mind, if the sole work that calls for it is the moving of the flexors of the body.

* Lectures, p. 127.

Let us proceed, therefore, to that last mentioned generalization, viz., as to Will in its other province.

## CHAPTER XXXIII.

### ATTENTION.

ATTENTION is Perception held in the mind by an act of Will.

The perception may be of any kind; of sense; of memory; of self; of not-self; of past; of present; it matters not what; if it pleases us; or if it does not please us; and on any account it pleases us to have it or to detain it in the current; then by an act of Volition we transmute a common perception into an act of Attention. There is nothing consciously present, therefore, except perceptions, unless Will can be demonstrated to be a separate faculty.

## CHAPTER XXXIV.

### ATTENTION THE ONLY PROVINCE OF VOLITION NOT MUSCULAR.

I SIT down to my desk to write a sermon. In the course of that sermon I exert all the powers of the Will, I think any one will admit, of which I am capable.

Eliminate now all the muscular struggles, the twitching of my hair, the moving on my seat, the fixing of my eye, and the muscular power to cast out a thought by distracting myself by some voluntary strain. Leave out of course all that is muscular in writing: and so let us take up those grander classes of intellectual acts that are concerned in the production of the sermon. Let us take up memory for example. What is there in memory, as a voluntary struggle, other than the fixing of the Attention? Consciously think of it! I want to recollect the word Mesopotamia, for I seem entirely to have forgotten it. Not so entirely, you will observe, that I have not something present in my perception that makes me know something about it, enough to desire it. Now what do I consciously do? I cannot command the absent syllables. I cannot say, 'Come,' by a direct act of imperial volition. I sit biting my pen and ATTENDING to the perceptions I have. I reach, perhaps, a part of the word—"Meso!" "Meso!" and I repeat it, or attend to it in thought. By the law of association I have experience that it will bring the residue. But I cannot command the residue. I can simply attend to the perceptions already possessed. And so in all the forms of elaboration, fancy, judgment, comparison; in all the acts of the mind; which, like the memory, we are yet in this book to reduce to the phenomenon of Perception; as respects the present point, we can see enough at once to admit that the sermon gets on by the mere exercise of Attention. I have a present thought. Its tendency is to suggest in order. As long as the order lasts I just gaze at it, and write it down. By the law of the Stronger Emotion the mind thinks to please me, and travels on for a page, perhaps, of just the associations. If they stop, I stop. If impertinent lines begin, I stop the machinery, like a mill operative who has broken a thread. I refuse to attend to one thing. I insist by attention upon another. I wait for that to start anew. I cannot order it to start anew. I cannot command an absent thought. But by the beautiful law of the strongest, and by the single act of Attention, I have experienced former success; and I confidently trust that the train will weave on to the close.

Now think of all the struggles of the will; on a battle-field; in the utmost storm of work; and think if I can do anything but attend and wait. I can brandish my sword, and rush upon the guns, and shout to my captains in the field, but can I do anything in thought but perceive what I perceive, and if I wish to perceive anything outside of that, attend to something I already perceive, and expect that to suggest to me the perceptions that are absent from my consciousness?

All this will be plainer when we come to speak of Memory; and will grow plainer afterward by our doctrines of Sensation; but the only way to establish metaphysical truth is through consciousness, and we appeal to that for any volition that does not move a muscle, or else secure a more attentive consciousness.

## CHAPTER XXXV.

### WILL IN ITS SECOND PROVINCE NO SEPARATE ACT AT ALL; ATTENTION ENTIRELY ACCOUNTED FOR BY THE LAW OF THE STRONGEST EMOTION.

HAVING proved the Will to be concerned in moving the muscles, and in nothing else besides except the phenomenon of Attention, we mean to lower it in its claim altogether, and show that the phenomenon of Attention is itself an instance under the Law of the Strongest Emotion.

Not, let me explain, that we are to hold that the word Will is without a meaning; nor that we are to cast it out from its place, or to deny it our thought as a correct and critical reality; but that we are to renounce it as an original act. It moves the muscles, and it spurs us to attend. So doing, it shakes the earth, and it scales the heavens. Nor can we exaggerate the measure of accountability to which it will be held. And yet it has but two provinces,—certain tissues of our body, and the movement to attend. And not only is it solely Perception, but, in the latter instance, Perception pure, the fact that we attend being only a case under the Law of the Strongest Emotion.

To prove this,—what was that law? That, out of the two storehouses of Sensation and Recurrence, the next thought that would consciously emerge would be the one that could produce the strongest emotion. If a rocket-stick fell, and should tumble at our feet, then that might wake us most, and would irrupt into our consciousness. Then the boy that fired it. So the thread would spin, each last striking thought marrying itself to the next, and picking from the stuff of Sensation and Recurrence the most shining woof for the fabric of our continued thinking.

Now perceptions give place as the stronger ones move up. Why? Because perceptions fade. But suppose we can prevent their fading. Why will that be? Because they are precious. What will that mean? Simply that they *have not* faded. For some cause they continue to interest us; and apart from some muscular motions by which we can throw out what disturbs, we keep to a line of thought by a superior wish; and what is that but the law of the strongest emotion?

We will to attend. What is that but a will for the present thought? We feel a need that it should stay. By experience it can. Experimentally it does. And that begets the imperial sense. We decide, or we elect, or we determine, that it shall; and, as in the instance of the muscles, we know that it will have to.

It is proper, therefore, (though we must not anticipate Ethics), that a man should be responsible for his wish as well as for his Volition ; one is but an instance of the other : that he should he responsible for his perceiving as well as for his feeling, since both are but an aspect of the same : and that Volition, merely moving the muscle or merely enabling us to attend, should not be set down as all our account, since the thoughts and affections of the soul are alike phenomenally responsible.

## CHAPTER XXXVI.

### ALL VOLITION PERCEPTION.

WE are better prepared now to understand exactly what Volition is. We were able to say in the instance of Consciousness, — All Consciousness is Perception, and all Perception Consciousness. In the instance of Volition we are able to say only one of these. We can say, All Volition is Perception ; but we cannot say, All Perception is Volition. Volition is the shape only of a few perceptions.

We have been able to show that Volition occurs simply in two provinces, the one the moving of the muscles, and the other the phenomenon of Attention. These, obviously, are very different. Will when I move my arm, and Will when I hold a perception, are so thoroughly distinct, that this alone ought to destroy their primordial character. And it will be very helpful to our consciousness to show where they agree ; to show where they differ ; to show how complex they are ; to show that they are emotional and cognitive ; to show what the complexity is ; and to show that the complexity consists in perceptions emotional and cognitive heaped up and interblended the one upon the other.

4

I have a perception, and I desire to keep it. That desire keeps it. Interpenetrated into that desire is an experience that it will be kept. That experience, as will be hereafter shown, is itself perceptive, and it lends to the desire an imperial or authoritative character. So much for Attention.

Now I have a muscle that I have moved from childhood; at first vagrantly (till I grew cognizant about it), like an infant fighting the air, the phenomena being (1) a desire to move it, (2) an experience that it will move, (3) a perception that it does, (4) a conscious sensational strain or stress, and (5) an imperial sense of control or authority in the matter. Now the first is a Perception, as we show when treating of Desire. The second is Perception, as we shall show when treating of Experience. The third is Perception *pro forma*, and as is above announced. The fourth is Perception, for it is only Sensation. And the fifth is a Perceptive confidence, made up of all the Perceptions combined, and giving assurance of the successful act.

Further; of the two acts, Musculation and Attention, there is absent from Attention the *nisus*, or instantaneous attempt, and all bodily sensation.* But there is present, the desire, and the choice (that is, the immediate imperial expectation), and then the immediate sequence instantaneous with the desire itself, not so clean-cut in the instance of Attention as in the instance of Muscular Motion, yet showing such powerful analogy, and connected, the bodily and the mental, so much in human accountability, as to show why these two things, Muscular Motion and the Act of Attention, determined by like sets of conscious emo-

* Except, indeed, certain incidental strains of certain muscles of the body, particularly of the eye, when we attempt mentally to attend.

tional perceptions, have set apart such perceptions, and labelled them Volitions.

## CHAPTER XXXVII.

### LAW V:—PERCEPTION AS RECURRING.

HAVING considered Perception as Incessant, Perception as Associated by the Law of the Strongest Emotion, Perception as Fading, Perception as Affecting the Body, I come to the Fifth great law of Conscious Perception, Perception as Recurring.

And this demands the very simplest enunciation. Being inexplicable, and utterly original, to try to give it a name even in semblance expressing a cause, would disguise the reality. Perception recurs. That is the whole of it.

To say that it is retained, and to call the power Retention; to say that it is impressed, and to call the power a power to receive impressions which endure in the mind; to call it Memory (a good word in its proper place, but) as a faculty directly to cognize passed events,—is all to cloud our Metaphysics with an imagined explanation, or at least the guise of one; when all the fact that comes up into our consciousness is that perceptions come back again. Why,—no mortal will ever discover: and it is unscientific to take anything but the fact. By a law of Nature, the kindness of which is all that can be established, a perception, once had, may or may not come back again. There can be probabilities found out; as, for example, where the thought has been deep and pungent, where it has been held fast to by an act of the Will, that is, in conscious Attention. But experience discovered this. The naked phenomenon apart is, that Perception, when it has once occurred, recurs, and that without the sound and without the sight and without the scent that originally engendered it.

This makes the shoal of possible perceptions that the Law of the Strongest Emotion does so eternally fish up.

Let not the fact that perceptions differ as they recur, suggest that there must be a power of Fancy that new combines the material before their advent. The law of association, i. e. the Law of the Strongest Emotion, is that flashing and immediate influence. Let but the selvage of an old thought come up, it rushes into new arrangement; that is, it calls up a set to meet it. The mind does have new pictures that it never had before. But why? Grant but two things, the power to recur and the power to suggest each other, and perceptions will be varied endlessly. Each smallest one, having the power to come back, will choose its fellows; and the result will be a mental kaleidoscope. The law of association will choose the one by which we will be most entertained, and the result will be endless combinations of thought out of the old material.

## CHAPTER XXXVIII.

### LAW VI:—PERCEPTION AS CONTINUOUS.

I MUST interpose at once some account of the last law of Perception, viz. that it is Continuous. It would have been easy to omit this, it is so unobtrusive. And yet it would have been convenient to have had it earlier. But I postponed it; not that I did not feel the want of it in treating of Association, but because it would delay the thought. In expounding Memory, it becomes altogether vital; and therefore, as it must be somewhere interposed, we will let it come in in the very happiest place. Like the long staple of which the manufacturers speak, the law of continuance, like the long fibre of cotton, helps to strengthen the thread which (granting the Law of Recurrence) connects the present with the past in the phenomenon of Memory.

The law of Perception as Continuous is, that, as a primordial fact, Perception continues a little, and does not flash upon the mind and die with no conscious duration. It melts slowly like a glow-worm in its gleam. Sensation corresponds in this. The eye is inert in seeing. It sees on after a vanished vision.

So of the ear. A note of music does not die instantly.

So of the smell. There is a lingering on the sense.

If I take a brand and twirl it, it will make a ring of light, showing that the light and the coal do not get out of the way together.

Now all of this is not physical; it is partly in the mind. The mind takes some time to think. And without attention, and without anything to breed delay, thought does not flash in an absolute instant, but glides in a conscious period; and this fact, like the thread in wool, helps to spin thought, and carry on a train. It gives edge to connect pictures. It gives the waiting moment necessary to get the next association. And, therefore, I said it would have been convenient to be known at the time when we were speaking of the progress of an orderly suggestion.

Perception as Continuous, therefore, is the law by which Perception as Fading takes an instant to fade, that it may join itself in the current to others.

## CHAPTER XXXIX.

### MEMORY.

When I look at a distant house, I see a red brick, or a white painted, surface, and if any one should say I had a primordial faculty by which I cognized that house as distant, and just so distant, he would contradict consciousness, and all the later metaphysical teachings. I cognize the color as a sheer sensation. But the out-ness of that color, and the length of that out-ness, is the accretion of many perceptions. I *learn* it as we shall hereafter see. And now, when I behold a house, perceptions in an associated order flash along the intervening landscape. My eye has been bred a land measurer. Experience teaches me the distance. And more than that, certain deepness of the hue, and certain focus of the eye itself, and certain thousand other things, aggregate as tests, and make the decision facile and perfectly immediate.

Now precisely this, *MUTATIS MUTANDIS*, is the phenomenon of Memory. For the brick house I have nothing but the instrument of Sensation. For the past event I have nothing but the instrument of Recurrence. Sensation announces the brick house, and a glance over the intervening space, and those other things, announce it as distant. Recurrence brings back an ancient thought, and a glance over the intervening time, and certain other things, announce it as past.

That is, a thought comes up by the law of bare Recurrence, which we have described as primordial. It comes with no label on its back, and we have no power such as everybody has been imagining, to cognize it as past. But the very law of Association that brought it up, has already probably connected it. That is, the oat-field and the wheat-field and the grass lawn, by which we give distance to the house, serve no other purpose in the matter of space than intervening events do in the matter of time. Nay, time has two advantages. Time can borrow also a measure by space. I see a house; this time not actually, but as a matter of Recurrence. I see it is my neighbor's house, in ten thousand ways. The intervening fields show it; measuring the distance of it, as though by sensation, right up to my door. The familiar face of it; its connection with all my life; its thousand tracks of associated thought,—all fix it in an instant. And just as the hue of a building, or the focus of my eye, are those "other things" of which I spoke a moment ago, so there are lesser things that attend Recurrence, like the deepness of the print or the familiarity of the look of an idea, by which we learn by experience * that it is remembered, i. e. that it has been in the mind before.

The dogma, therefore, that Memory is a primordial power by which the mind directly cognizes the past; or as Sir William Hamilton describes it,† "a knowledge of a present thought, involving an absolute belief that this thought represents another act of knowledge that has been,"—all theories of the past as directly known as the past by one act of original intelligence, are *de trop;* and, therefore, fanciful. The whole can be explained far short of that. And this analysis of Memory which makes it perfectly on a par with Sensation as applied to distance, is a wonderful philosophical

* The teachings of experience will be analyzed when we come to the Book on Logic.

† Wight's Phil. of Sir W. H., p. 178.

relief, because it removes the bar that has stood in the way of many a metaphysical elucidation.*

There is a law then that perceptions, once possessed, come back again. The law is naked and perfectly inexplicable in any other way than that it is a good law, and highly consistent with the goodness of our original Creator. They come back unmarked and undiscriminated and undistinguishable from others, except intrinsically, that is, as fainter and other than perceptions of direct sensation. This power to recur is a store-house in an inexplicable way like Sensation. I say like Sensation; for thought may be liable to recur and never do it, just as light may beam upon the eye, and sounds pelt upon the ear, and scents bathe the nostril, and be store-houses of sense; and never sensation. Consciously we do not see or hear. Consciously we do not remember. We see some things. And we bring back some things from the store-house of the past; but infinitesimally few things in contrast with the enormous crowd that are ready to come into our consciousness.

Suggestion, indefatigably busy;—or rather, to speak in more measured terms, Perception, by its law of the Stronger Emotion, is emerging into consciousness from either store of our unconscious perceptibilities. It picks its thread from either distaff; and now a house, and now a past event, and now an abstract fragment, is drawn into the staple of the thread, leaving the myriads that are beating on the sense just as distant as the throng that is clamoring for Recurrence. Let it seize a house, Suggestion immediately places it in space by a flash over the field of vision; or is it a past event,

* See Mill's difficulty which he gives up as insoluble. (Exam. of Sir Wm. Hamilton, vol. 1, p. 262.)

Suggestion immediately flashes over the past till it places it in time. Memory is nothing but this. And a recurrent thought would have to stand out in the cold, for any power we have to cognize it as of the past, unless it can rouse some other thoughts and bridge over the space and know itself by intervening histories.

Of course the whole contents of consciousness recur. The very idea of thought as past, by whatsoever way I get it, may then after that recur. And thus in ways hereafter to be more fully sketched when I come to speak of Intuitive Belief, *pastness* may be learned just like *distance*, but, when once learned, may recur along with the thought, and may be at once concluded on as a part of its recurrence.

## CHAPTER XL.

### RECOLLECTION.

MEMORY being only the power by which a recurrent thought is recognized as past by its simple associations, and having no other claim to be a simple power than that which reveals to us distance in the instance of sensation, Recollection is nothing more than Memory with the Will annexed.

Experiencing the law of Suggestion as recalling thought, I use the Will in it. Recurrence is the mere emerging. Memory is the recognition of the emergent thought by quick associations with the rest that give it its place in history. Recollection is an effort in all this, that is, the use of the Will in its second province of Attention, I mean attention to something already perceived, and I mean in order that that perceived something may suggest a thought, a thought of which we know enough already to know that there is such a thought, and then further than that that it is a thought waiting for recurrence.

## CHAPTER XLI.

### IMAGINATION.

No separate *Fancy*, therefore, is required. The Law of the Strongest Emotion makes pictures to please us. It uses the store-houses of the present and the past. Out of the past it is really Memory. For though we may paint a goblin, and can hardly say we ever remember one, yet the *material* is out of the store-house of the past, and the *grouping* is by the stronger emotion. The picture I form of Windsor Castle, when I stand and look at it, and the picture I form of the town of Man-Soul, when Bunyan speaks of it, are both by the Law of Association. Sensation furnishes me for one, and Memory furnishes me for the other. I pick out the "Castle," and I pick out the "Town," and I discard other things. I pick out the Castle and leave the rest of Sense, and I pick out the Town from all the other Recurrences; and though the Castle is made ready to my sight, so the Town is by the same flash of the Strongest Emotion that seizes upon the one just as it throws together the pieces of the other.

Imagination therefore is that grouping of perceptions which the mind got by Recurrence, and which the mind selects by the Law of the Strongest Emotion.

## CHAPTER XLII.

### ANALYSIS.

I have said (Chapter XV.) that there are no Simple Ideas; that is, Perception cannot be made so unitary that more truths than one must not of necessity be in it.

Dividing a perception, however, and distinguishing as far as possible its conceivable elements, is the work of Analysis.

## CHAPTER XLIII.

### ABSTRACTION.

ABSTRACTION takes these elements, and looks at them separately.

I analyze a sunbeam. I note its course and its color—its heat and its continuance—its light and its actinic influences. I *abstract* any one of these. Consciousness, emotion, and cognition are abstractions from any one perception. Nevertheless nothing is unitary. All stay mixed; though we think we abstract them. A course or a color or a time gives us more to think of than can be absolutely single. Consciousness grasps back at both its sisters. Analysis is a mere bungle: Abstraction never perfect; and the names and of course the definitions (see Chap. XVII.) which it is the office of Abstraction to bestow, a mere hint at a real difference.

## CHAPTER XLIV.

### JUDGMENT, COMPARISON, DEDUCTION, REASON.

WE mention these simply to glance at them. These are not different faculties. Each is the mind in its power to perceive. Each is the whole mind with names used as for mental convenience. They differ as perceptions differ. And they may be multiplied to any extent, the vocabulary of perceiving having all the room that perceptions have of being multiplied in the mind.

# BOOK II.

# LOGIC;

OR, THE

# SCIENCE OF PERCEPTION AS KNOWLEDGE.

---

## CHAPTER I.

### KNOWLEDGE.

A VERY subtle philological question might be allowed to hinder us at the very opening of this discussion.

A simple statement would be, that Knowledge is of two kinds, Conscious and Unconscious. By Conscious Knowledge I would understand that which a man has at the time, as when I say, 'I know that I have a sensation of pain,' or 'I know that light is beautiful, for I am looking at it at this very moment.' Unconscious Knowledge would be the Knowledge of Greek or Latin,—Potential Knowledge, or the power to know when the opportunity offers, as, for example, when I say, 'Such a man knows Logic, or the whole circle of the Sciences.'

Now the question to which I allude is, whether this last is not the only proper sense; whether power to perceive is not the universal sense of the word Knowledge. We are not willing to make the least pause about it. Metaphysically it makes no difference.

To make clear the statements, we will *adopt* the twofold distinction. Conscious Knowledge is something cognized at the time; and Unconscious Knowledge something I could cognize if the occasion should occur. Let it be distinctly observed that any difficulties of all this are simply difficulties of Philology.

## CHAPTER II.

### CONSCIOUS KNOWLEDGE.

Conscious Knowledge will be found to be of two kinds, Intuitive and Empirical.

## CHAPTER III.

### INTUITIVE KNOWLEDGE.

The three aspects of Perception were Consciousness, Emotion, and Cognition. The wonder might be felt that we did not employ these three as the subjects of Divisions. Psychology might have been the Science of Consciousness. We might have called Logic the Science of Cognition: and Pathics the Science of Emotion. There might have been some advantages of this. But there were disadvantages that we need not stop to mention. Yet simplicity will be achieved by saying now that Cognition is nothing more or less than Intuitive Knowledge. All that we said of it will apply to the subject of the present chapter. All Perception was Cognition, and all Cognition was Perception, and what is more important far, Cognition is nothing more than Consciousness. Therefore our definition in this place can be very distinct. I intuitively know nothing but the contents of my consciousness.

To show that I distinctly appreciate what I say, I mean that Intuitive Knowledge does not cognize self unless self as an object of knowledge is itself a consciousness. Please understand me literally. I mean to show hereafter that self *is* partly consciousness, as I mean to show by that, that that is the reason that we speak always of being conscious of self. I mean to show that it is an affair of language. Self as a mere thing of dictionaries, for reasons that might be stated, includes the passing consciousness that is with us at the time. When I speak of self I mean an *ens* and its consciousnesses. This is an accident of language—not an accident either as being devoid of sense. What I know intuitively is only consciousness. If consciousness were counted as the act, and self were kept out of view as only the agent, it would not be true that there were intuitions of self. This is mere vocabulary. We wish thus early to make a point of that. We mention it out of place; for Ontology is that which will introduce us to self. But we mention it to allay distrust. It might be thought contemptuously that we were not contemplating results. It will make our meaning plainer as to Intuitive Knowledge. We have no Intuitive Knowledge of self, if only self is considered as meaning what thinkers have universally imagined it to mean, viz. an inward entity. Of that we have naught intuitive. Self in its working sense, that is as the word can be seen consciously to be framed, includes the present consciousness; and *qua* that consciousness we are conscious of it, and that is all the way we are conscious of self.

So of not-self. We are conscious of it; but only because qualities have gone into it. As mere lexicon-work, matter includes blackness,—includes hardness,—

includes anything we see that we are conscious of as of it. Not Metaphysics now, but mere Dictionary, —very important in Metaphysics, because it uncumbers a difficult subject, yet not *in se*, but only as words go *in usu*, declares that not-self includes consciousness, because the pink and yellow of the peach go into the fruit, and my Intuitive Knowledge seizes the peach, but only as including these conscious seeings. So much to allay impatience. When Ontology is in turn, it will be seen that Intuitive Knowledge is sheerly Consciousness.

Nay I may go a good deal further. When I say I am conscious of the peach, I do not mean I am conscious of the peach *through* its qualities. I mean nothing of the kind. There is no such consciousness. I mean I am conscious of consciousness, and the dictionary puts consciousness inside of the peach. I have property inside the word, and merely go for it. Let the pink, which I consciously see, be kept out of the fruit, and the strictly constructed entity, viz. the atoms that *have* the hue, or the force that projects it to the sense, I am not conscious of. Intuitive Knowledge is simply of the contents of Consciousness.

## CHAPTER IV.

### GROUND OF INTUITIVE KNOWLEDGE.

If Intuitive Knowledge be Consciousness, i. e. the intelligence that each perception has of itself, the ground of the Knowledge is nothing more than the perception. The ground of any certainty is the reason that we have for its belief. As all that we believe in Intuitive Knowledge is that we have a perception, it is idle to battle the watch about the truth of consciousness, or the goodness of God in not imposing a deceit, as the ground we look for is found in the very proposition. If we have a perception, that is all we mean by Intuitive Knowledge.

## CHAPTER V.

### DEGREE OF INTUITIVE KNOWLEDGE.

THE degree of Intuitive Knowledge is as complete as the fact of the perception. The degree of Empirical Knowledge is not complete. It is never absolute. Intuitive Knowledge, as will appear in the sequel, is the only absolute certainty possessed by man.

## CHAPTER VI.

### EXTENT OF INTUITIVE KNOWLEDGE.

KEEPING it well in our memory that we are now speaking of Conscious Knowledge, or Knowledge at the moment in the mind, the extent of Intuitive Knowledge can be seen to be nothing more than the extent of the perception, that is the extent of absolute consciousness possessed by any beholder at the time. As Perception is never simple, and sometimes very varied, and always entire, I mean by that an entire perception of everything present in the vision; as, for example, I perceive light, and I perceive flavor and scent and sound and other things often all in one consciousness; though the perception be but a fleeting gleam and is always passing to the next, yet while it lingers, it has a manifest extent, and that extent is all the points and hues and sounds and angles, and emotional enjoyments, and immediate associations, and I may add, uncertainties, that are present in that one perception of the mind.

## CHAPTER VII.

### INFLUENCE ON INTUITIVE KNOWLEDGE OF THE LAWS OF PERCEPTION.

The influence on Intuitive Knowledge of the Law of Perception as Incessant is of course this much, that it makes it embrace in time a vast multiplicity of objects; but except for other laws which are concerned in weaving these objects together, each separate perceptive gleam would have little gained by it. Perception as Fading, Perception as Transient, Perception as Continuous, almost all the laws, unless all combined and perfected by the later ones that we mentioned in the list, would leave perceptions each standing by itself; and though they would be varied endlessly, yet Intuitive Knowledge being only the present perception, each one would be unconscious of all the others, and a man's intuitions would be a set of fire-fly gleams, just melting out in the night, not spreading into thought, and not rising into anything like practical intelligence.

But now, take all these former laws, and add to them the Law of Recurrence, and the Law of the Strongest Emotion, and there occurs Memory; and Memory we have seen to be the recurring of something in the past, and then the recurring by the law of association of enough of intervening things to serve as a bridge. I see a cottage on the plain, and enough all around it and between, in the same flash almost, to show me its position. I have a perception from the past, and enough all around it of other perceptions that it immediately suggests to bridge over all that intervenes. I see the thought mapped. And so my perceptions, though only conscious of my perceivings at the time, and only intuitively knowing my present consciousness, yet are so bred by my beneficent Creator that they come up in maps or connected pictures. They have something of the present, and something of the past; something of the near, and something of the distant; and these in every picture; so that recurrent past suggests the present, and the intruding present suggests the past. And thus my Intuitive Knowledge, though a mere perception, is nevertheless a conscious sight of a suggested chain that may link together the past and the present.

We shall see, when we come to the third Book, more of this effect of these laws upon our knowledge. We shall see how Sensation unites with them, and how Self and Not-Self both emerge to their full proportions. We shall show how Being, in all its idea, is built up by the help of these laws of the mind.

For the present, let us confine ourselves to a distinct progression. Knowledge is either Actual or Potential (Conscious or Unconscious). Actual Knowledge may be divided into Intuitive and Empirical. Intuitive, which we are now considering, is simply our knowledge of our own Perceptions. More distinctly, it is only the perception we are having at a time. Its Ground is that perception itself. Its Degree is absolute, for it asserts nothing but the perception. Its Extent is the extent of the perception. And what redeems it from a mere fire-fly gleam hither and thither idly in the night, is the law of the perception itself, as continuous enough and complex enough and then associated enough to make it move in connected pictures, and give conscious information of itself by Recurrence and by connection at the time.

## CHAPTER VIII.

### EMPIRICAL KNOWLEDGE.

We have seen how Intuitive Knowledge confines itself to immediate Consciousness. We wish to show how it can grow into Experience, or how it can arrive at anything else except that I am perceiving at the time.

In the town where I live is a chime of bells. Suppose I have a perception of one stroke of one bell. Suppose I have the same perception in five minutes again. Suppose I have the same perception in five minutes more. Suppose I have the same perception each five minutes all my life. I know that five minutes from the present stroke it will strike again: and in five minutes again. What is the ground of my knowledge? Simply Experience. What is the ground of my belief in Experience? Some say, A native principle. But let us examine that. What do I mean by my belief in Experience? Simply that what has always happened will happen again. Now suppose it does not happen again. Will it violate any native principle? Will it not only violate experience? We throw up our hands and say, We never knew the like before. The law is in the bell then, and not in the mind. It is a fact about the bell. We express it in the very usages of speech when we throw it into the form of a characteristic. 'It rings' (as a discovered experience of the bell, or a simple thing that we have perceived). 'It rings as the habit of its history once in five minutes.'

Now that is a type of all that we know about the universe except this moment's consciousness. This latter little gleam is my Intuitive

Knowledge. All beyond is but an endless repetition of the case of the bell, and is my Empirical Knowledge.

But let us look at this more closely.

## CHAPTER IX.

### GROUND OF EMPIRICAL KNOWLEDGE.

WE have seen that Intuitive Knowledge, or Consciousness, is cognitive in the respect of its extent of all the phenomena that are present in the immediate perception. If it is blue color that I perceive, I perceive its shade and any variety of its tint in one part of its surface or another. I perceive its surface and any angle that it makes; and if it borders a purple or a scarlet, I observe that. If it moves, I observe that. If it fades, that also I notice. The extent of my Intuitive Knowledge, let me insist, reaches *all* that appears. Now if a bell has sounded for twenty years, does not that appear? You may say, Not consciously; not as a matter of perception at any one time; and that clears the question, and brings it to a point of vivid elucidation just as I desire. I am not conscious that it has always rung, and, therefore, it is not a matter of Intuitive Knowledge. But I am conscious that it now rings; and five minutes afterward I am conscious that it rings again. And while I am conscious of its ringing again, I am conscious of the recurrent perception of its ringing the last time. And I am conscious of a row of such perceptions recurring like city gas-lights, fading back into the past. These things I intuitively know, for I actually perceive them. Now that the bell did ring in the past, or will ring in the future, is not intuitive. Yet I hold that, though it is not intuitive, simply because we are not immediately conscious of what is either past or future, yet that it is known without an independent faculty, and as a thing revealed in the Conscious Perception.

As this is difficult we will go to work with great method and in the following order:—

I. I will state, first, three examples of Empirical Knowledge.

II. I will make, second, a distinct affirmation of their empirical ground.

III. I will state, third, certain peculiar difficulties.

IV. I will state, fourth, how they are to be obviated; and

V. I will state, fifth, the single form to which all our Empirical Knowledge is to be reduced.

I. Let us suppose a house and a garden and a lawn and a lake and the man whose Intuitive Knowledge we are to start with, to be floating on the lake in a boat. We wish to present in his instance three forms of Empirical Knowledge.

1. In the first place he lies down in his boat and just thinks of the house, or remembers it. That is the simplest knowledge of the three. He has an image of the house though past.

2. In the second place he looks off at the house and perceives its hue and its distance. That is, he has an image of the house as though present.

3. In the third place, he begins with the lake, and raises his eyes by degrees, and predicts as he raises his eyes, the lawn, the garden, and the house. This is the most complex of all. It is cognizing a house though future.

II. Now my affirmation of each and all of these is that they are Empirical.

The favorite modern affirmation is that they are by

an independent faculty; that the first is by Memory, and that Memory is a direct cognizing of the past; that the second is by Perception, with the moderns an independent faculty over and beyond Sensation (the measuring of distance being, as they admit, in part Empirical); and that the third is by a belief that what has been will be, which some men make also intuitive, and also independent, as an original faculty of the mind.

1. Now my affirmation about the first is that it is a case of simple Memory, and that Memory is a recurrence of a past perception with our past convictions about it, and such an immediate tracking of itself by association with the present, as to show where it is in the past. With us the perception only is intuitive, and its connection with the past observed, and that by one line of experience which is concerned in Memory.

2. My affirmation about the second is that it is a case of simple Memory and of still another fruit of experience beside. I have to remember ten thousand things before I recognize a house as a house at all; and then, as to the distance, it is a remembrance of distances on which I build when I estimate it, and then besides this that other experienced fact, that nature is true to herself in these perceptions before the mind.

The first therefore is simple Memory; the second in fact Memory, but in two particulars: now—

3. My affirmation about the third is, that it goes further and is built upon Memory in three particulars.

I am bending my eye upon the lake. I say, When I raise it, I will come upon a lawn. Why? Because I remember a lawn: because secondly, I have experience of distance, or, in other words, shape and position; because, thirdly, what things have been will be. Or in other words I remember continuance in the past, and predict it therefore as my coming perception in the future.

My affirmation therefore is, that neither Memory when I close my eyes, nor Sensation when I lift them up, nor Prediction when I gradually raise them, reveals anything either of lawn or house that is not phenomenally perceived, or associated in a traceable remembrance.

III. I am to state now great difficulties in this arranging of a theory.

1. In the first place, where does the *affirmance* spring from in this account of cognition? I have a recurrence of a house. It instantly associates objects up to the very point where I am standing. It also associates events. Grant if you please that association flashes us a map, where the house that I conceive, and the spot where I stand, are drawn in their relative locality. Grant more than this, that time has its picture, and that the hour when I saw the house recurs by its intervening association. Where is the grip of actual belief? In other words, where is the affirmance of the house as actually of the past?

Recollect; we are shut up to a perception. What is not in the consciousness is not in the mind. My consciousness comes and is gone. What that does not teach is not taught at all. And I have refused to let it teach anything but by its own perceivings, and declared those perceivings to be annunciatory of nothing but themselves, or not in any intuitive way of facts or histories outside of what they experience.

Now grant a picture as perfect as I please. How

can I by mere Recurrence, which just returns me my thoughts so, with no mark upon them; and by mere association, which flashes those thoughts into connection with the present, affirm anything of those thoughts except their mere consciousness? How can I place them except in the present picture? How can I know so much in what is confessedly a fleeting gleam? And how, when I look at a house, or when I predict that I can look at one, do I get the grip of knowledge from what is confessedly a transitory consciousness?

2. Again: improvement; How do I get that? I advance in knowledge. Unless there are original faculties that are strengthened and increased, how does my consciousness to-day have so much more in it than my consciousness earlier in my history?

Remember, it will be said, you find all your knowledge of God and the universe in a passing gleam. How does that gleam get full? And how does this mere picture-making that connects, improve the thoughts into incalculable amounts of knowledge?

IV. Now we must recall our minds to the distinction of Actual and Potential knowledge, as before enunciated. Potential knowledge is that incalculable amount just hinted at.

Actual knowledge is that which is present at the time. But as nothing is present at the time of which we are not conscious, a man's consciousness at the time shuts in all his actual knowledge. So far then, for the steadying of the mind, we have something actually demonstrated.

The position, therefore, on the part of those that bring forward these very plausible and difficult arguments must be, that there is more in our consciousness than the phenomena we have mentioned, because, first, no beauty of association would *affirm* the past or future or the distant present, and because, second, no practice in mere tracking by pictures could accrete into one consciousness so much as we learn to know by one perception of the mind.

Now these are central difficulties, and deserve a most perspicuous answer.

1. Let me say first:—Convictions themselves are conscious, and are matters of memory.

I have a conviction this moment that there is a house beyond me. No matter how I get it, and no matter what I mean by it; that will come after (see Ontology). If I attempted to define it and say, as I certainly might, that it was a hundred perceptions, or rather a circumlocution to include a hundred points of consciousness in a sort of algebraic expression (for language lives by such things), you would easily entangle me in debate. But if I say, I know there is a house over yonder, you perfectly understand me; and you also understand me when I say, that this conviction is itself a subject of recurrence.

Now with what sort of a grip would the conviction, granting I once had it, come back to me?

Some may say, It would come back unrolled from its self-affirmation, and with no grip at all. But is that certainly so? In fact is it consciously possible? What is it? It is a conviction. It is a seeing, by indicia I have, that there is a house over in the field. Now what comes back? You say, a mere picture, or the mere idea, of a belief. What do you mean by that? The mere idea of the house? Then the conviction does not come back at all. Or do you mean the mere consciousness of such a conviction? Well, I accept that. Then you admit the mere consciousness of a past conviction, as recurring like everything conscious by a law of the mind.

But how does it come back? Of course with all its circumstances. The house recurs to me, and with it the consciousness of my first conviction when I saw it, and with that the additional consciousness of all that opens afterward. It is the harmony I wish to point out.

2. For, second, convictions being taken for granted as originated somewhere (we will not as yet say exactly how), they may be exceedingly obscure and feeble, and yet grow strong by mere reduplication. I have a conviction there is a house upon the plain: I look and see and find that it is the case. There recurs now a whole list of phenomenal additions. There recurs the old conviction. There recurs the new experiment. There recurs the fresh discovery. All these items of consciousness recur just as they were perceived. Nay, I try again; and try again. I multiply the experiment. The man in the boat looks up ten thousand times. The convictions all agree. They all aggregate. And this is the history of life. Life is an infinite experiment, as we shall see when we come to Ontology, in which a harmonious Providence confirms our convictions in ten thousand fashions; and it is out of these harmonious perceivings that we track sensation; that we track it to the senses; that we track it to the body; that we track it to self; that we track it to a not-self; that we track it to God; for all these are Empirical ideas, and all these easily flow if you will accord us the possibility of originating the first Empirical conviction.

3. Now as to that, (viz. how we get the first conviction), when I have a perception, it is cognitive. I

mean by that, it cognizes everything in the present perception; shape, color, everything, as we have said repeatedly before. Moreover, this cognition is an affirmance. It has every grip that we can imagine. That is, it is a conviction that everything is so perceived.

If you ask me, Is not this a separate faculty, the perception being one thing and the conviction another? I answer, Plainly not. The perceiving is a perceiving that I perceive, and that as an integral part, or rather the whole, of my perception. When it recurs, therefore, the conviction recurs with it, and that for the reason that the perception itself recurs.

When it recurs, however, there is quite an explicable reduplication. There is the old conviction and the old perception. They recur. Now they are the same; just as light and color; yet they are discriminate. Perception and emotion are one, yet easily distinguishable. In other words, emotion can be abstracted from perception and viewed separately. In like manner conviction is an aspect of perception, concretely inseparable from it, in compass commensurate with it, in origin the same, but so discrepant in potential thought that I can speak of the blueness that I perceive and of the sureness that I perceive it, without the risk even of entangling my speech in appearing to be announcing two separate perceivings.

When my perception recurs, however, the old conviction recurs, and with it flashes the intervening events. And this thing is redoubled endlessly.

I see a light, for example. Along with it is the recurrence of my seeing it before; along with that the old conviction; if you please simply in its transcript: along with that a new conviction. I close my eyes and open them again; and there is the light again and a new conviction. These things we are repeating all the time. And to say that we cannot spell out the past as past, and the distant as distant,* and the future as predicable upon the past, by the help of a complete return of old perceptions with the convictions that attended them, is to deny the perceptive clearness of each act and its full recurrent consciousness.

Besides, there are side lights from Sensation.

We cannot fully understand this till we come to speak of Sense in the next department. But we can go upon received ideas far enough to explain what we mean.

Suppose the recurrent conviction were a mere transcript, that is, the mere idea of a conviction, rather than a conviction itself. We are willing to suppose that, because we are willing to admit that the recurrent perception is rather a copy of the perception, and that altogether faded, than a recurrence of the perception itself.

Now suppose the sheer influence of such an instance of a mere copy of a conviction were originally only enough to suggest an experiment, and that with an infant it began with that mere tentative experience. Do we not see how rapidly it would grow? All nature is full of harmony. Little Chubby-cheeks, very bright as to sense, but very empty empirically, stuffs his fist into a pillow. Instantly it is a matter of memory. Now I do not believe he cognizes the touch as past by a primordial faculty, but that the cool feeling was pleasant, and has a power to recur. Moreover, a conviction recurs with it, or, if you please, the picture of a conviction, that it was cool and pleasant. Many actual

* This, however, cannot be articulately understood till we come to speak of Sensation.

touches would be necessary before he could build up the requisite experience; but each punch bringing its memories, and each memory aligned in a vista of convictions, and all convictions blended into one like the pictures under a stereoscopic lens, the child would begin to punch for himself, and would build up, before he became a man, his own complete circle of empirical predictions.

2. We are strong now against that almost overpowering objection, that a man must have the noblest knowledge in the form of some mere fleeting perception. Yes! For what may not that perception be? He may have a perception of the heavens. He may be in the night of a dungeon, and may just think of it. That is, he may have the recurrence of the stars and of the starry frame as one picture. He may have it with all its past convictions. He may run riot in trooping memories. And to say nothing of the changes of the thought, the picture at each conscious moment will be that of the Strongest Emotion to his mind.

V. Returning to the man in the boat, we will be able to answer to our fifth point, which is, the *Single Form* to which all our Empirical Knowledge can be reduced.

1. He lies in the bottom, and there simply recurs a house with lawn and garden, and all the attendant facts as we have repeatedly described. Here the form of Empirical Knowledge is simply memory: the recurrence of the house; the recurrence of intervening indicia of the house; and the recurrence chiefly and more important than the rest, of repeated convictions of all the cognitive realties. This shall be our first instance.

2. The second is of the man standing in the boat and looking at the house and judging of the intervening distance.

3. The third is of the man rising from the boat and predicting as he rises, in his glance, the lawn, the garden, and the house, just as they appear in the other instance.

Now I have shown that the first is a single, the second a double, and the third a triple, instance of the phenomenon of memory. In the first I remember the house. In the second (1) I remember houses (how they look, etc.), so that I perceive this to be a house,* and (2) I remember distances, and how objects help to measure them, so that I cognize this house as distant. In the third, (1) I remember this house, (2) I remember and judge its distance, and (3) I remember and predict that a house once perceived may at that point be perceived again.

Now what does all this teach? Why, at first glance, every one would say, that knowledge empirically considered, in these instances at least, is nothing more in the world than Memory. And so it is, in an instrumental sense. But, in its ground, Memory itself shares with it in something deeper. Memory itself is but an instance of Empirical Knowledge. As an instrument it does all the work. All Empirical Knowledge is an act of Memory. For, as all Empirical Knowledge is built upon experience, Memory, that gathers it up, is the active agent in every part of it. All experience is Memory, and all Memory experience; and though it will not do to say I remember that a thing will happen, or I remember that that house that we are looking at must be a mile off, yet it might do to talk in that way, and

* Of course all this is premature to any extent further than we design to illustrate, as we have not yet explained how we perceive a house at all.

would do beyond a doubt, if it were the *usus loquendi*. Both statements are made by means of what we remember.

If we will distinguish, accordingly, between the instrument of Empirical Knowledge and the ground of Empirical Knowledge, Memory is doubtless the former, and we remain free, as a distinct question, to ask, What is the latter?

Now the ground of our Empirical Knowledge is the orderliness of our perceptions.

If our perceptions were all sporadic, like fire-flies gleaming in the night, we could have nothing empirical. But, as it is, we have two orders. We have the order of external nature, which we will treat when we come to speak of Sensation, and we have the order of perceptive laws. Both of these beget the one order of perception. It is on the ground of the orderliness of perception that is bred empirical belief.

Nor let some one who doubts this as the final truth interpose the idea of the truth of our perception.

The ground of Intuitive Knowledge, it might be argued, is the veracity of consciousness. Now if the ground of Intuitive Knowledge is the veracity of consciousness, the ground of Empirical Knowledge is the veracity of memory; or as memory is so entirely complex, the veracity of those blended consciousnesses, recurrent and original, which make up that blended whole which is an act of memory. The veracity of consciousness, it has often been insisted on as evident, must be our final support in all our possible convictions.

But let us look at this very carefully.

If Knowledge of any sort is based upon the veracity of consciousness, it must differ as a matter of course from consciousness itself. Consciousness must be one thing, and certain facts that it veraciously teaches must be numerically another, or there is no pith in such a proposition.

But consciousness, as we have consistently taught, is itself the fact in intuitive cognition. All our intuitive knowledge is our present consciousness. Now to make the veracity of consciousness the ground of consciousness itself is empty to the last degree. And the only significant speech is, that our belief in consciousness, or our trust in our conscious cognition, is imbedded in the act itself. To know that I perceive is nothing more in the world than to perceive. And to know anything else than that I perceive, is not intuitive knowledge. And to build up that something else on what is called the veracity of consciousness is to evoke a figment, totally different I grant, but at the same time totally false as compared with absolute consciousness.

The ground of Intuitive Knowledge, therefore, is itself. The reason I have it is because it is itself the thing known.

The ground of Empirical Knowledge is the order of perception, just as the ground of Intuitive is the perception itself. The ground of Empirical Knowledge, therefore, is an order which I find to be.

Let us study this; and then we will be at the end of a long chapter.

The ground of any knowledge is the reason why we believe it. The ground of Intuitive Knowledge is consciousness itself. The ground of Empirical Knowledge is consciousness itself revealing itself in a certain order. The degree of Intuitive Knowledge is absolute. We are certain of everything that we intuitively know. The degree of our Empirical Knowledge is not absolute. Now, if both be grounded on consciousness, whence this difference, and how can consciousness, which is sure, be the ground of anything that is essentially uncertain? These are critical questions, and indeed vital to the possibilities of Logic.

I begin by asking, Can I, or can I not, perceive any order in my perceptions?

In my perceptions in space I can; for though we have not studied Ontology yet, still this much is a matter of consciousness. I look out on the starry heavens, and the order of moon and comet and cloud and the belt of Orion consciously appears to me. In fact, all that is synchronous in the current of whatever sort has its order when it comes into notice. But can I be conscious of order in my perceptions in time? Without Recurrence I certainly could not. For though there is a flux of the current during the conscious instant; that is, from the law of Continuance,* a flowing off and coming on during the moments in which the perceptions are lasting; still, if the perceptions leaped off and fell into the dark and never returned to us, we could know nothing essentially of order in time.

But how is it at present? Past perceptions come back to us with a suggestion of much that intervenes. They come back to us as images of themselves, but nevertheless with the conviction (or the image of it) that they were not images at the time that they occurred. They come back in all their order, like present visions. Then we have this much at least, that we have in our actual consciousness orderly images of the past coming back into the current by the law of Recurrence.

* See B. I, chap. xxxviii.

We have an order of perceptions in space; we have an order of perceptions in time; both, in our consciousness; both actual; that is, both absolute perceptions; but the first assertatory only of themselves as of the present moment; and the last assertatory also of themselves as of the present moment, but assertatory also of their character as images of the past. How do they get that last assertatory character?

Now to this we are ready to reply by six propositions:—

1. First; not only do past perceptions recur, but they recur with their essential convictions, one of these convictions having been of their being actual perceptions. As this conviction was conscious, and all conscious phenomena have the law that they recur, this conscious conviction may recur. And though it be a mere copy of a conviction, still what is that? and I appeal to consciousness whether it has not some affirming character.

2. Second; if it have the least affirming character, it becomes great by ceaseless and multiform reduplication. Grant that I see a house, and that each time I see it I am convinced of my conscious perception; and that that conviction, being conscious, recurs, like the perception itself; and that when the perception recurs conviction recurs, and with it the still earlier conviction, and so, like the two plates of the stereoscope, one adds vividness to the other, and so on in an endless progression,—and I think it cannot remain unapparent how convictions may *grow*, so that the mere sight of a thought may recognize it as passed, and fix it in time, just like an object in space by the tokens of present sensation.

3. This is still more easy to conceive under the law

of the Strongest Emotion, by which the recurrent thought pictures itself in its actual connections;

4. And yet again more easy by the bearing of sense upon memory. I lift up my eyes and see a house. I shut them and remember it. I open them and see it again. I can do this a hundred times. Each of these acts is conscious. Each of them, therefore, will be recurrent. All of them agree perfectly. The agreement is recurrent. All convictions that they agree, and that they recur, and that we have done the one and the other thing and asked the one and the other question, and that they have been answered in but one way, all blend in one recurrent perception. And that a man cannot in this way locate in time what correspondingly he can locate in space appears to me to be inconsistently denying the possibilities of the present perception.

5. When a conviction is once obtained it likewise is conscious and of course recurrent. It becomes general also. I know thought as past by its very glance, just as a house as distant. It has become an alphabet; that is, I mean, the very look of a past thought. I learn to know my consciousnesses, as a man does his flocks and herds, and simply by their looks. That tall image is a house. It stands there over the plain. You can touch it if you travel far enough. I know this by experience. Yon ghost-like thought, not actual, not really white or really square, but the image of such realities, is just the hue and guise of a thing remembered. I know it as such by the light of a life's experiments. I know a dream; and I know the memory of a dream; and I know a mere fancy, i. e. a mere fancied house, never actual, that is, that cannot place itself in any actual picture. I know each and all, as a

girl knows the keys of her piano. I know them in the same way. And I cannot insist too narrowly upon the light that is thrown upon recurrent convictions of what has taken place in time, by convictions of the external world, and of the place things occupy in space under actual sensation.

6. All moreover reduces itself just to one formula, viz. What has been will be. This is not an axiom either, but a mere fact. When it ceases to be so, knowledge vanishes. I believe I saw a house. Why? Because whenever such appearances recurred, when I went to the spot I found one. I believe it is a mile off. Why? Because whenever the field and the grove and the sky looked just so and so wide and so shaded as these intervening objects look, I have walked a mile and come to the object. I believe over there we will find a boat. Why? Because I have been to that sheet of water ever since I was a child and always found one. I believe the farm scene now before my mind is a dream and I dreamed it last night. Why? Because it looks like a dream (I mean the memory of one), and it has last night's surroundings.

Let the uniformity of perception cease and the things that have been cease to be, and a dream will no longer be known the morning afterward, nor a house the day after it was seen, nor a sunrise as a thing to happen to-morrow, nor any recurrent conviction. Man will have to learn the new system in the place of the one that resolved itself into the not-self and the conscious current. Perception has been a language to him like the dots of the telegraph, and he has learned to decipher it. It has led him up to God. Let that good Being give him no order for his perceptions, either sensational or recurrent, and they will teach him nothing. Intuitive Knowledge would be but a spark. And Empirical Knowledge could not even be imagined; for Empirical Knowledge is the discovery we make by the order of the conscious current.

The kept up order of that current is therefore the ground of Empirical Knowledge.

To prove it farther let us go backward. I go to the house. It is not there. Why? Has my mind deceived me? No: the house. The facts have changed. Nature has a different order. I look in my mind. The house recurs. I go to it and it is a different house. I recollect this last and pay the visit again. It is again different. What now! Is my mind deceiving me? That may be very possible. It is not deceiving me as to the contents of its perception. I perceive plainly enough. I perceive what I perceive, and feel what I feel. My intuitive knowledge is perfect. A deranged man has perfect intuitive knowledge, i. e. he perceives what he perceives. But my empirical knowledge is all awry. Order has fled.

## CHAPTER X.

### THREE KINDS OF EMPIRICAL KNOWLEDGE.

As Intuitive Knowledge is Consciousness, so Empirical Knowledge is grounded upon an order in consciousness, or upon a fact discovered in experience, that what things have been will be. Now, to be more precise in our statement, what things have been will never be again.

The things that come under the eye of our consciousness are perceptions. And it is the order of perceptions, discovered empirically, that constitutes experience. But it is *like* perceptions, not *the same*, that, having been, we learn empirically, do happen again. Empiricism is a great system of analogy.

Now of this analogy there are three sorts:—Absolute Analogy, Partial Analogy, and Analogy undiscoverable except by intermediate resemblances. They are all the same thing,—Analogy. They are all traced by the same thing,—Experience. They all employ the same instrument,—Memory. They all build the same system,—Logic. And they all point to this fact,—that conscious perception and its analogies, that is its discovered order, make up the whole of the knowledge unfolded to our species.

We must from the very beginning see clearly that these three are all monogonous. The first is often referred to Consciousness; the second, to Intuitive Belief so-called, a myth that has had a most wonderful place in modern investigation; the third has been given the whole of Logic. Now the harm has been inconceivable. It has kept us back from simple views; and prevented what I firmly believe easy, viz. the making of Logic to consist in the mere tracing of consciousness and its analogies. That when I see a horse it is the horse I saw yesterday, i. e. Absolute Analogy; that when I see a horse it is a horse—i. e. Partial Analogy (though the horse may be different from nine-tenths of the horses I ever saw before); and that when I see a bone from the pastern of an animal I perceive it to be the pastern of a mammal, though by intermediate analogies the steps of which I have forgotten;—these are the three species of empirical faith. And though so apparently diverse the one from the other, they are all in principle the same. They are all the dictum of consciousness, and the dictum of the conscious fact, discovered by recurrence in the way

I have articulately given, that perception has an orderly course, the bifold order (1) of what we have yet to treat in outward sensation, and (2) of what we have so carefully marked in the grouping of what is associatedly recurrent.

Now let us treat the three kinds more definitely and in an elementary light.

1. I brought in the chime of bells, and I intended them for this distinct service. I imagined one bell and one stroke repeated at a determined interval. The expectation of that bell would be a mere perception of a fact, or a LIKElihood as we significantly describe it; and if it did not ring, it would not violate a consciousness or a separate conscious act, but simply a fact about the bell. We would cry out, It has quit ringing! We are so constituted by the affirmance of our present knowledge, and by the recurrence of convictions that are redoubled, that we can note the habits of our perception, and mark that when it has sounded once it sounds again.

Now this is Absolute Analogy.

And I can go a little further and make it much more complex, and still not deprive it of this absolute degree.

Suppose that with one second between each of the bells the whole chime is set afloat in the belfry. Suppose it continues for twenty years. Here again is Absolute Analogy. If it continues at determined intervals and in the order of the scale, while it is not the same stroke of course, it is a like stroke; while it is not the same perception, it is a like perception; it is a prediction of what I have never heard by the light of what I have heard. It is not, What has been will be, which is therefore an imperfect formulary, but, The like will happen again. It is, therefore, an instance of analogy, and in this case of absolute analogy. The identical strokes are never repeated, but precisely similar ones, with the peculiarity of their note and in the order of the diatonic scale.

We might make the similarity, too, far more intricate, and yet not depart out of the category of absolute or complete analogy.

2. But, secondly, let the chime ring any notes of the scale, or at all hours of the day, but simply keep ringing. Suppose it had done this for twenty years. Suppose it did it scarcely at all some days, but never omitted it altogether. There would still be analogy, and still prediction, but it would be Partial Analogy, and this is a great track by which we climb to the being of the Almighty.

I see an animal in a gate. The gate hides all but her hinder half. I have never seen any other part of her. She has legs and tail, but unlike any other animal. They are not the legs of a horse, nor of a cow, nor of a deer, nor of a moose; but yet they are like all four. What can I tell? I can tell it is a quadruped, by mere analogy. I say, Let me go round the gate, and I will see head and ears and eyes totally unlike all I have ever witnessed, and yet *like*. The principle is just the same as if it were my own cow and I knew her perfectly. And if I went round the gate and found the fins of a whale, it would shock no intuitive belief, but only multiplied experience. If it seemed my own cow, and I found her a fish, it would be precisely the same. The shock would be greater. But it would only be the interruption of the order of what I have beheld. My mind by recurrence can take hold of the past. And I would express it all by saying, as the acme of the mystery, not, My Intuitions are failing, but, Did ever anybody see the LIKE?

3. Suppose the tower, like the statue of Memnon, chimed its own bells; and that, by action of the morning sun. Suppose I had it all explained to me, and had understood the steps. The expansion of the masonry on the easternmost side; that would be one analogy. Like happening to like, too, about some iron rods; that would be another. It might be a long catenation that no man could carry as a whole, but that any man could follow in its parts. Such would be the third species; empirical knowledge, but with the steps forgotten, just leaving the investigator with the fact; so that, coming up by recurrent conviction, he would be able to say, Sometimes (exactly when I am unable to state without going over the points,) that chime will ring of itself; and say it on the old ground of analogy or remembered order.

## CHAPTER XI.

### DEGREE OF EMPIRICAL KNOWLEDGE.

THE Degree of Empirical Knowledge will depend entirely upon the degree of the perceptive order. This might appear at first sight not the case. If a bell had rung every hour since I was born, and the sun had risen and no more regularly every day, I would believe much more in the rising of the sun, though it had occurred twenty-four times less often than the occurrence of the other.

But this will explain only more perfectly the doctrine of experience.

Experiences mat themselves together. Convictions are redoubled by borrowing from their kindred class. The rising of the sun belongs to an order of causation. Causation, as we will hereafter learn, is but a dictum of experience. And yet it links together analogous phenomena. The rising of the sun is a cause of causes, made credible by other facts that we fail to separate; matted together with a maze of probabilities. And yet it is precisely analogous with the bell. The ground of belief is identically the same. The bell may never ring again, and the sun may never rise again. And if either never do, the ground of surprise would be elementarily the same. Nay that either some day never will is a like prediction. And, as a universal fact, the Degree of our Empirical Knowledge depends upon the uniformity of the order that has been previously perceived.

## CHAPTER XII.

### EXTENT OF EMPIRICAL KNOWLEDGE.

BY this if there be intended the extent of perception at the time, of course it has been sufficiently delineated. But if there be intended (rather potentially) the classes of things that can become empirically known, I would answer, All past perceptions with their analogies. As this is a difficult subject, I will divide it into the two that are to succeed.

## CHAPTER XIII.

### INTUITIVE KNOWLEDGE AS EMBRACING EMPIRICAL KNOWLEDGE.

IT is now familiar to the reader that in the conscious current there is a phenomenon called Perception, which can be looked upon in the three aspects of Consciousness, Emotion, and Cognition. It is also familiar to the reader that these aspects are not partial but total; that is, that the whole of Perception is Consciousness, and the whole of Consciousness Emotion, and the whole of all or any, Cognition or any of the rest.

Now grant the truth of what we have established, that there is nothing consciously in the mind at any moment except one of these more or less complex perceptions, and we have the easy inference that Empirical Knowledge, if conscious, is a conscious perception. But if it be a conscious perception, it is entirely that and entirely conscious. Now if it be entirely conscious, it is entirely consciousness; and consciousness, by our very definitions, is Intuitive Knowledge.

We have, therefore, the ugly result that Empirical Knowledge, which we have started out to make distinct, reverts into the bosom of simple intuition.

Moreover, all that is intuitive we have already found is absolute or certain, and all that is empirical is in our very statement of its degree essentially uncertain. How then can conscious empirical knowledge be consciousness, and therefore absolute in degree, and yet according to the facts be CONSCIOUSLY UNCERTAIN?

Now fortunately this very last term is a fine key to the whole dilemma. Consciousness totally reveals all that is in its bosom, and reveals it intuitively. It reveals the exact appearance of the inward sight, whatever that may be. But of course part of the appearance of the inward sight is uncertainty.

If I see all that I see, intuitively, and therefore certainly, it does not impair the completeness of that sight, but rather enhances it, that I see things consciously and just as they are, if what they are is in its own nature necessarily uncertain.

I have but to preserve the same meaning for perceptive cognition, and make it always mean the perceptive aspect of an inward consciousness, and it would be always absolute, and always certain, and always intuitive, and Intuitive Knowledge would then fairly include the whole circle of our possible cognitions.

But Knowledge has slipped from one sense to another.

I see, for example, a pair of doves. I am perfectly conscious of the sensational impression. All that the doves work upon my perceivings and upon my conscious state at any one time I am articulately aware of. Nothing escapes me that is consciously present. Who shall say that all this is not Intuitive Knowledge? But one of the facts intuitively known is that one of the apparitions I call a dove, that is, one of the white surfaces or buff colored phenomena of vision, I care care not what you call it, may or may not be equal to the other. This I intuitively see. This is, in fact, the thing known. The knowledge in the case is a knowledge of uncertainty. And the corruption of speech is in taking the word knowledge, which might well be left for perceptive cognitions, and applying it to something else, that is, not to the perceptive cognition of a fact, but to the perceptive cognition of the greater or less probability of a fact, or in other words to the mere belief that a certain bird is bigger than the other.

When I say, therefore, I know that the doves are equal, if I supply the ellipsis, and say, I know that they seem equal, or am conscious of a likeness in the visions, I am translating the conclusion into the actual phenomena of thought. I keep the word knowledge for my actual conscious intuitions. I show that doubts and measured probabilities are part of the objects of my consciousness. I mark the genesis, so to speak, of all that is empirical. And I explain how, in the strictest metaphysical sense, apart from the use of terms, Intuitive Knowledge includes the other form of our alleged cognitions.

## CHAPTER XIV.

### INTUITIVE KNOWLEDGE AS DISTINCT FROM EMPIRICAL KNOWLEDGE.

It has not pleased the popular ear, however, to retain the word knowledge for what is conscious so far forth as it is conscious and therefore certain. But, there being conscious thoughts which are certain in themselves, as all thoughts are, but marked by certain uncertainties, which are consciously and hence intuitively known, and therefore matters of direct and absolute knowledge, it has not pleased the public to state facts that way, but to cut across lots, so to speak, and instead of saying I am conscious of a high probability that those doves are equal, to say I know they are; which means, I am conscious that they seem so, and take the seeming for a full cognition.

So, therefore, if we could discard this habit of the people, we could return to metaphysical strictness in this way:—We could say, I know that of which I am conscious, and nothing else. That would keep all things in their place, metaphysically, and therefore correctly. But among the things I know is the fact of certain uncertainties, which are just as open to my consciousness as blueness or fragrance or consciousness or certainty itself. This uncertainty appears before me in lesser or greater degrees, like blueness or cold; and I am able consciously to know a less or greater probability or uncertainty, and that as the very fact itself. Now, so long as I confine myself to facts, I can only say, I intuitively know the object of consciousness, that is, the uncertainty itself. And that is in fact all the phenomenon. But if I choose to translate it into other language, I can do so very usefully, not by employing spuriously the word knowledge, but by going off to other language altogether: by using for example the word belief; that is, by saying I am conscious that the hue of the sky seems the same all over; therefore I believe that it is the same; or, I am conscious of certain pictures and convictions that look like as though a perception had been possessed before; therefore I believe that it has been possessed before; belief not meaning, as it now sometimes does, my conscious intuitions, except those of this single case, where I am intuitively conscious of greater or less uncertainties of one of the facts perceived.

The question would then arise, Is belief in this case intuitive? I would say, It is. We might divide in this way then:—

I. Intuitive Knowledge.

II. Intuitive Belief. And this would have to include 1st, Direct Intuitive Belief; as, for example, where I see two lines abreast, and believe that they have equal length; and 2d, Empirical Intuitive Belief; which is now just that Empirical Knowledge which is so important in philosophy.

1st. Direct Intuitive Belief has no outgoings, and therefore is just what it seems to be at the moment of perception. It is no more than my simple consciousness of the state of the uncertainty when uncertainty is my phenomenal consciousness. I see blue all over the sky. I am conscious that it seems alike; but it may not be. I am conscious of what seems a point, but it may not be. It may be two points minutely separated. Beliefs like this are innumerable like the leaves of the forest.

But there is no outcome in them. That is to say (to explain this twice repeated expression), the moment we verify the belief, it becomes, as we shall see, Empirical.

2d. Empirical Intuitive Belief differs from Direct Intuitive Belief, in the employment of Memory. Direct Intuitive Belief, though we never get it entirely separate from Empirical, yet, in theory, would be my Intuitive Knowledge that those lines, for example, seem equal, or that that point that I have supposed seems one. This seeming is in the very glance, without any employment of other impressions. And if I go nearer to the point, and it seems two, this also is, in that newer seeming, a Direct Intuitive Belief. Moreover, if I had no Memory, it would be entirely distinct. An interval of time would have given me opposite and contradictory impressions. Moreover the actual impression in the case would have been true, as all matters of consciousness are. That is, the actual contents of consciousness, paring off everything aside, are absolute or undeniable. I am conscious of what I am conscious. I perceive what I do perceive. And if there was a fine white interval across the spot when I stood in the first position, and it was marked upon the retina, and might have been seen if I had perceived it, yet that does not affect the fact that all that I perceived reported itself just as I perceived it. And when I looked again, the two spots were just as I perceived them. And when I approached again, three spots might have been developed. Now each separate intuition is Direct. But if I put them together, and go nearer for a purpose, and still nearer to try again, and the former is corrected by the later, that becomes Empirical, and Empirical in many ways: that is, it depends upon the order of nature, first, as to the continuance of self, second, as to the reliableness of memory, third, as to the continuance of the spots, and a great many other things. The moment I recede from what is Direct, I cast myself upon an immense Empirical generalization.

The lines I adverted to are a similar instance. They look alike. But if I attempt to prove them alike, what do I do? I act empirically; that is, I employ a measure. I lose at once all Direct inspection. I launch upon a thousand uncertainties. And though they become practically what we call certain (and hence claim to be "Knowledge"), yet they are all uncertainties. The stick may have changed. The lines may have changed. The eye may have changed. The mind may have changed; and so the memory. I am conscious of what I perceive; but everything besides rests solely upon an order in Nature.

We are prepared now to note the difference between Intuitive and Empirical Knowledge. We cannot use that word Belief, though metaphysically it would be very accurate. It would be displacing old usage. Belief means sometimes consciousness; and consciousness means often belief. We could not dislodge such old peculiarities. We must be content to take language as it is. And we will understand Intuitive Knowledge as simply consciousness, that is, my act at the time by which I perceive what I perceive; and my Empirical Knowledge as also consciousness, as nothing conscious is not, but consciousness of intuitive uncertainties, which, of course, are very many, and consciousness of that class of intuitive uncertainties which are made less so by the voice of empirical recurrence.

The mind is conscious of some degrees in these uncertainties; just as it is conscious of some degrees of black and white. And it is my consciousness of these degrees, which is as natural as any other perception, that marks the boundaries of empirical conviction.

I am not sure that I have made enough of a certain stereoscopic quality that I have noticed. Convictions redouble themselves. Let us look at this more narrowly.

There can recur anything of which I am conscious. I am conscious of convictions. I am conscious of general convictions. I am conscious that when a house looks in a certain way, I have a conviction that it is distant. I am conscious when a thought looks in a certain way, that I have a conviction that it is past. No matter yet for the genesis of these facts; you admit that they are conscious. Now, all things conscious can recur.

But if they can recur when so general, they doubtless recurred when more particular. They recurred in their earliest asseverations.

Let me explain this.

I see a house. I have a conscious conviction of my consciousness whatever that consciousness is. I see it again. I have a conscious conviction again, and another conviction, viz, the older conviction recurrent. I see it again. Three convictions! I see it again. Four! I see a thousand other things. They multiply convictions. They mat themselves together. By the law of harmonious association they blend themselves into one. Like six thicknesses of tulle partially transparent they blend themselves into one brighter and more solid color. They blend themselves into universals of actual and instantaneous belief. And so perfect is it, this harmonious centring into one, that men call them original. It is the pride of modern philosophy to have found out this "Regulative Faculty," as Hamilton calls it. There never was such a superb figment. It characterizes the present philosophy more than any other one trait. The schools are full of it. It is the convenient pack for all sorts of metaphysical carriage. And in claiming for it antiquity of date, it is the faith widely most dominant in the thinking of modern times.

It cannot stand, however, this distinct analysis of Recurrence. The coal shows the fern-leaves. The man thought, who first looked into the measures, that it was an original rock, like flint-stone or granite; but the tell-tale print upon the seams hinted at last at the discovery. And so our recurrences, matted together like that ancient vegetation, abstract from themselves into universals, until the conviction that appears can hardly be realized as mere recurrent perception.

## CHAPTER XV.

### INTUITIVE BELIEFS SO-CALLED.

ARISTOTLE gained great influence over the Church; but in later times, on this very account, and by a mis-reading of Paul in the First Epistle to the Corinthians, philosophy has been at a discount; and yet, by a strange caprice, a certain tenet in philosophy in the last fifty years has been erected almost into a tenet in religion.

The Church and, in lesser degree, the Schools are like oysters. They shut more easily than they open. It is a provision of nature. By a law of the imperilled mollusk taste regulates its feeding, and taste is made by what it feeds upon. The oyster, habituated to the past, snaps itself down to new food, and opens to all that is old. We would not have it different. At the same time doctrines have to be dispossessed; and this Kantian belief,* which arrogates as original in the mind what is called an Intuitive Faculty, if it is, as we perfectly know, a fiction, gains by this habit. It has become entrenched in the creed. Theology will confidently tell us that the reverse is atheism. And, therefore, we must think with infinite care. Philosophy has had ill luck on the side of theism. Coming in she has been resisted, and going out she has been clung to as one with our salvation.

One device is always acceptable; and that is, to be perfectly fair with what we attack, and *that* we shall attempt religiously toward the faith in question. We will consider first what it is not. We shall consider second what it distinctly is. We shall consider third what it says for itself, and fourth what can be said against it, and fifth whether it be an unnecessary doctrine. The first three points belong to this chapter. The fourth and fifth to the two that follow.

I. In the first place, Intuitive Belief is not old-fashioned intuition. I do not *believe* the sky is blue; I see it. And to make this clear let me settle ambi-

* "Thus it is that Hume became the cause or the occasion of all that is of principal value in our more recent metaphysics. Hume is the parent of the philosophy of Kant, and, through Kant, of the whole philosophy of Germany: he is the parent of the philosophy of Reid and Stewart in Scotland, and of all that is of preëminent note in the metaphysics of France and Italy."—Hamilton's Lectures (Am. Ed.), p. 545.

guities. Blueness has three meanings. First it is a sense. I do not believe in there being a blue. I see it as an actual sensation. Again, blueness is on the sky, painted on it, and included in it by the Lexicon. The peach, as we have already seen, includes its ruddiness. The blueness is a part of the heavens. This is Philology at her work, not Metaphysics. The name heavens includes the blueness. This, therefore, is the same as the first. I do not believe merely. I see: and so am conscious. The third sense is merely empirical; and, therefore, not a consciousness, and not an intuition, but only the imagined power the air has to project blue upon the eye.

Then, higher: taste! I see a lily. What are we to understand by beauty? To prevent mistakes we must again distinguish. Beauty is either first, sensational, or second, what is mere dictionary-work, the sense transferred into the object, or third, a power. The last is not intuitive, but only the gift, empirically thought of, that the lily has to awaken the emotion. The first views the emotion itself. The second views the same thing precisely, only transferred by human speech to the surface of the lily. Each use is reasonable. But the first and second are mere intuitions. The third is an empiricism. So that there is no room for Intuitive Beliefs.

Again, a story higher. Let us come into the domain of right. This is not a color. It is mobile. It is the quality of an emotion.* Blueness is a painting on the air. Beauty is a painting on the flower. That is, they can be transferred that way. But right is painted on an emotion. There is another difference:—We may have an emotion at an emotion

* This we shall see hereafter (see Ethics).

in the respect of right; not in the same way in the respect of beauty. For example; I love others. That is an emotion. In that emotion is a conscious right. Again, I love that right. That is another emotion. Like blue upon the sky, right, whatever that consciously is, is seen to be upon this also. And now, the kindred ambiguities. Right is either the conscious nature of the good emotion, or else the conscious nature of the good emotion transferred as mere dictionary-work to an emotion looked at, or, thirdly, the quality of the emotion, or its imagined power, to awaken the sense of right, or breed the conception of it in the mind. These are mere differences of meaning. If we had more words, we could have a word for each of them. In either case there can be no Intuitive Belief. The first right is a consciousness, as much so as of blue or beauty. The second right is objectwise, but the same precisely as the other. The third right is the mere power to produce the others, viz. the fact about the emotion that it does produce a sense of right, as the lily does the emotion of the beautiful. We must wade through the dictionary, therefore, before we can reach the high ground, that right, like beauty, is of the contents of consciousness.

II. That Intuitive Belief is not old-fashioned intuition, will help amazingly in the inquiry, what Intuitive Belief really is. Old-fashioned intuition lays hold of beauty. It looks directly into it, as a matter of consciousness. It reveals it just as it is. It becomes aware of all of it just as it stands. For beauty is a certain tang of sense, like flavor of Johannisberg grapes, and there is nothing that can see it but intuition, and it sees it consciously, and sees the whole of it. But now take Causality. It is so different from beauty that Sir

William Hamilton could say (we think mistakenly)—"It is now universally admitted that we have no perception of the connection of cause and effect in the external world." *Lectures* (Am. Ed.) *p.* 541. Intuitive Beliefs lay hold of cause. See then the distinct difference between Intuitive Beliefs, and what we mean by old-fashioned intuition. Let me give other cases. Intuitive Beliefs lay hold of substance. They declare that qualities require substance. And this now will give us a fine opportunity to show what these credences most definitely are. Given qualities, which I most directly inspect; given, for example, red and hardness—of which I am directly conscious, and the mind has a believing faculty, by which it posits substance; though, as Sir William would declare, we have no immediate perception of substance in itself. Let us make this very clear. Given motion or sound, the sense of these things is directly conscious. It is therefore what we call an old-fashioned intuition. But the cause of these things we are not conscious of. We only assert it. We are conscious only of the assertion. The belief in this cause is an assertion in the reason. Such is the doctrine. We are born into this world with this appanage of thought. Given any experience of effect, we opine a cause. And we do so necessarily and by force of an original intuition, which believes that a cause has sway.

But we must be careful of our specifyings:—In the first place, men are not agreed as to these original truths. Their categories are endless. I have never seen two that were the same in every particular. In the second place, the Belief itself is pictured differently. I cannot define it, because Hamilton, for example, would denounce me as positively unjust. There has been a flux since the days of Kant. So that Reid and

Reid's commentator have been opposite in belief. This contrariety is indicative of mistake. And Philosophy may well come in like a mother upon two quarrelling girls, and snatch the doll from both of them. The account of Sir William Hamilton that cause is from an inability to think the opposite, and the account of Thomas Reid that cause is a square-faced original and positive belief, are so plain-facedly quite different, that it requires a good-natured polemic to unite them doctrinally.

We have, therefore, rather sketched the doctrine by example.

But we do insist most positively upon a third point. There has been a shuffle in the game. Eluding even first-class philosophers, a fusion has occurred of these so called intuitions with other positive intuitions, but which are of a far different class. It is like the sale of a watch on Pearl Street. The watch is really gold, and is of an uncommon value, and is sold for a song; but the buyer never gets it; for when it is the time that it should be delivered, there is a shuffle with something else.

We cannot move a step without making this clear.

That two and two are four is obvious, and we are born to believe it. That things that are equal to the same thing are equal to each other; that the whole is greater than its part; that it is impossible for a thing to be and not to be,—is intuitive enough. Call it what you please, a man had better be dead than not have some faculty to tell him such things as these. So the Regulative Faculty of Hamilton, and the *Vernunft* of Kant, and the necessity-belief of Leibnitz, things seriously different, and yet, as we have seen, claiming to be the same thing, have at least been the same thing in this, that they have swept into the same indiscriminated heap two entirely different classes of affirmation.

That the whole is greater than its part is one thing. That every change must have a cause is a very different thing. These two things are metaphysical antipodes. And yet the two have been swept into the one basket. I know not that any one has detected it. This undetected introspective legerdemain has had unspeakable results. The one sort of notion is necessary. We are forced to have it. It is, therefore, universal. And seeming to be born with a power to see such things, some native-born faculty seems to be confessed. If any one seems to hesitate about cause, some other fish in the basket is brought up, and some such truth as that it is impossible for the same thing to be and not to be is made to knock down opposition, if experience is pleaded as sufficient for that other asseveration.

The thing is a shuffle.

The remedy is to upset the basket.

Our right is to sort those fish out.

Here are two perfectly distinct classes.

One is of the sort,—It is impossible for the same thing to be and not to be. The other is of the sort,—that every change must have a cause.

ONE IS A TRUISM. That is now the solution. That the whole is greater than a part means that it is the whole. That things that are equal to the same thing are equal, means simply that they are equal. The thing is chop-logic. There is no aggression in the thought, and therefore of course a man is born to see it. But the truth that a change must have a cause is different. It is aggressive. This ought to have been the intuition aimed at. That those others are Intuitive Beliefs so-called, I cannot deny. That they are not included by Hamilton, I cannot assever. They are unquestionably. I can only say,—They ought not to be. And whether they ought or not, we at least shall treat them separately. One sort are truisms, and therefore are not Intuitive Beliefs, but simple consciousnesses. The other sort are discovered facts, heaven-wide from the first, and really the field on which the Kantian battle will have to be arrayed.

III. The second point, therefore, viz. What are Intuitive Beliefs? prepares us aptly for the third point, viz. What are the proofs of them? 1. And first we are told that we have this regulative vision, because we are conscious of its exercise. And here at once we must make a distinction. I know that I am conscious of the vision that two and two are four, and that an apple occupies space, and that perceiving occupies time. I know, therefore, that I cognize space and time. I know that the apple is extended, and I know that the extended apple is nothing more than the apple occupying space, and that the continuous perception is nothing more than the perception occupying time. Space and time, therefore, are consciousnesses. Moreover they are not beings: they are not entities; so that in existence they are nothing; they are mere abstractions, and, therefore, conscious thoughts, and, as applied to objects, conscious facts. Space is no more an essence by itself than extension is; or time, than continuousness is; and that they are infinite, means only what may be said of any consciousness; for sound and taste and angularity and tint and sphericity and surface may be made various in infinite ways, and endure through infinite dates, and be abstracted from for infinite varieties of idea. Whether we can conceive the infinite is mere child's talk. The peasant-man might scout it, if he merely had nerve to think. Infinitude is a mere made up idea. And having put it beyond conception by its very terms, viz. as devoid of boundary, half the questions that are built upon it are the mere dazing of the mind, as when we chafe and rub our eyes, and then amuse ourselves with the confusion of their first artificially palsied vision.

This obvious class are undoubted intuitions. And so of others that we mentioned before. That the whole is greater than its parts; that whatever is, is; or, set down with mere verbal variety, that it is impossible for the same thing to be and not to be; and an infinite horde of just such tautological expressions,—are undoubtedly Intuitive Beliefs; and that, because we are conscious of it. So that unquestionably this first proof does apply to these truistic expressions. But then we mention that fact simply to get rid of it. These beliefs are conscious simply because they are consciousnesses. And they are consciousnesses all through. They are not beliefs as the Kantians intend. They are not the mind projecting itself *ex se* by the force of an original belief, but merely the mind turning round upon a hinge, or rather exhibiting its consciousnesses when they are merely assertatory of themselves.

The force of the first proof, therefore, we only dignify with treatment when it applies to the second class,—truths that are really aggressive; and here it is stoutly pressed, encouraged though I feel sure by the confusion of this class with the other. 'Quality requires substance.' This is a specimen of the more genuine class. This the Kantian calls an Intuitive Belief. Let us state another. 'Change implies cause.'

This also asserts something. Now, says the Kantian,—Cause is not a consciousness, and I am not directly conscious of the cause itself; but I believe its existence. And the same of substance. I am born with a faculty such that, on experience of effects, I assert both cause and substance. And the first proof is, that I am conscious I do. This the first proof. And we lay it away in its distinctness for future refutation.

2. The second proof professes to be different.

Consciousness, these new philosophers declare, is an evanescent vision. It is not granite. It is not God. If therefore I am conscious only of my consciousness, and if now it is distinctly declared that consciousness fills all our thinking, and if this further is so much the case that consciousness is conscious only of itself, how prythee does it get beyond it?

3. This might seem to vary in a third proof. There is a cosmos: is there not? That question these philosophers may most rightfully press. If there be a cosmos, might we not have a need to know it?—to know God, if there be one? nay, to know self? Here the advantage seems to be enormous. If there be a universe, is it not better that I should believe it? The last argument was,—Do I not believe it? This argument is, Do I not imperatively need to? And now the whole presses,—How can I believe in anything, if it be cosmos, if it be actual existence, if it be abiding rock, or if it be Eternal Spirit, if it be demonstrable that my knowledges are cut down to what is consciousness, and I have no power *per saltum* to lay hold of being?

It is on this rock that the intuitionist scoffs at his empirical opponent. All seems a truism. Thinking is thinking and being is being. It seems as easy to make one out of the other as Cheops out of soap-bubbles. And it makes men arrogant. How can they be thought insulting if they refuse to argue? If we have built a high fence, and made the absurdity the more distinct, stating, till men have no power to restate it, that consciousness is everything that is in the current, and then following into the very region of relief, and cutting off all possibility of it by saying that consciousness can only be conscious when it is conscious of itself, we seem to have written our own fate, and to have announced that unless Cheops be consciousness we may stand and look at it and there may no pyramid exist.

4. Then a fourth proof, the argument of Leibnitz. Suppose I could see cause. Suppose Hamilton were wrong (Lectures p. 545), and it were not "universally [to be] admitted that we have no perception of the connection of cause and effect," we are now to climb to the very topmost argument as all these Kantian Intuitionists profess. Suppose it were admitted that we were even conscious of causality. The great invention of Leibnitz, so these men declare, is what they call the argument from necessity. It is the prince-dictum of modern times. It amounts to this,—that if we had seen substance, and been conscious of cause, if there were no difficulty in *foro conscientiæ*, but we had looked them to the bottom, still there is a *need* of them that the mere sight of them could never give; there is a ὅτι which quite transcends the simple ὄν; so that had we seen cause a thousand times, an averment would be missing that every change is bound to have one.

5. And now, one more formula of proof. This averment, we are taught, is Intuitive Belief. And another view is the doctrine of universals.

I see red. I see blue. I see both a myriad of times. Each time I see them something asserts gross particles behind them. That something is Intuitive Belief. And yet there is still another ground for saying so: at least so it is pretended; and that is the doctrine of universals. If I could see them without such a faculty, I would still need it in the gross, for there is something that asserts that the gross particles must be always present. I might see them a thousand times, and yet that experientially would not decree them universal. I see a sunrise a thousand times, and thereanent make no prediction that it will be always. But I see the red and blue a thousand times, and immediately assever, that universally the red and the blue will ever more require the presence of substance.

Hence, therefore, fifthly, there must be Intuitive Beliefs.

## CHAPTER XVI.

### NO SUCH THING AS INTUITIVE BELIEFS, SO-CALLED.

I. Now, the first thing we do with all these arguments is to pronounce them the same.

The first, viz. that we are conscious of Intuitive Beliefs, is the same precisely as the second. The second is, that we have arrived at the belief of being, and could not have done so without these intuitive cognitions. But that we are conscious of Intuitive Beliefs, and conscious of thoughts that could not have been obtained without them, mean precisely the same thing. That I am conscious of Intuitive Beliefs means that I believe, for example, in cause and substance. That I believe in cause and substance, and therefore must have just such beliefs, means in the

Kantian dialect simply that I am conscious of them. If any one doubts that this is so, let him try to put a knife-blade of difference between these two proofs after he has carefully studied them. Again *if there be* an external world, the *saltus* from the within to the without must be made by just such a faculty. But where is the force of this third proof? Simply an invincible belief. I believe that there is an external world, and therefore am conscious of such a belief. So Leibnitz's proof: a cause is necessary: there is an element of necessity in these Intuitive Beliefs. This is the fourth proof. But what does that amount to? This,—that I consciously believe so. But that was stated in the first. That I consciously believe there must be causality includes the second proof,—that I know causality, and the third proof,—that there notoriously is causality, and the fourth proof,—that there must be causality, viz. that it is consciously necessary, and now also the fifth proof, viz. that it is universal; the Intuitive Belief that the existence of a cause is necessary being identical in its very nature with the conviction that its necessity must be universal.

The proofs of Kantianism, therefore, are all a unit.

II. But so, in the second place, are the refutations.

I am to be taught that I know the *ego* by an Intuitive Faculty.

Or, keeping out still among externals, I am to be taught that I know cause by an Intuitive Faculty. Now, WHAT DISTINCTLY IS IT THAT I KNOW? That is the crowbar that is to pull down the building. To know a thing I must know it. To believe a thing, even though that be the phrase under which I hide the indistinctness, I must know, to some measure at least, what it is that I believe in. This was the tremor that had reached Sir William. He had confessed boldly,—"We have no perception of the connection of cause and effect" (Lect. p. 541). Nevertheless he admits that "we cannot believe without some consciousness or knowledge of the object of the belief" (Logic, p. 385). Whereupon he does not go bravely and ask (what would explode his theory)—'How then can we believe the connection of cause and effect?' But he does say, and that toward the close of his career,—"Just here is one of the most difficult problems of which Metaphysics attempts the solution" (Logic, p. 385).

Still, let us complete the argument. To believe in cause I must know something of what cause is. You may say,—No; it transcends idea, and is in the region of mere conviction. But you forget. Conviction of what? This is the difficulty that pressed Sir William Hamilton. You forget that c-a-u-s-e is an English vocable. To believe in five characters is to believe incontinently nothing. We force the answer,—What is it you intuitively believe? And there are few cases where a system lies so naked to the lance. A theory grown reverend with age is really quite open to a child's undoing.

To believe, I must in some measure see. The measure that I see is the measure of my practical conviction. Tell me how I see, and I will tell you how I get my practical belief. I cannot consciously believe till I in some measure consciously know. Now I may stammer in the genesis of this last, but no matter; I must wait for it. The thought must come up before I can believe about it; and when it has come up, I no longer need a Regulative Faith, but I get my belief precisely where I get my knowledge.

III. Nor will it weaken my point the least if I go through the five proofs, and diffuse my argumentation through every one of them.

1. It is said in the first place that I am conscious of Intuitive Beliefs. What does that mean? Does it mean that I am conscious of a Regulative Faculty? Hardly. It means that I am conscious of an exercise that points to the possession of such an original gift. What is that exercise? The exercise of believing is, of course, beyond all manner of question, simple belief. Now, as we showed, consciousness never gets beyond the contents of consciousness. What I intuitively know is sheerly the sum of the soul's perceiving. But there has always been an attempt like this,—viz. to *project* the consciousness; to confess what seems to be plain, that we are conscious only that we are conscious, but that one of our conscious perceivings is, that we look beyond our consciousness, and that we see things, or, to take shelter in a fog, that we believe things, that are beyond the contents of our consciousness: that this is the very thing we are conscious of. But now, like the plunger of a pump, the inquiry eternally follows, What is that we believe in? Sir William Hamilton confesses everything. "We can[not] be conscious of an act without being conscious of the object to which that act is relative" (Lect. xii. p. 147). But as Kantians differ, and bewilderedly refuse to follow any one leader, we will urge what all agree in in the second proof. They are forced to admit an object; and it is some knowledge of the object that is the ground for their belief under the second argumentation.

2. Now, what is that object?

The actualness with which I believe in the external

world is the ground for that scoff,—How can I build Cheops with soap-bubbles? Consciousness being an evanescent dream, how, if I know no more than consciousness, can I transmute that into granite? Of course I have a right to ask, What is granite? It is a difficulty that the *vernunft* men will have to meet. How idle to triumph over me, and say, I have dropped out the very universe, and, when I turn to be taught, find no universe; for undoubtedly Hamilton is right, that to be conscious that I believe I must be conscious of the object of the belief, so far at least as to have some idea.

3. And to make that plainer yet, let us go to the still grosser attitude of proof. There *is* a universe, is there not? Now, no matter for the belief. The object of these men is to press the issue of faith or scepticism. Let us not bother about beliefs. Such is their position. Is there not a *cosmos?* If there is, everything is manifest; for consciousness is not being; and to get intimations of the without, out of consciousness which is the within, involves the very *saltus* of Intuitive Beliefs.

So *cosmos*,—what is it? We have seen that names take in qualities. A chair takes in yellowness. A stove takes in blackness and rotund dinginess and shape. I mean that the genesis of thought has carried into nouns the properties under which the things discovered themselves.

So, of self. It has absorbed consciousness. This, which is but of the usage, nevertheless clears the metaphysic; for when I speak of knowing *cosmos*, I mean a thousand qualities in addition to the *ens*, whatever that quiddity may be. When, therefore, I speak of knowing *cosmos*, let it be remembered first of all, that

I am conscious of those myriad traits which the Dictionary has actually engulphed in the names of being.

Of the quiddity which is really in dispute this may be said, that it would be an amazing comfort if we *could* philosophize it under some mere believing. Men do such things. Lecturers in many a school relegate what they do not understand to some "law of nature." And we plead this as a positive objection. There was *too much* need for this doctrine. The mortar seems to have gone in because there lacked a stone. If the ghost could have risen unbidden, instead of in the creak and shuffle of the scenes, it would have inspired more faith. As it is, it is the very necessity of the belief, though in a sense grosser than that pleaded by Leibnitz, that becomes *prima facie* an occasion of misgiving.

That apart, however.

The paring down to the very quiddity itself, helps us; for it clears the question,—What is it that you distinctly believe? If I believe so consciously in matter as to make it atheism to deny the faculty, of course I must live up to so much boldness, and be able to show my neighbors what it is that I so consciously believe.

You may say, I do not know the *ding an sich*, but I know the *ding*. Well, what is the *ding?* In other words, we can force the Kantian to say what he believes. If he believes, he knows what he believes. If he does not know, he is trifling with us. If he knows what he believes, how did he find it out? Let him set that into the light, and there will be no need of a doctrine of original convictions.

4. But rallying to another point, he says,—what if he did know, that would not compass the doctrine of *Leibnitzian necessity*. He has in fact abnegated this.

For if he refuses to tell what he believes, its necessity or non-necessity are not a question. Still let us do all we can. Let us call the unknown quiddity, x. Now he says, if I had seen x a thousand times, that would not pronounce it necessary. This is the celebrated doctrine. If I had seen a sun-rise a thousand times, that would not reach the Leibnitzian affirmance, for it does not grow of repetition. But if I see an effect once, *presto* I aver a cause. Here is the triumph. I see the heavens blue from infancy to age; but if I woke up to-morrow, and saw them green, I could not complain. They are alike experiences. But cause,—that is a different matter. And so of substance. Suppose I could see substance, and it was decked with qualities, that would not make it necessary. Were it seven times a day, and seven times a day more, nay seventy times a minute, it would not begin to become necessary to thought. Where is the difference, therefore,—between a sun-rise, which I have seen a myriad of times, and a change which I may have seen never, and which yet, if I hear of it but once, I pronounce determinately to require causation? Where is the difference?

Why just nowhere. That is my answer.

And now it must vie in force with the single argument to which we before alluded.

Let us look at that.

The argument to which we before alluded was, We have none of these Intuitive Beliefs because they give us no means of cognizing their objects. Then, if we have no means of cognizing their objects, *a fortiori* have we none of cognizing the necessity of their objects; and this will appear on independent trial.

Let it be understood, we utterly deny any Leibnitzian necessity. If I see Orion a million of times, I do not say, Orion must necessarily have his belt; for I may wake up at midnight, and the belt may be no longer in the heavens. This therefore with most people is no Leibnitzian belief. But so it is in respect to effects. If I had seen an effect no oftener than I had seen Orion, my conviction would be the same. Effect is a mere experience. The thought that it looks for a cause by a congenital belief, is an absurd and impossible figment. It looks for a cause by every imaginable experience. And if any one says, Experience never can be total, I answer, Nor is the conviction. I deny that a jet of being is unthinkable. That bread should suddenly start up; that a loaf should spring upon my table; that rocks should rise upon my field,—are not things that my mind has visions about one way or the other. It has a mighty experience that such things cannot happen; but sheerly that they cannot, by the force of any native power to know,—I deny that there is any such consciousness. If any one presses the fact, it must be *discrimen simplex* between his mind and me. I have no such consciousness. In fact, to have consciousnesses they must be conscious facts. And to have facts, they must be conscious pictures in my experience.

But, to carry the war into Africa; how do you dispose of God? Is not He an effect? You say, No; an effect is that which is caused. O, then, I grant the truth of your proposition. Everything that is caused is caused; that of course. But if in effects we can include the greatest of all existences, viz. the Almighty, then of two things one; either the mind is a nice theological sense fixing God in His niche by an innate detection of His history; taking the most complex of all results, viz. the detection of such a Power, and finding the mind prepared for it by unexampled and immediate exceptions, or else God Himself and all His creatures are just matters of experience, and the laws of one and the laws of the other rise upon us just as they do rise, simply as a fact both revealed and experienced.

But says one, provoked by such folly, is there no necessary truth? And how does man ever discover it? Take the case that two and two make four, can experience teach it? Things that are equal to the same thing are equal to each other? Suppose we had seen that since we were born, would that be needful, or would that be competent, to explain it or to show it to be necessary? And how absurd, therefore, this empirical conceit, when all men in all ages have seen deeper than their sight, and more than the mere pictures of their phenomenal experience.

Now, here is a mixture to which we have already alluded. Philosophy has played false, and by a fresh shuffle has thrown in a new trick of conscious appearances.

They are not experiences. They are not the other thing. They are not one thing or the other as to having any philosophic pith or any bearing whatever upon the things at issue. They are mere truisms. And the slight is, to take things, of course intuitive, but which mean no more than blue is blue, or than joy is pleasant, and, because they are intuitive, to huddle them in incontinently among these other propositions. That the whole is greater than its part, means nothing more than that it is what it is. And to make that tally with every effect having a cause, is to bring live ducks down from the heavens by the plain wooden things that we throw as a decoy into the water.

The proposition, Things that are equal to the same thing are equal to each other, means simply that they are equal to the same thing, or simply that they are equal.

So that we might formally announce that the truths said to be original are of two classes, one simply of experience, such as that every effect must have a cause, and the other simply identical, as that black is not white, or that it is impossible for the same thing to be and not to be. Unquestionably these quite identical things require an original gift; but it is the same gift that it requires to see green to be green, or to see round to be not square, viz. the gift that it requires originally to see green or round.

4. The fourth argument,—that experience could never decide upon *universals*, is still easier to dispose of:—Neither could an original belief. In fact this mark of universality is mere rubbish after Leibnitz introduced the doctrine of necessity. The mark of universality is not one that men dream of contemplating in itself. The plea is: necessary, and therefore universal. All necessary truth is universal because it is necessary. All universal truth is necessary because it is necessary. Necessity, therefore, is all the mark. And universality, that is, universality in time, or universality in space, is not a thing that the mind can compass in itself, but can only dream of as inferred from its necessity. Necessity, therefore, is the only mark of original truths.

Now, distinctly, we admit necessity in the instance of two and two are four, and John and Robert are not Jim; and therefore we admit these truths to be universal. We profess to believe, and that originally, that it will always come out that way. For, though we have not seen all the Jims and all the Roberts, yet there is a necessity for our belief, and that simply on the ground that Jim is Jim, and Robert Bob. But that I have an innate belief that cause is necessary, and an innate belief that substance is necessary, and an innate incompetence to imagine a rock or a loaf as possessed of neither; that my mind originally evicts all possibility of phenomena without substance, and all possibility of a rock without origin just looming into space, are dogmas that we utterly deny. The mind has no rock and no loaf as an understood phenomenon at any rate. And when Sir William Hamilton perfectly revolutionizes the whole, and says our original belief is not an old fashioned thought of cause, but some Hamiltonian one that he would substitute, he shows how arbitrary is the whole conception. The mind, according to him, has an original belief in the sameness of the sum of being! that there goes out of the cause just as much as is lodged in the effect! and a whole parcel of other aphorisms, which are just as much true of the mind as that it is born with an original conviction of the proper length and breadth and thickness of a brick, or that it was born with an original norm as to whether there were nut-galls in the hand-writing upon the wall, or as to whether there were carbon in the angels at Joseph's tomb.

All this about necessity is absurd; and the way its advocates vary when they come to the categories of belief, shows that it is an unsound induction. Cause, like blue or green, is a thing that we have merely observed. If all things were blue, there are men that would enter it among the elements of thought. And if, as in the instance of cause, it could be predicated of the spiritual world, there would be men to argue that the creation required blue, or, perhaps, the Almighty required blue, and that we were born with that elemental belief.

For though I hold that no event, other than the continued existence of God, ever did happen without an adequate cause, I hold so from no native belief (particularly, as my very thought of cause is patched and imperfect and variously put together), but from an absolutely entire experience, which has had positively no exception; and from what I have *known* of cause; and from what I have *seen* of the requirements of its nature. In stating this in the next chapter we shall complete our adverse argument.

## CHAPTER XVII.

### THE DOCTRINE OF INTUITIVE BELIEFS NOT NECESSARY FOR PURPOSES OF EXPLANATION.

I. IF we go forward into a system of Ontology (Book III.) which shows distinctly how the idea of being could originate, this, if it say nothing of Intuitive Beliefs, must explode them better than any other argument. We might omit this chapter, therefore, and trust for its results to the whole that is to follow.

II. Again; the argument behind us! If the "Beliefs" we are instructed to imagine are not efficient, in that case too they are not necessary. The excursive leap, the *saltus* from the within to the without, may be ever so much vital, still if the Regulative Faculty will not make it, it is not the faculty that is needed. Here, therefore, we might pause also. A man's leg might have to be cut off; but if a knife is without an edge, that knife at least is not necessary. This chapter, therefore, is really superfluous, if we are punctual and complete in the rest of the argumentation.

III. But error is impatient. It settles itself in long dynasties. If error is prescriptive; if it has held the best minds of the world; if it has struck its roots into letters, and, what is more than that, if it has got itself ennobled as one with the religions of men, we must not wait for the leisure of our demonstration. The waters may burst a pipe, which, if they would wait, might be sufficient to carry them off. We must reply to the first gusts of displeasure. And here are two of them,—first that it is imprudent to cry, Nay, to some power which the world has certainly found to carry us from the phenomenal to the real; and, second, most especially impudent, when, not only as fact, but as demonstration, we have not dreamed of any knowledge of the real from what is phenomenal alone.

Let us look at this.

1. The world is certainly carried from the phenomenal to the real. There is that much of preascertained argument. Now grant, it may be said, that Intuitive Beliefs are hazily exhibited; still, there must be something. Consciousness cannot be being. Consciousness, if it only sees consciousness, cannot see being; and that it does see being having been the conviction of our race, there must be something (better or worse in its expounding) that answers to what we have been groping after in Intuitive Beliefs.

This is the first impatiency.

And the second is like it:—2. How do *you* arrive at the real? Demonstrably you cannot, empirically. Consciousness is one thing. Being is quite a different thing. Let us force admissions as we go. Consciousness is a perceptive gleam. Self is a real entity.

Unless there be a *gnosis* that projects me out of my thought, how can I conceive of self? Let us consider both impatient appeals to us under one.

(1) I may say, as belonging to the philology of the case, that all men conceive of substance as both phenomenal and real. A star, even to a philosopher, is partly a bright light. This we shall often advert to. As an actual fact (I speak now as apart from your philosphy) you conceive a chair as yellowness as well as scientific substance. In other words you put together all you know of it, and, phenomenal as well as real, the whole bundle you call a chair. And so of self. It is not the scientific *ens;* above all, it is not the Pantheistic Power: indeed, it is not the veritable I,—but it is the consciousness *and* that. Or rather, to utter the real philosophic fact, the veritable I, as we become entitled to call it by the usages of speech, is really, like the yellow chair, the *ens* AND its qualities. The philosopher (the very best) cannot fail to understand that his conscious meaning for the word *self* is a *painted* entity; that is, a ghostly entity with the consciousness annexed. So then, the very Lexicon entitling me to be conscious of myself, I must remember that carefully,—that I make the trajectory from the within to the without first of all by carrying the within into the without. This is not important philosophically: I mean, except in the way of correcting our mistakes. But it shows how error fastens. I really see being if yellow color is made a part of it. I really see self if consciousness, as with every thinker, sticks fast as an ingredient. But the chair aback of the yellow color, and the self as the *dunamis* of thought, metaphysically are something different; and when

these are in the case, Intuitive Beliefs are the things dispatched to go and fetch them.

Here comes the appeal,—'How do you empirical men dream of these hidden entities? You believe in God. Did you ever see Him? You believe in cause. Do you comprehend the whole of it? Nay, do you perceive the least of it? If "Intuitive Beliefs" are to be exploded just to the extent that we cannot conceive their subjects, how are any beliefs to flourish outside of actual perception?'

Now, there is the very point. The doctrine of this treatise is that no belief is to flourish outside of positive consciousness.

There is nothing consciously in the mind but Perception.

There is nothing intuitively known but Perceptions.

There is nothing consciously believed, except either first what I consciously introspect, and that I prefer to call knowledge, or secondly, as a part of this, so much of what I consciously introspect as is uncertain, and whose uncertainty can be measured in my consciousness, and thus become the object of probable knowledge, or what it would have been philosophical to call, simply belief.

The uncertainty of doves being alike has formerly been instanced. That they are alike is probable; that they are unlike is probable. The probability is present to my consciousness. So now (what is wider in its empirical range), the uncertainty that an order, if it is once observed, will be observed repeatedly. The uncertainty is empirical; the uncertainty is conscious. Here it is that the two theatres come together. It is the same with cause; only in the instance of cause the uncertainty is so diminished by the effect of repetition that the empiricism answers all the ends of positive and certain knowledge.

Carry this into theology.

I cannot see God, but I trace Him in an order hereafter to be explained. I cannot trace Him wholly, but so as I fail to trace, it is absurd to say that I believe. I believe more than I know, but I believe it nakedly in that shape, that there is something more than I know; and I believe that for conscious cause. I believe all the analogies I trace, just as I believe the ears and the head of the cow standing in the gate; * nay, I believe the ears and the head where I know it cannot be a cow, and that they are head and ears that I cannot entirely shape or conceive in my expectation. So I believe in God *like* a man, because I trace him through man's nature. I believe in God *different* from man, because I trace the need of difference. I believe in God higher and holier and something altogether beyond man, for that I have traced in the analogy of Nature.† And yet beyond the fact of this beyondness, that is, beyond the fact of more and wider, and this beyondness itself a dictum of solid orders already traced, I believe in nothing for which I have not an experienced reason. And, therefore, I believe in God no further nor other than in the way I know Him.

And so of Cause. I believe in Cause; and why? Because I have some idea of it? ‡ But do I believe no further? No. Except just in that shape: I do believe FURTHER. That is, from the very amplest tracings of analogy I believe there is *more* in cause than I am able to uncover. If you retort and say, Why not let

* See B. 2, chap. x.

† That is, as we shall see hereafter in the "Order of Perception."

‡ See Ontology

*us* have this ulterior belief? I say, For the want of grounds for it. I base this thought of more upon trains of consciousness. I *have* this thought of more. Whereas in your case you have absolutely nothing. By your own anterior reasoning you believe that of which you have no idea.

(2.) To come back to a more distinct answer to what has been asked, we take the leap to being by its ANALOGY with what we have seen in our consciousness. We will trace this in the Book that follows.

(3.) And, last of all, we add to it by the idea of MORE. This itself is a dictum of analogy. We have no intuitive belief that there are phenomena and more, but we have an experienced discovery that there are analogies traceable without; and that these trace still further analogies, and these further (dependent on the uniformity of nature), and these further still; till like the x. y. z. in an equation, the color fades out, and the result that our empiricism holds, is rather the counter for a thought, than any distinct self-conscious idea.

This, which we can now but faintly trace, will more distinctly appear under the head of Ontology.

# BOOK III.

# ONTOLOGY;

OR, THE

# SCIENCE OF PERCEPTION AS THE KNOWLEDGE OF BEING.

---

## CHAPTER I.

### ONTOLOGY UNDER THE LIGHT OF PSYCHOLOGY.

ONTOLOGY is the Science of Being. Being is either self or not-self. The doctrine of Psychology is, that there is nothing consciously in the mind but perception. If there is nothing consciously in the mind but perception, then self and not-self are perception, or they are not consciously in the mind.

If any one says, There is nothing consciously in our minds but perception, but perception of being is one of our conscious perceptions and therefore we are conscious of being, we turn to our former arguments. The whole of perception is consciousness, and the whole of consciousness is perception. If the whole of perception is consciousness, then we do not perceive being unless the self or the not-self is throughout a consciousness, because moreover on the other hand the whole of consciousness is perception, and if the whole of consciousness is perception, then we are not conscious of being, unless the whole of being is a mere perceiving.

Unless a part of being is perceiving, therefore, we are in no part conscious of either self or not-self.

## CHAPTER II.

### ONTOLOGY UNDER THE LIGHT OF LOGIC.

The doctrine of Logic is, that there is nothing intuitively known but perception. If there is nothing intuitively known but perception, then being is perception, or it is not intuitively known.

There are men who believe that we are conscious of all of self; for they imagine that self is a unit, and when I put my hand upon a stove, they believe that the feeling of warmth is a consciousness of myself as feeling it. But there are no men who believe that I am conscious of all of a not-self.

I see a peach.

No one dreams that I see all of the peach, or that I see all of any part of it. I do not see or hear or taste or smell or take-in any even phantom of the peach, except a mere superficies of color. Even that I can divide,—because the very word color means an impression upon my sense, or it means a pigment upon the peach. Now, press any one to his last results, and he will confess, that, if he is conscious of the peach, he is conscious only of a part of it, and that that part consists only of this light upon the sense, and hence that this light must be the peach or that it cannot be said to be intuitively known.

Now, is this light the peach?

I may have been delivering an answer which has surprised the pure metaphysician when I have said that it is.

Our first impulse was to say that it was not, or

rather to say, that the peach of the scholar, and above all, the peach of the Christian, was different from the peach of the peasant, and proved itself empirical by the different versions given at different stages of empirical development: for example, that the peach of the peasant was little more than qualities: and so of self,—that the self of the peasant was little more than consciousness: and then I meant to advance upon our learning: the scholar looking deeper; the theist far deeper still.

But when I came to consider, language asserted a far different signification. Language stood with the peasant.

The simple eye of a peasant-race looking out upon the world had seen being with its qualities. The idea had become conglomerate. They had seen self with its consciousness. They had never separated them. And I hardly mean that the peasant-man got the start in our vernacular: for the scholar finds it convenient also. Who ever dreams of substance *pure?* And this is no mean fact to bring out in our Ontology; for that which has the right of names has the correctness of aphoristic statement. If being includes qualities, and if, when I speak of self, I include consciousness, then of course, as a mere statement out of the Lexicon, I am conscious of self, just as far as the working name of self includes an ephemeral consciousness.

But then, see! This may be quite important to explain,—but it is not important to deep investigation. There is a scholar's self, and, moreover, deeper still, there is a Christian's self. *Ab extra,* there is a scholar's peach, and a Christian's or a theist's peach. I care not a particle whether they are ever called by the name; and I know they never are. The conscious self and the purple peach have long ago got possession of the words.

But there is a metaphysical reality, viz. the *ens* without the quality. It is either I or not-I. We might call it this name or that name. The name does not interfere with the reality. It is in self what is thought of as the unconscious mind. It is in matter what is philosophized about as substance. It is this which under the light of Logic is by clear demonstration not a consciousness; is, therefore, not perceived; is not intuitively known; being, therefore, not certainly demonstrated; but left to be inferred; and opening the whole field of empirical investigation.

## CHAPTER III.

### HOW COULD PERCEPTION BEGIN?

Perception could only begin by a sensation.* If any man thinks differently, let us proceed inductively and ask for that other perception than a sensation with which a man's perceiving might consciously begin.

Let us suppose Adam just born, or a man swept, as to his past thinking, by an entire oblivion; and let the statement be of some thought, other than a sensation, that might set on foot the conscious current. Suggest any. Nay, even dimly describe the mere ghost of an idea that could be obtained for such a beginning of perception.

* Sensation has not been treated of yet; but Metaphysics is an interlapping scheme; and a system cannot be promulged without anticipating some of its parts. Sensation is enough known popularly to meet our purpose; we have already been obliged to allude to it, in ways, however, requiring no assent except what all will give to its general idea.

The reply that might come back upon us would be, that we might be conscious of self. But think! how could we be conscious of self, without some conscious perception? And if any one promptly replies, Why, the conscious perception is a conscious perception of self, we beg to get him ready for dealing fairly with his position by certain plain reminders. The self that he is to suppose conscious *ab initio* of itself, is a self by agreement destitute of all sensation. It is not clothed in flesh; or, if clothed in flesh, it is to be destitute for the moment of all sense-consciousness. If the Adam is sitting on the ground, he is to be unconscious of any pressure by reason of weight, or of any glow of muscular sensibility. His flesh-sense all over him is to be for the moment dead. He can have no recurrent thoughts; for he has had, up to this first thought, of course, none to recur. Now give me some idea of self that a man may have before any sense or any desire or any perception other than of self itself has intervened to give the scaffold on which the idea of self may climb into his view.

Asking how angels manage is a mere *interpellatio difficultate*. Angels are not men. They may begin with sensations just as we do; getting them from matter without a body, as we do, with a body; moving matter without a body, as we move it with a body. I do not say that sensation is necessary to thought, but that God has chosen that ours shall begin with it, and that men, who are to sit as kings, shall have their dwelling in the dust, and, like a child's kite, are to be tied to to it as their only chance of rising consciously to something higher.

## CHAPTER IV.

### PERCEPTION NOT IN A CURRENT NO COGNITION OF BEING.

PERCEPTION not in a current is perception nakedly by itself. Perception in a current is so uniformly our experience of perceiving, that we asked the question how perception could begin, that we might look at one perception in its most naked and original isolation. But we may conceive of it in any way. All we ask is, the simplest possible perception.

And let us think of one. Let a man lie upon a tower, and get a glare of sky, with no sight of anything beside. Or, to make it simpler, take a probe, and touch an optic nerve, and give the idea of blue. Or let it be an odor, or, if you choose, a harp-note. All that we ask is that it be single. The body is to lie dead, and the mind is to have no recurrence from the past. The blue glare is to be all, and we are to treat it as it first spreads upon the sense. I am conscious in that gleam of no idea of being.

I cannot demonstrate what I say; for, when I have seized the thing, and held it up in this very delicate segregation, each man must judge for himself. But let any one who cannot submit, tell his own story, and say what consciously happens. Being is either self or not-self. Does the blue gleam give the idea of self? or does it give the idea of not-self? or does it give the idea of both? If it gives the idea of self, it gives two ideas. It gives the idea of self and one articulately different, viz. the blue gleam. Now, is it consciously anything but the blue vision? If it give the idea of not-self, then the glare upon the nerve and something else than the glare upon the nerve are distinctly to be made different. Can consciousness do this? Shut a man off from everything else, and give him just a simple color. Can that thrill upon the nerve be translated into anything but itself? And if being be considered as both self and not-self, can that instant of his fragrant sense divide itself, like a triple ring, into three ideas, and without any suggestion from the past to give shape or number to his consciousness, can that one smell have a threefold discrepance, or indeed any possible plurality whatever?

'Yes,' a man may say, 'it has plenty.' (For now mark the thing that misleads us.) 'When all our experience matures we see the tell-tale sense on both ideas. Take men consciously as they are, and let the odor come in the midst of our natural experience, and we see the odor on both self and not-self. How did it get there? Not troubling ourselves with an attempt at forced simplicity, our thinking, naturally, as it comes, shows the odor on both self and not-self. Now, if it gets there at all, why may we not suppose it to have been dual at the beginning? And why are we not forced to feel that the blueness, if it appear in both self and not-self now, did not originally appear so, as it is unchanged in its relation to our being?'

Now, this will help us very much toward our own particular discriminations.

Blueness appears in both self and not-self, because both are highly complex ideas, and sensation is found as a part of either. I did not say, sensation is not concerned in exhibiting being; but shall teach the contrary. I did not say, sensation in a current is not called being, and that inveterately; I have said the opposite. I only averred that the moment that the current starts, the gleam that begins is nakedly itself. It is not I; it is not Not-I. It is a whiff of fragrant delight, that is exhibitive not at all of either. And if it wear a tell-tale look as it rides afterward upon both, it only helps to show how the idea of being is made up. There is nothing intuitively known but perception. If, therefore, being is intuitively known, it must be perception. If it be in part intuitively known, that part must be consciously perception. If any part of it be not intuitively known, that part of it must be empirically discovered. This is the genesis of ontological thought. And, therefore, the riding on the idea, at the time, of a present consciousness like a blue vision only expounds the conscious reality. The blue gleam may come to be noticeable in both self and not-self; but that does not show that it would be the least of either, if, as an isolated gleam, it had just arisen.

'Nay!' the retort will come, 'you have missed the argument.' And there *is* a point in the case that we are now ready to consider. If there be possibilities in a single gleam to enable it to appear at any stage of the current in both self and not self, how can it be said that that one gleam has no duality in the beginning? If in its original rise it was not subjective and objective in its very nature as a gleam, how can it become so in any stage of our experience? The I and the Not-I are unquestionably two: how can the gleam, if indivisibly one, appear in both of them? Is not a sense of Ego and a sense objective to the sense a sense thus consciously inferred in the most isolated and original sensation?

Now our whole Book will be an answer to this in its successive chapters. Suffice it now that we challenge the boldest consciousness to see any duality in a gleam. We claim it as originally one. How it appears experimentally two it is fair to treat as a question when the subsequent consciousnesses come in. The bold denunciation of its doing so, as of necessity absurd, we may, however, roughly reply to by a case in mathematics. Is not a point one? With the utmost compass of invention can I impart to it any duality? Let it alone, and it is one individual unrevealing point. But I move it, and it traces a line. Or I let it alone and draw a line through it, and it appears in that line. Then I draw another line through it, and it appears in that. Does that make it originally two? Metaphysics can have but little light shed upon it by such mathematical conceits. But still, till we get on into the facts, it is enough to serve as a breakwater to hold back the attack. The point appears in the two lines, and the gleam appears in the two beings, for precisely similar reasons. If the point began the two lines, it would be in both because they start there, and if the gleam began the me and the not-me, it would be in both because they start in it. The sense that is consciously present is the starting gleam of both varieties of being.

## CHAPTER V.

### PERCEPTION NOT IN AN ORDERLY CURRENT NO COGNITION OF BEING.

IF perception not in a current could be no cognition of being, perception not in an orderly current could not be such a cognition.

Perception not in an orderly current is hard to think of, if that want of order is to be entire. A building that falls into ruin is not an indistinguishable heap. The maddest maniac has some harmony in his continual perceivings.

But let us suppose perception banished of all its

laws. Suppose it to be not Incessant: then an irruption of gleams would be no better than one single one, in which we saw there could be no idea of being. Suppose it not Transient, and also not Recurrent, and also not Associated, or, as we explain it, not marshalled forth by the law of the Strongest Emotion. Suppose it to be utter jungle, and that, with no continuous influences to chain my consciousnesses together: we defy any man to think of any other result in Ontology than would arise from one gleam.

If there be no leaping memory, or power to cognize the past, passed objects must be orderly mapped to see them in their position, and present objects must be orderly mapped. If, therefore, our original positions are correct, we are following what necessarily results when we say, that if one gleam can give us no ontological thought, ten million cannot, if they are breaking around us like sparks with no harmony and no memory together.

## CHAPTER VI.

### PERCEPTION IN A CURRENT OF BUT ONE ORDER NOT A COGNITION OF BEING.

If perception not in an orderly current can give no idea of being, perception in a current of but one order can never give it.

This may excite surprise.

We speak with reserve too, because we are imagining an impossibility.

Perception with but one order could never begin.

The order of perception traceable to the laws we have noticed could not begin except with another order, and the reason will be found to be, because perception cannot begin without a sensation.

It will be better for us, however, to explain at once these two orders. How one would be barren will appear more definitely when we come to describe the fecundity of the two. And that one cannot start by itself need not really interfere with the conviction that, if it could, it could not be prolific. The fecundity of ontological thought is due to the duality in our train of consciousness.

## CHAPTER VII.

### TWO ORDERS OF PERCEPTION.

I LOOK off from the top of an unsheltered tower and see nothing but a blue glare. We have used that place because it helps us to conceive of the simplest possible sensation.

But, really, one sensation is never by itself. The eye looks out from a body all full of nerve sense. If I were bound upon my back, and held fast to that single vision, other consciousnesses would break in. Sounds would steal up; or at least pressures upon every limb, or general sensations of my flesh, would rise to my thought, even if this had been the very beginning of my being.

Of course then the current would set out. Just as through all eternity, the first thought would fade, and the next would weave to it by the law of the Strongest Emotion. Now, a child can see that two harmonies would begin at once.

There would be but one current. Nothing through an eternal age would lie outside of that linear unity—I mean nothing conscious; but in that consciousness of mine would be immediately revealed two accreting harmonies. (1) Thought would go on, harmonious through the law of the Strongest Emotion, and yet (2) with pieces of harmony supplied otherwise, such as the harmony of Orion's belt, or such as the harmony between sensation and recurrence.

It matters not now to say how. We are seizing a fact. The fact is beyond all cavil, that the man with the azure glare starts from that simple point, and there accretes to it two orders, an order of the strongest emotion, and an order bred otherwise, that is an order forced upon his eye in ways not wholly by the laws of thinking.

These orders are immense,—the one for all time, and the other for all space and for all the reaches of possible recurrence.

And yet how simple they are!

A little baby wakes to the beginning of thought. A cherry hangs before him. There is a harp in the casement, and a fragrance from a vase of flowers. His little thought begins to travel. It instantly gathers two separable arrays. He looks at the cherry, and afterwards returns to it. He hears the harp, and afterwards hears it again. He smells the flowers, and has a sense of them a hundred times afterward. All is very dreamy yet, but two orders are waking in the single current. One is leading him from harp to cherry and from cherry to the fragrance of flowers, and regaling him by variegated thought, and feasting him by its calm continuance. The other is the order of the room. But we must be careful about such matured thought. What does the baby know about the order of the room? The order of the room is a high empirical discovery. The embryo of the order of the room is an order of analogy. If the baby saw novelties every time, the cherry and then a lamp and then a fire-fly and then the moon and then its mother, and moreover had no remembrance, but spun an eternal line with no analogies, the fact would be entirely different; but he sees the cherry and sees the cherry again; he hears the harp and hears it afterward; there is a room-full of analogies that recur. They are not the same things at all, but the like. The harp-note is not the same sound, but a totally different sound made by new undulations. And the cherry not the same light, but a totally different light that left the lamp after the other. Still, as the absolute reality with the child, he sees things LIKE. He would not know that fact but for the fact of recurrence; but, as we have already explained, sensation recurs. The new sight fits down upon an old recurrence. The child has not gotten over grasping at the moon; but in his eye (for it is too soon yet to speak of it as in the room,) he sees old faces. Analogy is his very earliest life. There are two orders, the order of emotional thought and the order of recurred analogy.

And so the man upon the tower. Suppose Lethe blotted out the past. Starting from a point if you please, viz. one blue gleam, two orders like two lines emerging from a point would begin at once to travel. They will never be young again, not even through all eternity; but will fill themselves with endless maze; one the order of continuous thought, and the other the order of observed analogy; * one the emotional line of remembered consciousness, and the other the emotional world of remembered like things; one not all inward, for it picks material from without, the other not all outward, for it blends its pictures with what is within;

* These are but proximate expressions; for the order of continuous thought is itself also, in another view, the order of observed analogy.

in fact neither inward and neither outward, but both in the line of thought; inwardness and outwardness being both conscious perceptions, but one order being the conscious succession of the current, and the other the conscious stability of like recurrences.

## CHAPTER VIII.

### ONE ORDER CONTINUOUS IN THE CURRENT, AND PRODUCED WHOLLY BY ITS LAWS.

One of the orders in the current of perception is unbroken in it (unless we consider sleep as breaking it), and is nothing more than the order of association, produced in ways that we have already considered. The law of the strongest emotion makes it really an order, choosing for it agreeable pictures, and making it deal in wholes not in fragments, and in groups not in monads, and in lines not in glimpses, and in logical results not in casualties of no distinguishable interest.

## CHAPTER IX.

### THE OTHER ORDER, IN THE CURRENT, BUT NOT CONTINUOUS IN IT, NOR PRODUCED WHOLLY BY ITS LAWS.

To show that there is an order in outward nature and an order in inward consciousness; that is, (to treat the case by an easy example) that there is an order in a spangled sky and an order in a current of perception, —this, which is really an advanced stage of dissertation, is not our object in these chapters.

Our object in these chapters is to show that in conscious knowledge, that is, in perception this moment as it may arise, I discern two orders, an order continuous in the current, and an order in the current but not continuous.

The order continuous in the current is what I may perceive by present sense, or any other present perception, with what I see redoubled upon it in the way of recurrence. For example, as a harp-note slides along (and it must not be forgotten that perception before it fades is consciously continuous) it not only weaves into our consciousness from some other thread of sight or sound that just preceded it, but what is more, it weaves into some other thread just as it fades. There is thus trodden a conscious track. Only a certain part is conscious at the time, but it may be any part. The thread in the region out of which recurrence comes is continuous. It may recur in great lengths. It may recur in myriads of ways, and, more than that, myriads of times; reduplicating myriads of instances of conviction. At last, no length of it can ever recur without reduplicating upon it former consciousnesses; till the mind becomes aware of a current; and this is what we mean by saying that there may be perception of continuous order at any conscious moment in the current.

But now, my sight of the starry sky brings back another starry sky, and lo! it fits itself upon it; and again, myriads of starry skies. I have shown how these years of harmony mat themselves like ferns in the coal measure. It looks as though coal were an original formation, just as though coal were an original gift. But Orion grows familiar in the sky, just as feelings grow familiar in the current, by repetition. At any rate (for we need not grow so explicit yet in all that we behold), the harmonious heavens can be lost to me, so that they are not continuous in the current. A sound can lead me off, or some pain that twitches at my knee; and when I come back again, the heavens spread upon my eye, and then another heaven, and another, stereoscoped all into one. And then so orderly becomes this train, which is not in the current, that it covers all space.

Just as the train continuous recurs from a single track, and may report from any part of it, till we become satisfied there is but one; so this train in-continuous grows into heaven and earth. It takes in all sense. It is found to be perfectly combined.

> "The mountains look on Marathon,
> And Marathon looks on the sea."

It blends all that is recurrent into one. And as each conscious length reports itself backward and forward through the current, so, each conscious breadth spreads over all that is seen, and finds no break in harmonious recurrences.

Let the reader however grant but this; we will take up other developments as they arise:—There is an order each conscious moment in the perceptions that we see, as concerns those that weave to them as they are passing off, and as concerns those that weave to them as they are passing on. There is an order, therefore, continuous in the current. And there is an order each conscious moment in the sensations that we have, not simply that the pictures remain in order while they are passing before our mind, but that they recur analogously, the old picture and the new picture fitting upon themselves, so that Orion's belt (to speak of what is a conscious spectacle) recurs as Orion's belt, and so that, if the belt recur, we may open our eyes and actually fit it upon a new sensation.

There is an order, therefore, not continuous.

## CHAPTER X.

### PERCEPTION IN ITS CONTINUOUS ORDER SELF TILL MORE IS ADDED TO IT.

NOW perception in its Continuous Order is Self until more is added to it.

It will be seen that we avoid saying that Self is nothing more than perception. We believe the contrary.

But as perception is not even Self in its first simple sensation, afterward it is all the Self we see till more is added to it.

We have described a certain track, lengths of which are kept in view by every recurrence. That track is Self, till other more complicated recurrences and analogies come in.

If you shudder at such a thought, remember that it is an error to supply others when the facts already noticed supply all the realities thus far in the case.

For example, I have a certain perception: it is bright, clear, and complex. It is conscious of all that it perceives. We have already seen that by itself it would give us no idea of Self. It is just as bright though as if we had had a thousand. Suppose we had had a thousand, but leave off for a moment ideas of Body and Will that we are afterward to consider. It would be seen weaving itself out of a perception past, and lingering for the company of the perception yet to come. This weaving goes on. It is pleasurable. The pleasure is in a continuous thread. When a pleasure fades from consciousness, it goes into the enormous store out of which are to travel back innumerable recurrences. They come back conscious of what they were.

They fit innumerably upon the new part of the thread. Now, knowing, as I do, that God could create me this moment, and yet supply me with all these analogous recurrences, *and, therefore, that the evidence of a past self is not intuitive to me like my present consciousness*, yet I see that this conscious inweaving of recurrences would connect the present with the past, and give the first idea, that I am to notice, of self as one form of being.

We see, too, how the present thought belongs to it. It is the great attaching centre. Past thoughts are gone, and are never to come back again. It is the present perception of which it is the law that it paints itself with the images of the past. It is the present perception that is our first self. And it is so rich and continuous in its feeling, because those recurrent images make it so. To see the invisible God, and to see the invisible self, are about equally impossible. And, therefore, that neat alphabet of recurrence is what sets itself in order, and is about the best news of self that perception at its start is instrinsically able to give us.

## CHAPTER XI.

### PERCEPTION IN AN ORDER NOT CONTINUOUS THE NOT-SELF TILL MORE IS ADDED TO IT.

As in one sense we are not conscious of Self, and in another sense are conscious of nothing else (because it takes all our consciousnesses to arrive at our idea of it), so we are conscious and not conscious of external being. We wish it to be distinctly understood that our evidences of Self and Not-self are precisely similar.

I look off from my high tower and see the broad

blue. We have long ago attempted to show that this could give no idea of Being. But the first consciousness, which is a mere light, and which, if it be all my consciousness, must be all of myself that I wot of in that first moment, soon moves upon its eternal journey. The blue gleam from my tower passes into a distant harp-note; that, into a pain in my leg. The current starts off upon its track, and it will not be long before the baby, even, will find out that the sights are to be depended on as alike. The red patch that she sees before her eyes, *stays;* and she has two ways of being conscious of it. The patch that she sees before her eyes, and that *I* know to be a cherry, does not flash and disappear, but hangs there through the moment of her consciousness. She thinks away from it to the ivory of your teeth, as you chuckle and laugh, and she thinks back to it again perpetually. She has the brightest recurrent thoughts. And without saddling ourselves with all the processes, her consciousnesses, which are thus early perfect, reveal to her by necessary steps those orders in themselves.

The order in the behavior of the cherry is all she knows of it step by step.

This order will be very slow; but hastening it, as it is all the same, the coldness and the redness and the roundness and the smoothness and the hardness and all about the cherry can become conscious. How such thoughts can become perfect, it need not matter. Generically they are all isogonous. They are things in consciousness, with one marvellous help, that they all agree, and that, from no order in the mind other than from that second order that is not continuous.

Not only does the cherry hang out till recurrence touches it again; but it is a consciousness where sense is harmonized. I see where I touch, and touch where I see, and smell and taste and even hear concordantly; and though these are most advanced modes of expression, yet they tell a tale of our very merest consciousness. The cherry is an assemblage of my sense, and that, meeting all in harmony, is a necessary part of that baby's actual perception.

Now, would it do nothing for her in the way of a Not-self? Strip off from her all "*Perception*" in that most baseless and modern sense. Conceive of her senses as fresh and bright, and that she sees as we do, only without experience. Know that she will have that track of recurrent consciousness which we have spoken of as the first order, and the ranges of heaven and earth harmonious and one before her; let me ask, Will she learn nothing? Shut off the idea of Intuitive Belief, and say, Will she not see things precisely as she does see them? Do we not know that she sees the cherry round and red? Do we not see all her other consciousnesses? And, as those consciousnesses are in strange harmony, is it too much to ask that where those harmonies are the harmonies of the Not-self in its appearance to men, that she consciously see them, and learn that much of exterior being?

If we can suppose that that baby can find out in the cherry all that is in the most perfect sensation, and hold on to her recurrent sights till other sides and other phenomena of the fruit have blended themselves all together, unquestionably she will have (by help of other lessons, too, that she is taking, in other visions) a harmonious cluster of sense, which she consciously sees; and that I aver is her first idea of being.

The track of continuous consciousness, therefore, initiating a knowledge of Self, is like the breadth of harmonies that are not continuous, initiating a knowledge of Not-self.

## CHAPTER XII.

### THE LAWS OF PERCEPTION, GIVING RISE TO THE CONTINUOUS ORDER, GIVE RISE TO THE IDEA OF BEING.

SUPPOSE there be such a thing as being, apart from actual perception, what a special instance of the power, wisdom, and goodness of God, to frame the Laws of Perception as the only possible occasion by which it could be traced!

Being must be a shadowy conception, or the finest minds would not have been so much at sea. No one can doubt the superior intellect of Berkeley. Now, if the ideas of being are so singularly plain and simple, why all this noise about them?

We have shown the nicest arrangement of Perceptions. No one can have read all that has been said about original laws without receiving at least a part of them. Now, with half of this strangely artificial system—Perception as Continuous—Perception as Fading—Perception as Recurrent—Perception as Associated, and that in interesting forms by the Law of the Strongest Emotion—if, with these singularly adapted laws, being sheds such a dim light upon the best minds that strive to comprehend it, how would it be if these laws did not exist?

Sensation would be but a passing flash; or make it Continuous, then it would be but a passing glare; or make it orderly, who would take note of the order? or make it Recurrent; unless the laws of perception were exactly what they are, there could not be built up those two orders of recurrences which the veriest enemy of our system must now admit must have something to do with discoveries beyond us.

## CHAPTER XIII.

### SENSATION.

THERE being nothing consciously in the mind but perceptions, and perceptions being endlessly different and multiplied, sensations are a certain class of perceptions, that are found to be connected with what we call the body. It would be useless, in studying the current, to study the nerves and organs by which these parts of it are produced. The nerves and organs do not show themselves, except empirically, in the constitution of the current. Neither need we tell all the history of what men have thought about sensation. Indeed it would be better to exclude all else but the current. There are certain perceptions in the current. They are very peculiar in their vividness. They are our only connection consciously with things around us. They are the only start conceivable of thought within us. And yet they are but five simple consciousnesses. A smell and a sound and a taste and a sensation of light, and then a corporeal feeling or nerve sense of some kind or other, are all the alphabet of this amazing and all-including revelation.

The splendor of philosophy here is that it is so conscious. A sound holds itself up before me till I hear exactly what I hear. A smell floats till I have discerned all of it. I am sure that the consciousness in the smell stands perfectly revealed. What my eyes take in is but parti-colored light. And what my flesh reports is what I am conscious of as felt. This, and nothing more, is all that is meant by my sensation.

If any one conceived that it was less material than this, he errs; and yet, it is not material at all. A sound is a pure perception. If an odor floats upon my sense, it is perceptibly a mental consciousness. Light is in the current; so is my zest for good eating. If there is anything that goes abroad in my sense, it has learned to do so afterward. The beauty of sensation is that it is so mental. Light is altogether lighted up. Its colors and its shapes and its surfaces are all revealed in it. And sensation is so thoroughly among our consciousnesses, that it is emotional like all the rest, and weighs and judges and compares, like any form of possible perception.

If any one therefore thinks sensation not intelligent, let me deal with him specially, as I take up each special sensation of the five.

## CHAPTER XIV.

### SMELL.

SMELL is nothing more than what I am conscious of in any one familiar instance of the sensation. How vain, therefore, to multiply words about it.

And yet a smell is so intelligent that it grades itself with the nicest discrepance. I never have more than the first generic scent, if I continue to use my nose for ten million of ages: but then, perhaps, all that time I never have two odors passing to my brain that do not report either in strength or flavor some sort of intelligible variation. The mind becomes aware of all these differences; but, as the mind is but the name for the empirically discovered self, the smell must be considered as intelligent, just as much as any other, isolated or gregarious, of our perceptions.

We have pleasure in it; and seek knowledge by it. We measure distances and detect objects by their smell. It harmonizes with the order not-continuous, that grows into that grand creation, the not-self. And though it is a simple odor, and never gets-by that nerve-state, it is a mighty helper, when it comes to be found perfectly at one, in carving out that mighty universe without, when it comes to be shaped of these endless harmonies.

## CHAPTER XV.

### TASTE.

We would not object if Touch, which is the fifth sense, were allowed to embody Taste, which we have here numbered as the second sense in the series.

Touch is a very slack-twisted generalization. Hunger and sexual delight,—in fact warmth, and different sorts of pain, keep but slender company with the usual results of touch.

But, for our purpose, it is all excellent; and Taste might go with them. Metaphysically there is the same great lesson. We are conscious of what is discernibly felt, and we are conscious of every part of it. We are intelligent in all the changes through it. And whatever is to be learned of what is consciously revealed, we learn of course, and we learn alike, in all the forms of actual sensation.

## CHAPTER XVI.

### HEARING.

Sound does not differ from Smell or Taste. It differs entirely from both, if we mean to consider the nature of the distinct sensation. It differs so much from either, that in the case of a deaf man it is impossible in its least conception. But in the relation it bears to thought, it bears itself identically like all. Light does not differ. I have upon my nerve a distinguishable odor. I am conscious of nothing beside. But I exclaim with confidence, that there is a dead carcass in the woods. If I am called to give my reason, I say, I smell it. Consciously I smell nothing but an odor. And while all will admit that the carrion, as the cause of it, is only an empirical belief, we refuse to be so easily persuaded as to either a sound or a vision.

I hear a horn away up in yon distant Alp. As a sound upon my ear we are slow to treat it as a smell upon my nostril. It seems to be up in the hills; and I point to it as the very seat of the sensation. And yet how impossible! The child would hear it at his pillow; just where he sees the moon. I am sure of the triumph of this fact, that noises are mere sensations; that what we learn of them as to place is as we learn of odor, a mere experience; that the Alp-boy in the hills is tracked like the nearness of the carrion; and though five million of sounds have been present to my sense since the beginning, they may be endlessly different, and beautifully arranged in their expression, yet they are eternally sounds; generically they are but one sensation; empirically they are the whole of speech, but actually they are the pelting of a nerve, which returns but one kind of perceivable impression on our consciousness.

## CHAPTER XVII.

### SIGHT.

We have been thus particular about Smell and Sound, because they introduce us in the happiest way to the facts of vision. Here, the odor in the nose and the sound on the ear are identical in mentalness with the light upon our vision. That peerless sense that reveals to us the starry heavens, is nothing more than a nerve-sense like the rest, dealing in its own easily discriminated sensation. The reek that is felt from the carrion is isogonous with the lights that are taken from the sky. Both are unitary, generically never to be different. I may see things for a thousand years, and my eye will have but a kaleidoscope of lights. If they are red and blue, so the smells are good or putrid. If they are broad or bright, so are the sounds shrill or constant. If they are beautiful and in graceful swells, so are the melodies. The neatness of this generical research is that it is so perfect; for sight upon my eye, and sound upon mine ear, and smell upon my nose, are incontestably alike, mere nerve-senses for a thousand years; and yet, so varied, and so delicate, and so conscious, that is, intelligent of themselves, and so harmonious, that is, reporting in one great system, in which they all agree, that though literally but light and odor, they combine into a frame which becomes the sum external at first of the not-self before our minds.

If any one points me out qualities that he calls Primary and Secondary, I admit them as having distinctive traits, but I ask him where is the flaw in these pictures of my consciousness? If he says, What I see in the light is there where I fix it, and much more plainly than what I smell in its odors, I do not hesitate a moment. Smelling a thing and seeing a thing are very distinct indeed in their exactness. One sense may be much more useful than another. But, come back to where we are flatly conscious. Smell a thousand years, will it be anything but a smell? and will it not be an act of perfect consciousness? So gaze for a myriad of years, will you get anything consciously but light? Will it not be an eye-surface like a bed-quilt patched over with colors? Do you not see the whole of it? And if you do, leave not me absurdly in an error. I see nothing all the time but light. Tell me what you see that can be more. I see it move. I see it square. I see it fade. I see it beautiful in figure. My vision is perfect in its sense. But it gives me nothing but light. And if I find out a universe of things by its colors, I do the same by the mere noises and smells that fall consentaneously with my vision.

I see a distant city; but the houses are out there, and the steeples are off far, only as the Alp horn is, because I have learned to translate. And all you tell me, that the eye actually places the city at the spot, I answer by remembering, so the ear does, so the nose does, in a much more imperfect way. The Alp horn sounds precisely where it is; and I can hardly persuade my ear that she has learned to do herself injustice by her use; that my hearing is not off yonder among the snows, but close at home; and that the eye and the ear have nothing more than one way and one place for their sensations.

## CHAPTER XVIII.

### TOUCH.

Touch does us so much good in many metaphysical ways that we might fear that a perception so versatile in its effects might fail to be traced to the same simplicity of sensation. But Touch, more than any other sense, is almost brutish in its plainness. What a child feels when it touches a cherry, it feels generically in everything.

Now I do not deny that Touch has immense advantages:—

1. It fits in so nobly with vision. I stand by a shelf, and look at a silver goblet. The sensation of sight is a mere consciousness of light in the goblet's shape on the hemisphere of vision. I touch the cup, and a harmony of fact is at once perceptible. I rap the cup and there is an agreement of sound. Taste and the other faculty of smell might be each arranged to bear a perceptible relation. But of all these harmonious facts the first is the most immediate. The eye and the finger meet at the same surface, and without staying to ask what language we shall use to describe this early agreement, the fact is conscious. The light upon my eye and the touch upon my nerve are a visible result, and that result may be as untutored as you please, it is obvious in both, that they stand related in some way harmoniously together.

2. So Touch has an immense advantage in respect to surface. The eye has but a narrow inlet. So has Taste. The nose and the ear and the palate and the optic nerve, all have a limited dwelling place. Touch revels over all the body.

3. Moreover, it has wonderful variety. It feels warm, and it feels hard, and it feels smooth, and it feels pain, and, what is more, a muscular stress that it will require care to represent as only feeling:

4. Because, next, Touch is connected with the empire of the will. I choose to smell, but the power with which I draw in the scent is a power of muscle, and reports itself to Touch before it reaches the pleasure of the odor. My Taste must be muscularly through touch. My sight, and above all my hearing, must be involuntary things, unless a motion, which is in the theatre of Touch, opens the eye, or moves the ear, into their theatre of pleasure. Touch, therefore, is an imperial sense, less magnificent than sight, but more singularly rich in its reports of Being.

## CHAPTER XIX.

### SENSATION AS IT CONTRIBUTES TO THE IDEA OF NOT-SELF.

THOUGH the Eye and the Ear and the other instruments of sense report consciously nothing but sensations, yet those sensations appear consciously in shapes, and those shapes marvellously agree together.

That silver urn comes upon my eye as a mere patch, the absolute sense being one of a mere surface. I have an eye-full of variegated lights, and this silver urn is simply one of them.

But then I have seen this urn before. The mind, in its recurrent power, is not like sense, but may deal in many surfaces. I have my vision all on one: and though sense is far brighter than my memory, yet it has to confine itself to its absolute plane. I see the urn, but, as an absolute sensation, only a color. But the mind, by its recurrent law, builds an urn upon that face. It saw the back of it last week, and the inside yesterday. Or, if it never saw that urn, it has seen a thousand. Or, if it never saw an urn, it has seen things just like it. It puts its recurrences together. Now, you would rather help me if you would deny one resource or two, for they crowd upon me till I cannot build conveniently. They crowd upon me in amazing order; and the back and the side and the bottom of an urn all come in in place. What, as an actual sensation, is but a patch of light, adds to itself recurrent parts of it.

Then my finger comes in. I touch the urn. Grant me my mere conscious sense. I smell it. I take my finger and wake it into sound. I take my tongue and it has a taste. Now limit these consciousnesses as much as you desire, there is an amazing harmony of sense, which does actually build itself fair and round.

Say, all this would not produce the urn. I grant it; and have a tale of much more. But it would produce something; and you may take the laboring pen and tell what that something is. We are conscious of nothing but sensations; and those sensations are nothing but colored lights, smells, tastes, sounds, and feelings. But those thoughts, though bald in sense, are very rich in recurrent combination. And all recurrent senses, consciously perceived, do give enough for an urn; for there is no discovered part of it that was not sometime visible.

Now this urn, thus made of images; thus built of harmonious sense, and lost sometimes to immediate consciousness,—comes finally to be identified at once. A spout will show it, or its topmost acorn. It breeds recurrence at a glance; and the mind delights in it as a whole by the law of the strongest emotion.

Now, if any man demands, Do you think this the whole of Not-self? I answer, No. I am yet to speak of Body, and I am yet to speak of Will. But I say, This is a conscious something. I go up to the urn and put both hands upon it. It is cold and hard. I tap it on the top. I smell it, and taste its surface. I gaze at it, and it is covered by my hands. I step back from it. It is an image in its place. I say, All these things are conscious: and if you will do me the favor to take out from them everything but sense (save only what may be recurrent), something will remain: now it is that something that I pronounce to be some thought of Not-Self.

## CHAPTER XX.

### SENSATION AS IT CONTRIBUTES TO THE IDEA OF SELF.

IF perception could not begin without Sensation, Self of course could not emerge; because, as we have seen, the mind could not become conscious without perception.

If perception could not begin without Sensation, Sensation must have an important rôle all the way through. Self, therefore, being revealed to us by a continuous orderly current, what Sense contributes to the current it contributes to our idea of Self.

## CHAPTER XXI.

### BODY.

IN the region of the Not-self lies a something which, curiously enough, is all mixed up with the absolute Ego. The Eye and the Ear and the Nose and the Tongue and the whole net-work of nervous tentacula are parts of what we call the Body. Bodies are unveiled through instruments that are parts of themselves.

Two things may be said of Body:—

1. First, that it is, like the urn, cognized by the nerve sense and completely in the same methods. I look upon the urn, and precisely with the same perceiving I look upon my body. It seems to me round and full, and I build it up with recurrent sights of it, just as I do the other. I strike the urn, and so I strike my body. Sound and smell and taste and tactual sensation can all be experienced upon this hulk of flesh, precisely as they can be experienced upon a lump of gold or upon the silver goblet. Let it be understood, therefore, that, if the body differs from the silver urn, it differs in the direction of plus, and that, quite consciously as respects sensation.

It belongs to the external world as distinctly as my raiment. But then it has another whole mass of facts, which have only to be *added* to those that belong to everything.

2. It is found that this something behaves double in respect to all my sense. The eye that looks out upon my leg finds itself carried about with it—nay, looks out on it from a position in the body. The nose not only smells my hand, and drinks the perfume on it as on a rose or on a bean, but is found in partnership with my hand, the smell itself finding its centre in my nostril. My tongue tastes my finger, and my finger feels my tongue, and both that instant in the current. The current seizes them in one. And the whole wilderness of Touch has this double action. I touch the urn, and it is simple. I touch my hand, and it is a double effect. It is the wakening of two sensations; and the sound and the smell and the taste and the

light and these two sensations and the whole crowd that can be packed into my present consciousness, are found to be blended into this:—that they are in one perception of the current, and in one accord in this thing called Body.

## CHAPTER XXII.

### BODY AS IT ADDS TO THE IDEA OF SELF.

NOW it can be imagined that in the infancy of thought Body could be supposed to constitute the Ego. And it does not involve the peril of that genesis of Self that I before considered.

Order in a continual current, with the power to have that order back in the way of recurrent threads of it, a path re-beating itself again, until a foot of it flashes back in glances of a mile, this is that loitering consciousness that we learn to speak of under the name of Self. But yet no mortal can fail to see, that that oneness of body which we feel to our very sole, helps the report of consciousness; and that a something (1) shaped to us like the urn, and then (2) knit to us by every sense, must be consciously united, first (1) as the urn is by single-handed sense, and second (2) in a double way, by what is equally our mere sensation.

This unity, therefore, helps our idea of Ego.

## CHAPTER XXIII.

### BODY AS IT ADDS TO THE IDEA OF NOT-SELF.

BUT in a still more striking way the sensations of Body unveil the external world.

1. They help the idea of *outness*, which has been so much talked of by philosophers.

Now, I do not mean the rude reality, that the body unveils the universe because it carries the senses. That of course. Nor do I mean, what is a more pertinent claim, that it carries us to the scene of our sensations. I do not mean that it opens the eye, and draws in the odor, and moves the tongue. I do not even delay to show its dexterity of feeling. All these things will be known of and thought of of course. I mean, that the mere sense that unveils a body, the mere sight that ranges from the eye, and the smell and the taste and the wide-spread tactual impressions, all of which have conscious sensations of position, sketch that body forth into a figured shape, like the urn or goblet; do it by usual sense like the urn or goblet; but do it over again by sense utterly unusual and different; that is, frame my body precisely as I would the urn, by sight and touch, but do it also, as I can frame no other thing, by double consciousnesses, not only the set by which I know the urn, but a set, just as consciously perceived, by which the smell feels itself at the nerve, and light at the optic threads, and the taste and the sound and the touch at each conscious point of the sensation, by which the whole feels itself in the current, and by which this whole shapes itself upon our material frame just as consciously and just as mechanically as the urn by my sensations. And I mean that when the body is thus set forth by nerve perceptions, the *outness* from it of other things is a mere sensation.

Why should a man admit angles and admit shapes as open to our consciousness? Why should he confess they are consciously before my eyes—an absolute sensation; and not admit that externality is just the same? Here is the leap, that has puzzled men so much, from the inward to the outward. But is not outwardness just as much a feature of our sense, as blueness, or pitch in sound?

The urn I noticed is either outside or inside my body. If it is outside, is that not consciously my sensation? And is not the interval between, like intervals of any sort, a strong reality of vision.

2. Again, the idea of body by its *unity* leads me to a more intelligible world outside.

The idea of unity is triumphant in the body. The harmonious nerves lap all round it, and bring intelligence of sense from every corner. Each square inch of sense reports; and, what is more, reports from every inch may come almost each instant. The body is unified in almost every consciousness.

Now, as the body besides all this is visible, also, like the urn, it is easy to see how the unity conscious in the body suggests unity in other objects. Color and sound and smell and taste and all tactual impression are themselves adequate *quoad* the urn to ideas *quoad hoc;* but recollect, we claim every atom of conscious perception. And accumulating everything as we go along, we say, that what simple sense begins, the body, as sensible, adds to and knits together. And carrying about this sensitive and harmoniously reported hulk, I claim all that it perceives. It is a great mass with harmoniously reported sensations; and I say that, consciously thus unified, it helps to the idea in objects that are spectacled around it.

3. Again, it has *inward* feelings. It feels all through as well as all over.

It is perhaps imprudent in me to attempt categories of comparison. I am much more zealous to hold clear one fact, that Being is piled up by our perceptions;

that it grows in all we wot of it by downright consciousness; that it is immensely heaped together by one perception and another; and that what our perceptions do not make of it out of all that is consciously combined, is not Being, that is, is not Self or Not-self, in any way that we can dream of or believe.

Sense actually carrying to us *inward* feelings, we just add those as we do the rest. The heart and the lungs and all the interior viscera report themselves. I feel all through what I call my person physically. Now, what I want confessed is, that these things, which are consciously perceived, give notions accordingly of other being. The urn and the body are both similarly perceived. The body is perceived also additionally, and in a way dissimilarly to the urn. This way gets noticed, and gives me feelings of substance which I attribute to the urn. And in the old Hindoo theology, and in the every-day experience of children, inside facts are attributed without, which are actually over-reasonings. The urn is supposed to feel. The clod is invested with *too much* of our inward life. The little hideous gods are preached of as only samples of this inward and universally existing sense. I mean, all matter is supposed to feel; and beyond all shadow of a doubt, *our* thoughts of matter are but slenderly right, even though we may have taken out of them a great deal of pantheistic prepossession.

Now, to repeat my idea, matter is just what we have sense to make it. I do not mean that it is not more: on the contrary we have actual sense for making it what we consciously perceive,—and that very thing—*more:* but beyond what we consciously perceive, including this very idea of *more*, matter as a *noumenon* is nothing but the sum of my perceivings;

and body in all its traits, and sense in all its outgivings, all the myriad differences of vision, and the rest, and all their harmonized recurrences, make up my ideas beyond me—beyondness itself being a mere reality of my working consciousness.

## CHAPTER XXIV.

### WILL, POWER, AND CAUSE.

WE have already exhibited Perception as resulting (in two conditions of its consciousness) in certain very imperial effects.

1. When it desires the stay of a thought; that is, when it is so strong in its emotion that the thought coming in by that law continues to be pleasant, and, as the effect of a whole experience, desires and expects and *sees fit*, as men philosophically express it, to continue in the mind, we call that the phenomenon of attention, and we have already established the fact that Will has but one other province that can possibly be divined.

2. That other province is muscular motion. Now this obedience of the muscle gives, in its shadowiest outline, the idea of Power. My thoughts go sailing along, and one of them with its peculiar emotion moves a muscle. It is in fact a thought to move that muscle, or, to speak less learnedly, a thought to do a thing which the infant as he kicked and fumbled learned would be done at certain thoughts of it by the mind. Able to say, therefore, what shall be done, the infant moves one step further in sense, and experiences Power, but Power only in its earlier gleam of desire as it determines motion.

Separate altogether from this is a nisus which is

conscious in our sense. And hastening at once to terms, I say, this nisus is a physical pressure. Let me be understood. I do not disown the sense that it is a nisus; but the nisus is not the sense. I teach barely two consciousnesses, one a desire, the other a pressure. The desire may be dismissed at once as already treated. The pressure is all that is left in this conscious sensation.

Now let us understand it. A timber lying on my leg exerts, as we are conscious, only a tactual impression. We call it pressure: but confine yourself to the simple thought. A finger touched upon your nose, or a feather wafted to your cheek, are not generically different from the timber in their touch sensations. Now articulately then you will understand the speech when I say, that the pressures bidden by the will are precisely of a piece with the squeeze that is felt from the timber.

Anatomically, I know there is a difference. But metaphysically, there are but two facts, a desire and decree and choice long ago put together in these chapters, and, secondly, a mere sensation.

If any one asks, Is there not a strain of some kind? I say, Yes, upon the muscle. If any one asks, Are we not conscious of it in our mind? I say, Yes, as a sensation. If any one asks, But is it not a sensation of a strain? I say, Yes; but, metaphysically considered, the strain is not generically different from a pressure.

Let me explain this now critically.

I have what we have combined into the complexity of Will. I have what follows as the swelling of my muscle. The first I am conscious of as Will. The second I am conscious of as a sensation. I do not doubt that interposed between the two there are physiological facts of nerve and cerebellum. That is not the question. We are talking of what we are conscious. Our study of the facts is entirely in the current. Now I say, after we have desired with the Will we only *feel* the pressure consequent.

If I could will to weigh down the timber, and, without a hand upon it, I could make it press at the direction of my desire (as perhaps angels do), I would imitate, generically considered, the feeling about the muscle. That is to say, There are present two consciousnesses, the consciousness of an imperial Will, and the consciousness of a sensational pressure, with no consciousness between, and no knowledge, reported to the sense, of nervous messages that may fly between them.

Now I clear off a great deal of doubt by one pertinent reminder,—that what may be generically the same, specifically may be very different. The pressure of the timber is one specific thing; the pressure under the muscle is multiform and diverse in its sense. For example; this cannon-ball! Here I am raising it in my hand. What do I experience? First of all a swelling pressure at the muscles. I need not picture it; for a man can strain his arm, and try it for himself; second, a leverage strain of a very peculiar sort, undoubtedly a cultivated idea when we speak of the lever of the arm, but a mere conscious one in its peculiar pressure; lastly, the mere timber over again, that is, weight and touch, or, in other words, the ball, as it is raised, touching and pressing in the fingers.

Besides, there is more than this; there is fatigue, like hunger, and a sense of effort uneasily submitted to as a form of bodily pain; and I do not for a moment question that other attributes might be added to the list. Touch is a badly generalized sensation. But all the discoveries that might be made whatever, would bow to the consciousness, that, when I lift the shot, the strain is all sensation. Outside of the dictum of the Will there is nothing that can be traced but what generically is like tactual impressions.

But though I have thus carefully enforced this generic sameness in the sense, I shall be able all the more usefully to employ the specific difference.

There is a strain upon the muscle which, though sensationally pressure, consciously is peculiar to itself, and in connection with the Will initiates our idea of Power.

As before, I only ask consciousnesses. They are rich beyond even our need.

I am conscious of the imperial desire. I am conscious of the immediate strain. I am conscious of ulterior results. The total; what is it? In your own language, it shall be, *usque hoc*, empirically my idea of Power. And if any one says, Consciously not so; for the nexus is the thing we want; and you have developed only an *order* not continuous in the current,—I say, One thing in the order is an idea of Power. It is not mere antecedence and consequence. The muscle's strain is a reality in sense. The will before it is an ancillary consciousness. The cannon ball that moves is the absolute result. And I say, these things together, peculiarly the first, give us in shadowy form an idea of Power.

I need hardly make a separate treatise on *Cause*. Philology employs the terms. Their difference is philologically great. Their employment is mechanically necessary. Nay, their theatre is but partially the same. But metaphysically we have explained them both.

That every effect must have a cause means simply that this ball-raising is a universal experience. If any one says, Nay; that is an intuitive belief,—we put off that question to a subsequent chapter. But if he says, as a ground for there being an intuitive belief, that there is no causal nexus, meaning by that that there is no idea of cause possible in the mind, that brings us exactly to what we have been saying of Power. The causal nisus and the muscular nisus take their very expressions from each other.

The cause in the wax, that melts it under the shining of the sun, may be mysterious and practically invisible. But men learn like children. The little infant gets an idea of *strain;* wrinkles its little face under the effort to rise up from his crib. Ten million of repeated thrusts must give him some idea of strength. And it is this stress continually on our sense that would be hard to dispossess of some gleam of this wonderfully agitated matter of causation.

At any rate, we will show the folly, in a subsequent chapter, of an intuitive belief where we have no possible idea, and be all the more careful now to show that we have an idea.

The wax melts not at all for like causes with the lifting of the ball; but let it be remembered we were dealing with the springs of thought. The child is to live a score of years. The first weights that he may lift give him a shadowy sense; but he is to lift a million. He is to see a million lifted by other men. He is to run against brute pressure, and to have piled upon him material weight. And in the midst of it all, he is to have his own imperial will, and his own muscular strains, to pattern forever what is to be meant by these causations.

Now I know that the wax does not melt that way. But how does it melt? It melts, you say, by some causal nisus. Very well, he has generalized all that. He has observed ten thousand powers travelling out from his first lessons in the cradle. The grand central ones were more mechanic. But the list has been enlarged. He adds now everything to it. He found motions and liftings had to be produced, and he looks further; till the circle of what he calls Power has been increased to the very extreme; till changes unrelated to the first are found just as certainly to show causation.

Science comes in to tell us what makes the analogy more complete, but we did not know that all the time. In our intermediate state we called that thing Power which had the very slenderest similitude to that which we felt upon the muscle.

I am to be held to the strongest accountability at last (Chap. XXXVIII.) to tell whether all these things are ONLY perceptions; but before that reckoning day comes, I wish to teach boldly, that they are all perceived; and that though, with all the rest, they are what we perceive *and more*, still the MORE that they are is itself also a dictate of Sensation.

It is a bold ephemera of thought to teach, as this century does, that there are beliefs where there is no perception.

## CHAPTER XXV.

### WILL, POWER, AND CAUSE, AS THEY ADD TO THE IDEA OF THE NOT-SELF.

CALLING back, now, the idea of two orders, the order of interior thought, and the order of external harmony, it has been seen how each particular sensation, though originally one, appears on both these harmonized groupings. The blue color appears on that harmonized assemblage that we call the sky, and in that interminable current that we call our consciousness.

Now, we might anticipate the like in anything so conscious as the strain of muscle.

And blueness being a simple consciousness, and Power being conscious, as we have seen, we can understand it all the better. The Will being a conscious thought, and the nisus being a physical sensation, and the idea of Power partaking of these two, we can understand how it should attribute itself within to our inward consciousness, and how it should attribute itself without as belonging to our body.

The more might this become the case because body for a long time would be mixing up with self. The infant would hardly get them separate. The man of adult years would incorporate self undoubtedly, and give to it ideas of body. And while this was so, Power would be shared between them. And if science carried such a sway as to convince the man that body was altogether outside his consciousness, it would still preserve of course its ideas of Power, the muscular stress being a better thing to translate into our ideas of body, than blueness or smell or any other of our usual sensations.

Parting with self, however, the body would cast off the Will. As we became cleared in our intelligence the nisus would stand out more separately. We would retain the shadow that Will had helped to give, but mould it with a continual difference; till the various strugglings of the flesh, incessantly perceived, would make Power more visible, till we came steadily to attach it as an attribute of these muscles of our system.

But, obviously, there would be shadows of it without. The ball, when lifted in the hand, would have its nisus. Its pressure downward would be felt like the pressure upward of the muscle. This would be witnessed every day. The tree bent over by our nisus would bend back with all its force by a nisus of its own. Though Will would vulgarly perplex this thought of Power, yet ultimately we would get rid of it, and have left pure force suggested originally with the Will, but divested at last of all idea of it.

Still, Power would be but a shadowy idea. And what I mean now is this. Consciously there can be nothing but perception. Perception as alleged of Power began by being Will and nerve feeling. And the shadow that arose from thence was a conviction that there must be MORE. The consciousness of the Will, and the conscious immediate strain, and the conscious visible results, and then the conscious pressure of the ball, and further still the strain that is from the tree,—all are perfectly conscious perceptions; but then they are consciously different, and that leaves a shadow over the whole. There seems to be a strain without Will, and a nisus absolutely independent of the Body. And that leaves an idea of *Power;* something more than a mere associate of Self, and something else than consequent upon any usual volition.

What is that, therefore?

Plainly, a shadow. Plainly a thing hinted at rather than discovered. Plainly an empirical belief; and, to place it just in the position where in a future chapter we will make it generically stand, it is a thing discovered by consciousness itself, but discovered to be uncertain; that is, discovered to be probable by something that we are conscious of as its like; discovered to be a-wanted in a chain where in another chain a link just like it is consciously supplied; discovered perceptibly by its effects; but then not on the principle that of *necessity* there must be a cause; but on the conscious fact that in a million instances the effect has had one.

Now, therefore, to the main subject that is in place we are prepared to speak in saying,—that Power, being thus evolved, goes out from the conscious Self, and attaches itself to trees and balls. Of course it adds to the idea of Not-self. The Unity that was borrowed in a previous chapter from the Body, is made more complete in the rock or in the urn by this harmony of Power. Indeed, it takes new aspects. Externality, figured forth, gets more vital, as though conscious of itself. Indeed too much so; for it was not always in the history of men that the ball weighing down was not imagined to have will, and the tree snapping back. The standing out independence of things, *quoad* our consciousness, seeming only to be images, is immeasurably helped by these multiplied introactions of what is outward and our muscular volitions.

## CHAPTER XXVI.

### WILL, POWER, AND CAUSE, AS THEY ADD TO THE IDEA OF SELF.

BUT matter, with its new gifts, returns to help its comrade. Matter without Power, seeming only like an image, when endowed with force seems to get still further off from us. And this force is endlessly different. We have seen in a previous chapter how it gets generalized into everything that will make results. The muscular nisus of the arm gets generalized with the action of a mirror. The likeness is of the most shadowy sort. No marvel! Blueness and smell have no likeness; and so, shape and melody. Will is a conscious thing: motion is a conscious thing: strain is a conscious thing: weight is a conscious thing. These leave their prints, and are reported back into our consciousness. Then, as we travel out, things of diminished likeness—the pressure of the wind; the waving of the forest; the pelting of a storm of hail; these all throng innumerably. Of course consciousnesses are had of them; and these consciousnesses contain two things, first, direct consciousness of facts, and, second, direct consciousnesses of evident resemblance. The mind by its amazing harmonies groups all these; and, as its result, Power falls heir to a huge class that bears but a small analogy to original musculation.

Now, armed with this thought, the Not-Self helps the Self; that is to say, the mind, having learned to count its own images without as independent powers, returns with them to edify itself.

*A class of these powers it finds wakening sensation.* That is, all sense moves, so the mind discovers, at the beck of Not-Self. Hearing dies if there is nothing to provoke it. I scrape a light, and then I see. I ting a lyre, and then I hear; uncork a vase, and then I smell; touch my forehead, or I cannot feel. Self, therefore, gets this incident from Not-Self, that it is a consciousness that can be acted on. In other words, the Not-Self, being only an order, or, to talk more vulgarly, being at first only an image, gets an independent stand from certain attributes of Power; and so the Self, being at first only a current, gets a shadow of consistence from finding that it can be *acted on.* Not-Self gives sensation and *something more;* and so Self feels sensation and something more; that is, as we shall now increasingly explain, Being, though revealed by consciousness, is revealed as possessing more than consciousness, and that by conscious analogies traced in the resemblances of consciousness itself.

Meanwhile, to sum our chapter:—Will, Power, and Cause add to the Idea of Self in this, that beyond its being a mere order of consciousnesses, it is found to be at least such an order as this, that it can be acted upon, and caused by moods that it does not will, in the condition of the other order not continuous.

## CHAPTER XXVII.

### THE IDEAS OF SELF AND NOT-SELF AS THEY ADD TO EACH OTHER.

AN idea very valuable in all my ideas of Being, is the idea of Continuity.

Where do I get it?

I look at a rock, and it prints itself upon my consciousness. I look at it again, and it comes recurrently; that is, my sensation that is fresh, has fitting itself upon it a sensation that recurs. Now I conclude that that rock has stood there; and why?

Observe, I have no evidence of it in my sight. I have but immediate consciousness. When odors fade from my nerve, what tell they of anything continuous? Besides, I may be the victim of a mistake. The rock may have been crumbled up, and carved in like fashion again. The principle of the "same sum of Being," * is mere shop-work to account for difficulties. The idea that a grand mountain remains, is not a native one, and must be learned by experience. Now, as I cannot watch all mountains, why, when one heaves in sight,—why am I so pat in the conviction that it has been there all the time?

* Hamilton.

Obviously, here;—Self lends to Not-Self.

The order in the current is continuous. There is an order not continuous, as, for example, where the mountain comes and goes again in its harmonies before the mind. But there is an order that is continuous, because, though consciousness is an immediate thing, it recurs; and by its recurrences weaves back a chain of Self in the way that we have considered. Now this chain of Self associates itself with the Body, and knits all that into its chain of continuousness. Not that I am willing to teach that the Body is never forgotten (for even the mind may be, in sleep); but that it is so associated with sense as not possibly to be severed from it in the idea of our own continuousness.

The body though, like the secular men among the monks, goes out to mingle with the world. My hand is just as earthy as the rock. If my hand continues, so, by analogy, all. And my frame, therefore, becomes a scaffolding of thought by which I climb to the permanency of all that is external.

Permanence, therefore, is one of the great facts that the Self offers to the Not-Self.

But now a serious consequence! If the mountain must be permanent, it is permanent without consciousness.

The continuous idea of my Self is made easy because my consciousness continues; and this truly is the great attribute of Ego, that it never parts with consciousness. But here certainly is a great stride without, that what began as a consciousness, comes now to be something utterly without it. The clamor of a horn was mere sense. The glimmer of the urn was a mere patch upon my vision. The carrion pelt was a mere fume upon my nostril. But it has come to this, that these consciousnesses have so well agreed into themselves as to stand out in conscious images. Though the present puts in the front, and the past comes in with its recurrences, yet the urn stands urn-like in my consciousness, and my nose and my finger wander to it and have also their harmonies. And yet this harmonized consciousness (adding also power and other bodily ideas), gleams at last into something unconscious; that is, a continuance of the image after its hardness or its blueness have absolutely faded from the mind.

Now, call not this belief simply. There is some idea. This thing has traced itself, and earned its Being. Flesh, having reported itself as continually conscious, there is a manifest likeness between the flesh and the rock. My first impulse is to call the rock conscious. But driven from that, what follows? Why that *something* must remain ; and like the body it must be something of Power, and, like the body, permanent in shape and figure.

We see, therefore, at a glance, what an immensity is done by Self for the entity of the Not-Self.

But, now, obversely:—Of course the outward, being seen as cognizable in permanent being, reflects that thought upon the inward. If rock may be something fixed, so, travelling back, must be the body, and so, travelling back, may be a mind. If rock lasts when it is unseen, so *something* may when we are in slumber. If Ego seems a mere conscious journey, the facts that it finds out, viz: its action upon body, and the action of body upon consciousness, must all be showing their analogies. If body lasts, so may mind. If body may exist unconscious, so may mind. If body be possessed of power, may not mind be? Order continuous in the current, and order not continuous, started as mere perceptions. They were conscious as harmonious groups. They partook of sensations with each other. They gathered each to each immense accumulations. Now, if one by that singular sensation of power, and by its likeness to the body, retrocedes out of a passing consciousness, and claims an abiding entity, why may not the other, acted upon by this and claiming common facts, arrive at the same idea of corresponding Being?

## CHAPTER XXVIII.

### THE IDEA OF OTHER SELVES AS IT ADDS TO THE IDEA OF SELF AND NOT-SELF.

It might be an easier plan to show how the being of self could be supposed, to remember that, in the cruder form, Self is included in the Body.

The wandering Goth had perhaps no other idea. Now, as a continuous something attaches most easily to the Body, especially when it has suggested (and then returned from doing so) the unconscious continuances without, it would be perhaps far the simplest to say, that the body, having the idea of continuousness, and being supposed to include the mind, gives that the idea of Being, and Self, once existent, never loses the idea.

If Self be nothing but a round of exercises, certainly it thinks otherwise, and thinks falsely to a large degree; that is, our ideas of Self are largely corrupted by the body.

Our existent entity, taken up primarily from the animal frame, takes up many of its coarsenesses with it; and perhaps, therefore, the most philosophical account of all is, that self begins with a conscious order, advances into a physical awareness of itself still further in the body; adds afterward the idea of power; and, being possessed of an easy sense of continuousness in its physical frame, retires out of that, only when the most reduplicated analogies lead it to more interior imagination of Being.

However it ends, therefore, certainly the permanence of matter makes our largest *éclaircissement* of an unconscious entity for mind.

This being so, how wonderfully must it contribute to the result, to see other bodies, and to argue from them other minds; especially to see animal bodies, and to infer from them other resemblances.

Unquestionably the idea of brutes helps our ideas even of our Maker.

But, in respect to man,—the rock having borrowed continuousness from our ideas of body, hands it on again with large interest when we see other figures heave in sight—the very image of our material frame. Possessed of sensation all through Self, and all through body, which, in coarser minds, is part or the whole of Self, it is impossible to see a leg without thinking of its sense, or an arm without ideas of the nisus; and thus other men's senses come of course to be considered; with this important difference, that it is no longer conscious sense that is perceived, but sense imagined to be conscious in a consciousness not conscious where it is conceived: I mean by that, consciousness conscious but in another man. I repeat: worlds of addition is made here to the idea of entity; and I want it felt, as these consciousnesses are stated, that each adds its trait; that each piles the already accumulated assemblage; and that, if the bitterest sceptic would only tell us what each of these incontestably experienced consciousnesses adds to the assembled group, we would be prepared to use his terms for the genesis of the ontological idea.

Not only men, but brutes; not only brutes, but trees; not only trees, but rocks,—these forms are all unquestioned in our vision. Now rocks, seen in visible analogies with all the three, borrow their attributes, and in the end lend them back, and in the end multiply them by diverse relations and impressions, till Power and Will and Continuousness, and all the *legomena* of sense, speak together, and shed their reflected lights, and all upon the idea of Being.

A body becomes not my body but one like it. Its senses become not my senses but similar and seriously different: its consciousness, if we but look to the primary idea, no consciousness really at all. The otherness of all this is in fact a new and strong idea, and helps in unnumbered ways our important point,—that all that can be learned by consciousness, whether ontological or not, must be either intuitive or empirical; that is to say, must either be consciousness barely, or else, what is a wider field, what consciousness discovers to be its *like*.

## CHAPTER XXIX.

### EFFECTS OF THEOLOGY ON THE IDEA OF BEING.

I WILL not anticipate the origin of the idea of God, and, therefore, can dwell but meagrely upon the effect of Theism upon our Idea of Being. I want it however thus early to fix our point, that Being is a great accumulation.

Being, among different people (and of course by that I mean, the *idea* among different people), is this or that largely according to their training. If Being is solely, according to the true account, what men can gather up into it empirically by reduplicated observations, it takes-on this or that additional construction, according to the facts that men have brought into their consciousness. To the Fakir it is all perceptive, even to the rock and to the clod. When he leaves his person, instead of travelling to plants and mountains as things that unconsciously exist, he just travels on as though the whole were conscious. He steps upon the earth as though it felt his trampling; and, therefore, he gathers up a little portion of it into a god, to represent by that little fragment of it its whole intelligence. He makes no difference sensitively between the rock and his finger.

Theology, therefore, must operate marvellously.

Through all the journey that we have thus far been describing, if we travel at last to a Deity, it is easy to see how entities would recede under the truth. We would grow modest in the end about imagining ANYTHING BUT POWER. And though the difficulties of that would continue back into the Deity, still it would give all a shadowy phase. We would trace the mystery of matter to the invisible God; and knowing that He is unseen, we would yield better to the invisiblenesses of matter, and to the shadowy *Power* to which we seem endlessly at last to trace it.

## CHAPTER XXX.

### EFFECTS OF SCIENCE ON THE IDEA OF BEING.

THE Self and the Not-Self tracing themselves back further when we get the idea of God, so they do when we get the ideas of Science.

To the Hindoo, even when not Buddhist, body may well seem himself. And as he travels out to what is external, it may be hard to divorce matter from sense or consciousness. The best of us in our lazy moods, and perhaps the best of us forever, make body include our-Self, and make matter automatic like the body. Science however, at least, influences this. The educated man gets matter more entirely dead, and gets mind far backward out of the body. And yet Science holds up the fact of the meagreness of sense. It tells us that there are but five gates to do all our journeying to the outward. It tells us that there is but one way to communicate with every sense. It tells us that every one requires a propulsion on its organ. It tells us that the residuum in every search is finally the idea of Power. It tells us that light must impinge upon a web, and sound upon a drum, and smell upon a couple of nerve-plaits, and so of course touch and flavor, and then, therefore, that varieties of Power are all that can be traced in exterior Being. Like things are pronounced upon the Ego; and though all these facts do not take us out of the court of consciousness, yet they affect our whole thought, and make an addition to our views of Being.

These we must again repeat and, therefore, take from all things; and it is the amazing harmony of sense (that is, the order not continuous) that makes it pile up so, and so endlessly subtract as well as add, while the idea of Being is being put together.

## CHAPTER XXXI.

### THE WORD BEING.

CONSCIOUSNESS, being so very express, and reporting so very consciously, would bring its reports most necessarily through the verb '*to be*.' Most naturally would this be so if the verb '*to see*' should begin to fail it.

If I looked upon the urn, and found it most stubbornly in place, and felt it and smelt it and found it harmonious in my vision, I would part with the idea, '*I see*,' and deal in the fact, '*it is*.'

In other words, walking and sleeping and coming back, there would be the urn again,—grant, now, merely an image. And while consciousness would put in its face in immediate sensation, recurrence would put in its back, and touch and sound would complete a harmonious impression. This impression consciously as I look, I can realize this instant. It *is*, whatever I reason about it; and call it image if you will, I cannot strip it of absolute BEING.

## CHAPTER XXXII.

### THE WORD EXISTENCE.

BUT not only does it BE in spite of what we think of it, but it EX-ISTS; it STANDS OUT. This stereoscopic *rilievo*,—though it is empirical, yet it is made up of the clearest dictates of consciousness. Grant that it is a mere image (with Berkeley), still its *thereness* learned from the body, and its *outness* seen from the body, and its distance measured by touch, are all apparent. It EX-ISTS. If it be the ghost of a fancy, still these particulars can be known. And, therefore, aside from Perception, there is a name for this abiding harmony.

## CHAPTER XXXIII.

### THE WORD SUBSTANCE.

AGAIN, it SUB-STATS.

And I had always thought that this was a difficult word for a mere empirical observer. I had always thought it meant, It stands under, and might allude to to a *tertium quid* bearing up qualities—too early a conception, it struck me, of Qualities as opposed to Substance.

But, in looking at some old dictionaries, I found that *substare* meant to resist, and *substantia*, something that resists; and I saw immediately its primordial explanation.

The urn, visible before my consciousness, has this fact about it, that, if I touch it, it resists. The image is all apparent without that trial of touch; but this consciousness which BE'S, and also EX-ISTS, has this separate phenomenon, that in its *outness*, and its *thereness*, i. e. just at the margin of color, it SUB-STATS, i. e. it RESISTS the finger that is pushed out toward its surface.

Like a guide-post, therefore, the word points, not to Intuitive Beliefs, but, like *outness* and *thereness*, to conscious experience; a downright resistance of touch which finds itself encountered in harmony with vision.

## CHAPTER XXXIV.

### SELF AND NOT-SELF HIGHLY COMPLEX IDEAS.

BEING is either Self or Not-Self.

I. Not-Self is either that which is entirely material, or else it is other selves.

That which is entirely material is either perception, or else it is not a matter of consciousness (B. I. Chap. IV.). Now sensation is a perception. Let us begin our inquiry as to the true idea of being by asking (1.) whether the not-self, considered as matter, is all or any part of it sensation.

This, at first view, will be scouted at as utter trifling.

Sensation is a print upon the nerves. It is true it has two meanings, one the potential faculty, the other the print as it is perceived. But this last sense, which is the one which is questioned, is so fleetingly a mental act, that to ask whether sensation is matter, seems to be trifling with the whole metaphysical theme. And yet query now, What are we asking for? Are we asking for the meaning of a word? or are we asking for an unwritten thought that may please philosophers or men of very abstract ideas? There is doubtless a naked quiddity bereft of traits that would be convenient to think of under some proper philosophical term; but this quiddity is not matter. I am speaking soberly when I say, that a cherry is matter. I am speaking more soberly yet when I say, that a cherry is in part sensation. Here shall be again a time to tell what I mean by that. I do not mean much metaphysically. And yet I do mean much in the way of clearing metaphysical idea. When I ask, What is matter? I mean, What does that word portend? I do not mean, What ought it to portend? or, What would be a completer or more advanced sense to agree upon under that vocable? I mean, What is *matter?* And with whatever metaphysical refinement I state that which it does not really mean, I inflict a wrong, for all these appellatives have an unbounded right to be philosophized upon in the absolute sense in which they are consciously conceived. For example, a cherry. What do I call a cherry? Do I conceive a naked *ens*, that bears the red color, and is cause of the round shape, and that lies metaphysically under it? Or do I, philosopher though I were, include the red surface? It is a question of the use of speech. And I answer it without a moment's hesitation. A cherry is a cherry, not as a metaphysical *ens*, but ruddiness and all; I mean by that, when I say, A cherry, I mean a ruby surface as part of the idea that I put into the very term.

You may say, This is a mere question of philology. That is the very idea that I wish to impress. When I speak of matter, I mean, as my habitual sense, the *ens* WITH its qualities, the cherry as partly color; I mean by that, as I look upon the fruit, My sensation in the conscious sense is an actual part of my working appellative of cherry. We have reached therefore this far at once, that the not-self in the sense of what is entirely material includes sensation, and, therefore, is partly a consciousness (see B. III. Chap. II.) and therefore intuitively known (see B. II. Chap. III.) just to the extent that the speech we make of it takes in our senses.

But now a cherry takes-in our senses to a very small degree. If I stand off and look at it, there is a patch of ruddiness. That patch has breadth and surface and varieties of hue. I am conscious of the peach that much; and I say, conscious of the peach, because usage has actually chosen to put that much in the peach as a part of its meaning. If any body doubts it, it is mere logomachy. We lay the stress simply to be clear. Men talk of consciousness of self, and intuition of an external world, simply from this usage, that from the peasant up, always as we shall hereafter see, they choose to put consciousness into their idea of self, and pink and scarlet into their idea of the external world.

Ruddiness, however, is but a small part of the peach. How do we form the rest? (2.) We resort to recurrence. How does recurrence build for us? This is a pleasant side-question. Does it put-in actual recurrences? Or does it transmute them into imagined sense? We think, the latter. The back and sides of the peach are imagined ruddinesses like the front. And here let me assert again;—These are actual parts of the peach. The front was a sensation. It was, therefore, the directest consciousness. The back is not a sensation. It is not even a recurrence. But it is what recurrence was helping us to of an imagined red. And these, let me say, are actual parts of the peach. Now take in all other senses. We have been speaking only of color. We have prepared the way that all may crowd in. Imagine touch with all its remembrance,—and scent, and sound. Our word-making seems to part with nothing. Consult your consciousness. In the very meaning of the peach you pack all you think of; the color, and its interior look, the hue it would have if you should open it, and the hue it would have behind it, and the grain, and the touch, and the surface;—inspect your consciousness; that is the most prudent test as to what you put into your meaning of a peach.

(3.) Now, as the actual fact, these images are all in *order*.

A bullock in a pasture is known to lick his flesh, and to lick the flesh of his companions, till a great quantity of hair is carried into his maw, and, usually, with no other effect than what might betide any other foreign substance. But sometimes, as a rare result, the hair adds to itself the attribute of order. By a strange felting process, that Darwin might envy for his protoplasm, the hair takes on a form. That which piece by piece is but a hair, webs itself into a cone. It is but hair after all. But who shall say that this exquisite shape is not more? Ideally I mean, the hair and this growth of the hair have the divinest differences. And so now in matter; the baldest sense, a single ray shot here, or a single touch felt there, are very different ideals from that *felted* sense which binds these five messengerings together.

(4.) And now we rejoice to note exactly what the old thinkers meant by *species* or *images*. They meant truth. The moderns who discard it all have fallen into error. *Images* are precisely the way in which the mind arrives at external things. Images moreover are real. That is to say, not only does the mind frame an image of external things, but it throws the name over it; that is, arriving at a cherry by having its image, I put the image in the cherry; that is, I give the name to that which includes the image.

For example, I see a cherry. That is my first consciousness. It might have been touch. It might have been taste. I might have shut my eye, and some baby-trifler might have fed me with a cherry. It matters not. Eye or hand, my first thought is a sensation. That first thought is the cherry,—I mean, a part of it. What care I what the philosopher says? He may say, My eye has never seen the cherry, and my hand has never touched it. And he may prove all he says. That is to say, descanting upon molecular realities, he may show me that hand and fruit molecularly have been hedged away. I care nothing at all. What I am descanting about is the name. The name cherry, even with the philosopher who talks so well, includes the sense. The ruddiness on which his eye falls, is part of the fruit; and when he takes it in his hand, the sphericity that resists his touch is the boundary of the thing. That is, the bundle of its traits is swept into his speech, and is included under the definition that is made.

Now this bundle is the *image*. Like the cone in the ox it is a something that is more than the hair; not more in essence, but more in thinking. The *image* that I frame is either, first, sensation, or, second, the thought of it which I bring up by recurrence; and though each gleam may be of small effect, like each hair in the maw of the ox, yet, felted into one, it makes an image; that image is by an order that is in nature; that image is of the most conscious that I possess; that image has been the dream of the past; and that image is the true philosophy: when I look upon this stove, the working word, STOVE, keeps in it the front and the sides that I put in it by sensation and recurrence.

(5.) But now, having such an image, an immensity is added to it by an empirically discovered *permanence*.

This is the progeny of recurrence.

Having a sensation of which I am directly conscious, it was noticed how the rest was put into the cherry by recurrent memory. Shifted, however. I think I am conscious that it is not a memory that I put into the fruit, but an imagined copy. I see the front: I imagine sides that shall be like it. But the more beautiful what memory does do in fabricating *permanence!* That is an immense stride in idealization. The *image* as a flash is a wonderful harmony; but if the image lives! The stove with its black bulk,—that seems more to think of than any one feeling of its surface; but if the stove stands there! And see, This is really nothing but perception. The cone in the maw of the ox is nothing but hair. Let us look at this suspiciously. The stove!—it is in part a bundle of images. And when we speak of permanence, what do we mean by that? At first, but a permanence of images. I see a house. I have learned distance in space. I remember a house. I have learned distance in time. And all the intervening length whether of time or space is filled up by experience. We are not going to teach that all being is perception; but see how we can go very far without putting anything into the name but sense and recurrent permanence.

(6.) But now permanence begins to mutiny. Permanence is a thing that requires food and clothes, and something more solid than mere perception. The image of a stove is a very solid looking thing, and the remembered image of a stove is very real, but what does it do for itself when no one is looking? That it drops out of existence we cannot think, for we believe it permanent just as we believe the analogy of the bells (see B. II. Chap. VIII.). It is not a consciousness, but an experience; and if it should not be permanent, and we looked and it had entirely vanished, it would only be a stoppage of the bells after a century of ringing. But if permanent, what lasts? Certainly not the idea; for there is no one looking. We are *forced off* into Ontology. Being is not idealized. We are not conscious of it. We are not looking at it; I mean as ultra ideal; but that word SOMETHING describes its origin. Mill dared wildly to say, that *possibility* was the word,—that self was a *possibility* of sensation,—that the peach was a *possibility* of being seen,—that the stove, in order to live between-whiles, was a *possibility* to be seen when we felt free to look at it; but, alas for Mill! this is but *tantum per tanto.* It is scarce as good as our word *something;* for while *possibility* is but a repeating of the case, *something* is a modest disclaimer of our being able to say much: it is a convenient trunk, into which we can pack many an understood analogy.

7. For example, *power*;—that begins to toll us off from pure and mere idea.

*Power* is conceived of in our consciousness (see B. III. Chap. XXIV.). Then it wanders off from there, and is seen in its analogies. There is power in my arm. That I feel. There is power in another man's arm. There is power in the wind. There is power in the heat. How vague the analogy at last becomes. Finally there is power in the cherry. I saw it last night: I see it again now. Has it existed all that time? Yes. Did you see it? No. Has anybody seen it? No. How has it existed? Why, surely not as a consciousness; but as a *something*, and as a something with *power*. And though the *images* no longer serve us, rotund and solid though they seem, yet they have done the arguing for us as to something permanent; and though we have to drop them out of the picture when the stove ceases to be imaged, yet they leave these vague analogies of *power* and of *permanence* and of *something* that continues to be there.

8. Nor must we go on from just this spot in Ontology without setting in its right shape that much abused term of *quality*. It is indeed three terms, the first two meaning the same thing numerically, the last meaning nothing of the kind. The first means a quality of the sense, as when we speak of the shrillness of a certain sound, or the sweetness of a certain taste; and even then we must state that it is the heard sound and the felt taste; for these words wander incessantly in objective ways. The second means precisely the same thing, but turned objectively. There is a tendency we have seen to put our sensations into the object. Thus blue

is blue, and all the dictionaries in the world cannot make it anything conscious but a color. Yet the color is imputed to the heavens, and that as a consciousness. It goes as a paint all over it; nay, dictionary-wise, right into it. There is a second meaning therefore to the term. The same color is a quality of my sense, and a quality, by the habit of men's speech, of exterior matter; though the same conscious blueness, numerically meant, is that which is present in my mind and painted on the sky. Palsy my power of sight, and the two would fade at once, proving their identity. But the third would survive. And this will make things a great deal clearer. The third is the mere power to awake the others. There is vast confusion from not having detected this dictionary-difference. The first and second are a sense. The third is not even a consciousness. And yet they are all called qualities. A quality in the third sense is a mere imagined potence to project the blue, or to awake the sound, or to produce the taste upon the healthy organization.*

Therefore at this stage of Ontology, if a man says, we are conscious of qualities, but we are not conscious of substance, we must ask him what he means. If he

* Now, one word here. We have said that consciousness goes into our idea of self, and that ruddiness goes into our idea of the cherry. So, let it be observed, these three dictionary-meanings of quality are more or less fused together. The mere consciousness, color, trajects itself we have seen, and becomes object-wise; and the more genetic meaning, viz. that which produces the consciousness, like the cherry itself, becomes suffused with the consciousness itself; so that all three meanings are with difficulty abstracted from each other. It would be difficult to say that color is not a sensation, and yet we rather say, Sensation *of* color; so obstinately does the mind speak object-wise of its different sensations.

Let me entreat, however, attention to this fact;—these are dictionary questions; not points about which consciousness differs outside of our speech.

means qualities in the earlier senses, we have nothing to say; but if he means qualities in the third, he is utterly at fault, for we *are* conscious of substance as a dictionary thing, for it includes qualities in those earlier forms; but we are not conscious of quality at all, I mean of quality in its third sense, that is, simply of the power by which a thing seems blue, or is the instrument of God in projecting the blueness or projecting the sound or enkindling the taste upon the mind.

II. We are not ready for our last assertions, and, therefore, we will go on, and close this chapter with what is the second great head of it, viz. Self.

(1.) SELF INCLUDES CONSCIOUSNESS. This is the great philologic fact. We have seen that the cherry includes ruddiness. These are things of the Lexicon. We do not say that they might not have been different. When I say, I am conscious of self, I mean conscious of self understood as that word must mean. And when I say, I see a cherry, I mean that I see what that word cherry answers to; and I must know what that word cherry answers to, before I know whether I really see it.

Now that I see a cherry depends upon the fact that its ruddiness is a part of its idea; with the cherry a very slender part. The ruddiness is a mere patch of light; and a vast deal idealistically has to be fabricated from the region of recurrence.

It is not so with the ego. The ego is all the consciousness. Let me be understood;—The word *ego*, or to speak more plainly the whole idea of myself, includes my consciousness, and not, as in the instance of the cherry, a patch of sense, but the whole contents of the spirit; the whole existing consciousness goes by the law of the Lexicon into myself at the time.

In the instance of the cherry, recurrence brought up and finished the fruit by imagined sensations. In the instance of self, all goes in directly. Whatever my mind is conscious of at the time, enters for that time into my idea of ego.

Do not debate now! Deny or reject or declare that this speech contradicts your dictionary. That is the direction which we are now travelling. But if you admit that practically it is actually the case,—that is all I care for. I say, that, as my mother taught me, I have learned to count self, conscious self. And, therefore, when I speak of self, I am not remembering whether some other self would be more for science, but I am speaking of the self I know. The self I know, includes the thoughts.

(2.) Now, though recurrent thought is conscious, and, therefore, makes up my consciousness, yet it does more for the felt ego than this. It not only adds its volume to the consciousness which is self, but it also tells facts about it; that is, as in the instance of the stove, it brings out the idea of *permanence*.

(3.) In like manner, *power*. The stove is permanent. Why? Is any one looking at it? No. *Possibility* is the word with Mill. The stove is not looked at, but it has a possibility to be looked at. That is its permanence. But we, claiming a vast many other experiences, lay emphasis upon the fact of power. It has a power to be looked at; and that helps the thought of being. And so now in the instance of the ego;—not only is it all our consciousness, but, if forced to give up that, and if a race should arise that should change the dictionary and shrink self into a naked *ens*, we would make much of the idea of power. The stove has power to be visible. I never knew it except visually;

or, otherwise, never, except tactually; but I know by likeness that it has a power. And if the stove has power, why not I? I never think stoves if not in part as images, and I never think self if not in part as consciousness; but if the stove has power to project these images, why not I to receive them? and, moreover, if the stove sends images, and has therefore efficient strength, why have not I also? for as the stove sends images to me, so do I to myself in those perpetual recurrences which something or other is printing and sending to my eye.

Now this is all very slender, but it will help what was more fully treated before. It is very slender, because we have singled out but one sense. The stove is a hulk of images, and the ego a maze of consciousness. Nevertheless one is just like the other. Both, as words, take in consciousness. Neither, as things, is confined to it. Both are like in travelling out from it. And neither could advance an inch but on that principle of the bell (B. II. Chap. VIII.), which, beginning with the sense, travels out empirically on the strength of likeness.

## CHAPTER XXXV.

### EFFECT OF LANGUAGE ON THE IDEA OF BEING.

MERE language makes self include consciousness, and makes the not-self, so far as it is material, include the instant sensation. We have no questions to ask as to whether this is for the best. "Vox populi, vox Dei." In all languages, so far as we are aware, the words for being include the consciousnesses that reveal it at the time.

To men of perfectly sharp minds this would make no difference. The philosophic entity could be treated, whether cherry included its red color, or whether ego included my existent consciousness, or whether it did not. It is only a question of the Lexicon; though the formation of the Lexicons of all language indicates in the most striking way that path of thought which enters the domain of being.

All men have not sharp minds, however; and in the maze of Metaphysics no man has a particularly sharp mind; and, therefore, the meaning of terms, though it can be conventionally agreed, has had a most potential way of warping knowledge.

I. In the first place, self, including consciousness, and yet coming afterward to be dreamed of as a naked entity, has started with a sort of scorn at any one who has spoken of it as not conscious. If I were to declare, You are not conscious of yourself, you would cry and stop your ears. And yet this is but the effect of language. Ever since the world began, self has included consciousness; and now, when metaphysicians dig and conceive an *ens* inside of our conscious thinking, that is seized upon as though it were the genuine philosophic self, and, not remembering that then language has to change, we utter an outcry of horror if a man says we are not conscious of the ego.

II. And so of the non-ego. These are useful words even in their popular sense. The non-ego, in the cases where it is wholly matter, takes in, as we have already seen, the mere sensation. It takes in the whole bundle of recurrent images. This is a grand help. (1) It gives unitariness to our speech; and (2) it introduces the peasant by easy stage to the idea of being. But it has proportioned evils. It breeds chapters of mistake. It has seduced men since the time of Plato. Having intuition of a cherry; being sure that I see it; having consciousness that I am in its very presence; so long as a cherry includes sensation, my dictum is complete; but thought steals in and cuts off the quiddity, and sheers away what is conscious from the fruit, and yet still spends its time in inquiring how I have certainty of the cherry.

The remedy lies in the speech. Changing the speech, I must change my intellection. Taking hue out of the peach, and looking at it in metaphysic guise, I must cease to see it. And so of the ego. Robbing it of consciousness; I mean by that, taking out of the word a thought-current as part of its signification; and we relegate it into the inane. After that it is not conscious. Then it becomes a spirit like God. We believe in it, like angels. And for a man to say he is conscious of himself, is a mere tripping up upon the old idea.

## CHAPTER XXXVI.

### CAN WE BE SAID TO BE CONSCIOUS OF THE NOT-SELF?

WE are ready, therefore, for all those questions about the domain of consciousness.

It seems that matter is an object of consciousness because, as the actuality of speech, the word matter includes sensation. I am conscious of matter because I am conscious of its hue; or I am conscious of matter because I am conscious of its image, and its image, grouping all that is sensational together, is an integral part of the defined reality.

Other parts, however, are not sensational. The image is mostly made up of the past. Of the ruddiness of the peach I am distinctly conscious; and if that is the peach, I am conscious of the peach. But of the back of the peach I am not conscious. It is made up of images. They are fashioned from the past. And though they are integral parts of the peach; I mean lexically: yet I am not conscious of them; for they are not like the ruddiness I see, actual facts, but they are *likelihoods;* that is to say, whether they are ruddy or white I cannot settle till I actually see them.

So of *permanence;* and so, above all, of *power.* They have drifted further from consciousness. We will explain how far, under another chapter. So, above all, of *entity.* When the philosopher comes in, and sheers away all that is of the image, an entity is conceived, and of that there should be no pretence that we can at all be conscious.

## CHAPTER XXXVII.

### CAN WE BE SAID TO BE CONSCIOUS OF SELF?

If the appellative, self, includes our existing consciousness, of course, as we have already explained, we are conscious of self. And as consciousness is very large, we are conscious of very much of self,—far more than of the not-self as matter.

Ego signifies all of consciousness. The non-ego does not. Hence in common language we are said to be conscious of self, but we are not said to be conscious of a cherry.

We are conscious of a cherry just in a patch of ruddiness, a sort of umbilical feeding of the main idea. We are conscious of self all over. And this is the answer we give to the above inquiry. We are conscious of self as a dictionary word including all our consciousness at the time. But as a philosophic *ens*, if thought succeeds in divorcing it from all our consciousness, we are not conscious of it at all. But as a thought-bearer, just as a stove may be conceived as an image-bearer, as an original *esse*, inside of consciousness, and yet outside of God, and given by Him efficiency to breed our thinking, it is dead as Dido; it is outside of all our image-making: we have no look into its face: we look into its being as we do into God who made us.

## CHAPTER XXXVIII.

### IS BEING NOTHING BUT PERCEPTION?

THIS seems an obstinate going back to an offensive scepticism; but we are guilty of it in order to gather up every crumb of the required empiricism.

All that man knows he must perceive. All that he perceives he is conscious of; moreover his perceptions of whatever sort, as was long ago determined (B. I. Chap. VIII.), are throughout a consciousness. Therefore, if we perceive being, must it not be all perception? inasmuch as all perception is all a consciousness? We are at a state when this difficulty can be gotten over, and, we think, finely and finally.

A cherry is being. Ruddiness in our conscious thought of it is part of it; and, therefore, so far as a cherry is ruddiness, it *is* a perception. But ruddiness is but a small part of it; and there are back and sides and juice and pulp and pit and ten-thousand-concourse of images. What are these images? Sensations? They are not even recurrences. They are images of recurrences; and what our mind asserts when it fits them to the peach is that they are parts of it like the ruddiness. But am I conscious of them? Let me ask another question. Am I conscious of the ringing which having continued every five minutes for a thousand years I *perceive* will ring the next minute? Behold the answer!—Perception is the unlucky term. I really mix things when I consent to use it. I do not really *perceive* the ringing that is to be the next moment. If I did, it would be all a consciousness. The ringing this moment is all sensation, and of every wave of it I am squarely conscious. But the ringing that is to be is a faith. Now let me transfer this, and we can become very lucid. The patch of ruddiness is the peach, that is, according to the vocabulary, it is a conscious part of it. Therefore that much is perception. But of the back and sides of the peach think a moment. It is just like the ringing of the bell. The ringing next moment is a faith. The back of the cherry is a faith. I do not even know the color of it. No, not the fact of it! I have a sensation of the front, and that sensation two things,—first, the hue of it, and, second, the fact of it. And now of the back what have I? Decidedly a consciousness; and that consciousness is all a perception. But a perception of what? A perception of the exact mental phenomena. What are the mental phenomena? They are conscious recurrences. Is that the peach? No. What more are they? They are facts about these recurrences; for of all the facts, as in blueness and redness, we are supremely conscious. What are these facts? First, their conscious analogies. What more? Second, the order that they keep. Give us, therefore, four things; first absolute consciousnesses; second, among these, conscious recurrences; third, among these, visible likeness; and, fourth, among these like things, conscious order,—and Ontology becomes a thing of prediction. The front of the cherry is a consciousness; but all beside is predicted probability,—which might actually deceive,—a framing of faith on the base of experienced recurrence.

How, still it may be shouted out, does anybody get the *ens* from the image? the granite from the soap bubble? Thought is one thing. Iron is another. Where does the latter come from? And our antagonists may press in upon us, and crowd us in this extremest moment with the question, Where did you get the iron? Our answer is, We have not gotten the iron at all. Thought is all mine. I see every part of it. Iron is not all mine. I see scarce any of it. What I do see is thought. Beyond thought I do not see the iron. By thought I get a faith in it. As thought I have seen power. As thought I have seen permanence. A bundle of thought has made an image. The iron would be mere thought, were it not that discovered order, and experienced analogy, and detected difference (all these mere thoughts), had pushed me beyond thought into the region of empirical believing. A rock first reports to me as light; but when I infer permanence where there is no light, I am forced to conceive of *something* not light that abides in the absence of my vision.

This something I am not conscious of. It is a made up thing. I do not possess it sensibly, as I do my consciousness. I assert it as I do the future ringing of the bell. And if any one says, Yes, but it is an entity; and that is very different from perception,—I say, Yes, but the *difference* is what perception asserts. And if he adds, It is so different as to be genetically incapable of such a birth, I bring him to pause by asking,—Specifically what is it? He soon begins to describe it in terms of consciousness; so that when power and hue and bulk and weight and permanence, all of which are consciousnesses, all combine, he has nothing beyond, except SOMETHING, that he can assert of being.

And that *something* is just the same discovery in the instance of the *ego*. The *ego* as consciousness is of course perception and nothing more. The *ego* as something that has consciousness is an empiric functionary, permanent because we trace it when out of thought,—powerful because acting and acted on, these being simply consciousnesses,—a being, because it IS all that it is consciously discerned to be,—an existence, because it stands out in imagined separateness like matter,—and a substance as some men call it, as though it did really resist, and had power for impinging upon the body.

Now these are all shadows. They go by the tether of consciousness. They go as far as that will lead them. That fact is seen in the very terms that we employ. And when consciousness leaves them, we embrace the ὅτι rather than the ὄν. We no longer see anything direct. But like a hand holding us out of the window, consciousness holds us out into the inane, that we may affirm by analogy and experience *that there is something more and different* to what perception itself can squarely bring under its eye.

## CHAPTER XXXIX.

### IS THE IDEA OF THE NOT-SELF INTUITIVE OR EMPIRICAL?

INTUITIVE and empirical are terms of Logic. That is intuitive which I know directly. Whether the not-self is intuitive, depends upon the question whether I know directly all or any part of it? That we have settled already. It makes little difference inherently; but philologically our minds are conscious that we do attribute to the word *stove* a patch of the present sensation. So far therefore our question is answered. The idea of a not-me is intuitive so far as it takes in a patch of the present sensation.

But how is it, farther? Here let me divide. We go farther by asserted analogy; and we go farther, beyond a doubt, also, by asserted difference. Both of these assertions, let me be careful to say, are not by any separate faculty, but by mere experience.

We go farther by asserted analogy. I see a black surface, and it is part of a stove. I fill up behind it, and that is the other part: but the first part I see. The other part I only think of. Moreover I only think of it in analogy. The rotund back is as much the stove as the rotund front, though both are images; but the one *is* just as I see it. The other is in but uncertain analogy. It may be brown. It may be rusted. It may be broke; I cannot tell. It is a mere analogy. Nevertheless it is a part of the stove. And it is a part aimed at by analogy, such that I dream that if I stood where I could see it, it would be a part of the image, and as such (as an ancient *species*) would make part under that vocable, *a stove*.

But now a deeper part comes in by difference.

We hug sense for one. We dream out away from sense to supply the other.

For example, the stove. It endures when we are not looking. Why? Because we endure. And we learn that largely by the body. We trace its permanence. It comes out by facts of consciousness. The indicia are immense. We will not repeat them. We are forced to have signs of permanence without consciousness; and that sets us at what? Why, at asserting likeness with difference. These are the thought-carriers. We are carried by likeness to the limits of consciousness, and then we are projected off, and forced by what we have called intermediate analogies (B. II. Chap. X.) to assert a *something* of which we have no consciousness.

The not-self, therefore, is in one single patch intuitive; in the rest of a rotund image it is by partial analogy: as a metaphysical essence it is more empirical still, and results from tenuous likeness carried the very farthest off and there forced to assert a difference in a needful something that must have permanence with no consciousness at all.

## CHAPTER XL.

### IS THE IDEA OF SELF INTUITIVE OR EMPIRICAL?

ALL is plainer in the instance of self. The idea of self is intuitive so long as men persist in putting into it the idea of consciousness; but when it gets to the launching-off place it has to shift as in the instance of matter. It is bred of likeness. It is bred likewise of asserted difference. I think of self as conscious in the past. There of course it is analogy. And there of course it is empirical. I do not see the past. I am not conscious of what was conscious then. It comes up to me by recurrence. And though, like the back of the stove, past consciousness goes in to my image of myself, it is a matter of empiricism. I no more see myself in my existence yesterday than the back of the stove, and may make the same mistakes about it as to its minuter consciousness. But now the stove, when I am no longer looking, and my body, when I am fast asleep, and my neighbor, who has his own separate consciousness, all cluster their evidences upon me, and force me to think of a self that is not conscious. How does it look you may ask me? It does not look at all. Then of what is it conscious? It is not conscious at all. Then what is it? Genetically analogy and difference. State that more carefully. Well, take that sentence,—*a self that is not conscious;* take ten thousand other sentences; take all the facts that are bred of a countless experience: try to sink them as a boy does when he tries to go under; consent to my terms that they are not conscious *ens*, and try to annul them such as they are; and when you see that like the hair they are webbed into a cone, and all agree to the very uttermost accord, take that for self, that is, the asserted *something* that must endure in the absence of the present consciousness.

## CHAPTER XLI.

### ARE WE CERTAIN OF OUR OWN EXISTENCE?

TAKE self as partly consciousness, and we are certain of that much of self as is constituently conscious: but take self as a metaphysical *ens*, and we are not certain of it at all.

If I am asked, Are you certain there is any such city as London? I would say, Yes; because, for practical purposes, I am sure enough. But if any one begs me to speak definitely, I would say I am not certain of it at all. And if any one begs me to give my logical intent I would say, It is impossible to be certain of anything but my immediate consciousness.

Now my belief in the City is precisely akin to my belief in myself.

If any one exclaims at this, let me ask:—Might I not be mistaken? London is a tale. To most people it is a mere averment. Do men never tell lies? Suppose all the world had united to deceive me. You may say, That is not possible: and I admit that, in the sense of the highest conceivable per cent. There is not the ten millionth of a probability that the world has vitiated its maps. Nevertheless the conception is possible. The world may have been in conspiracy ever since I was born to deceive me on this subject of London. Moreover, I have been there. God may have deceived me. I mean by all to show that consciousness is a direct intuition. God cannot make it true that I have not the experience of light as I mark these strokes upon the sheet of paper. But empiricism is a faith built upon order. The order *may* deceive me, and things cease to be predicable upon that base which has been a sheer experience.

So now of my own existence. Is it consciousness? Ah then I know it certainly. Is it a substantial *ens?* God might be utterly deceiving me. He might make my present consciousness by the flash of an immediate power. Can any one deny it? He might make my immediate consciousness and nothing in the world beside. And in that consciousness is memory, which would be a mistake, and sensation, and image-making, and belief in the past, and belief in self and body and all my present harmonies, and yet it would be all a lie, God having chosen to create a consciousness like a flying seraph with no basis of life on which it could sit down.

You may say, He might not deceive us. There again is empiricism. Confidence in Heaven is never the terminal fact, but confidence in consciousness: when that is past, conscious probability is all that is left, higher and stronger like the likeness of the two doves, or like the probabilities of the bell that has been ringing a thousand years.

## CHAPTER XLII.

### ARE WE CERTAIN OF ANYBODY ELSE'S EXISTENCE?

THE cherry as partly ruddiness we are absolutely sure of. All beyond, not so.

I might go into a house. Who says I am certain of the house? I am certain of my consciousnesses, and nothing more.

I might own the house, walk its porches, sack its pantries, feel its fires, yea, have all my growth from infancy to a dotard's age inside of that house,—and never be sure of a single timber. Nay I will force you to admit it; for I have only to ask, Could not the Almighty make me believe I had a house? Could He not raise Samuel when there was no Samuel there? Could he not come as a tired man (Judges vi. 11) when He came as a God? Could He not wrestle at the Ford Jabbok (Gen. xxxii. 24), with no molecules in His form, and with no flesh upon His bones? And in my life-long home could He not make it all a dream to me? He could not make me conscious of that of which I was not conscious; and that is the bourne of the intuitive; but He could make me dream of any not-me, and fill up all its consciousnesses as of a score of years, and there not be a back to any front, or an instant of existence beyond the point where I was looking on.

The not-self, therefore, is well defined. Where it is sense, I know it. But as a physical *ens*, it is only empirically believed.

## CHAPTER XLIII.

### INTUITIVE BELIEFS, SO-CALLED, UNDER THE LIGHT OF ONTOLOGY.

We are now prepared to dispense with that jury-mast in metaphysical sailing, viz. Intuitive Beliefs.

We are now prepared to charge it with three incompetencies. First, it is *not conceivable*.

It is intended to make the trajectory from the me to the not-me, and of course, that is very essential. To do so it cuts away all other tackle by which that journey can be made; and that might seem very reasonable. In doing so, it denies that the journey is made with any *terminus ad quem;* I mean with any professed arrival at a conscious idea. Causė, for example. I believe it; I do not see it. And so of other examples. Our great averment against the system is that it is utterly inconceivable.

We must set a guard, however. There has been a false synopsis. That two and two are four,—that is conceivable. Regulative Faculty or not, the mind undoubtedly perceives that much,—and that a whole is greater than its part. If you like that style of getting forward we are willing to admit, that we were born with that much faculty, viz. a faculty, if we know that a thing is, to know that it is, which is all that we can get out of the axiom that it is impossible for the same thing to be and not to be. Such things are the baldest truisms. And if it were left to these, universals never could have reigned so long in Logic.

It is those other maxims,—that quality implies substance,—and that changes require efficiency,—that have made the Regulative Faculty seem at all worth while; for while these truisms have seemed to make it precise, these later maxims render it aggressive. That the whole is greater than its part is sterile; but that quality requires substance is philosophically prolific. Now, I say, there is no such Intuitive Belief: first, because, by the admission of its friends, there is no conceivable idea. This is the thought that will pull down the castle. Substance, what is it? S-u-b-s-t-a-n-c-e is a file of letters. Put an idea in it, and it is a matter for belief. But it is a weapon for a child that will arm him against the most honored reasoners if he is able to ask, How can I believe in that of which I have no idea?

The first argument therefore against the system is, that it is in terms *meaningless*.

II. The second argument is, that it is practically *false*.

Here are Moses and Elias on the top of Tabor. These men exhibit, so the doctrinists say, certain phenomena about their persons which are merely mental; that is to say, I, looking on, see, not Moses, but certain colors, and the fact that there is a substantial patriarch is by an innate faculty, or, as these scientists tell us, by an Intuitive Belief. But query now, *Is* there a substantial patriarch? Elias was carried to heaven, but Moses died on Nebo. It is sane to think that Moses was disembodied. Suppose it were so. These men distinctly aver that qualities imply substance. They will not leave it to empiric steps, but leap toward it as a fact universal. Now, abandoning our first difficulty, that the thing is inconceivable, let us press this last. How can I be born to certainty that qualities imply substance, when here are two saints, the very thread on whose vestments seems alike, and yet one may be bones and flesh, and the other a floating phantasm of whatever sort may be put forward by the Almighty?

Nor can it be replied that this is a fine illustration of the very doctrine impeached. These men may say, We have confessed we have no idea. What Moses was, and what Elias was, we have no conception. That is the very nature of the belief. That Moses is the same as the other, we can never know. But all the better does it illustrate our doctrine, that the mind reaches to universals, and asserts that neither patriarch is mere phenomena; that underneath the color of his hair there must be an actual something; and that neither figure can be a mere floating sense, but must have a ground to stand on in some group of material efficiencies.

But let us not be too bold.

The hand upon the wall,—did Belshazzar see it? In all that part that consists in consciousness he certainly saw it, and that is all the part that he did certainly see. He certainly saw all that my hand seems as I look at it now as it moves over the paper. And yet what did he see? These men say, A phantasmic something. No, not certainly that. All quality implies substance, and these men say there is something efficient upon the wall; and yet there may have been nothing upon the wall. We may pare down the reality until we see that there is nothing we can assert except the bare consciousness that had arisen in Belshazzar's mind. Nay, we who are mere empiricists can assert more than the advocates of universals. For universals are all or nothing; while we who are empirical in belief can have probabilities for faith outside of the domain of certainty.

III. Therefore a third argument. A third argument is, that this Faculty has no pretence for its main proof, viz. that it is *necessary*.

We argue this in several ways. (1) In the first place, that is not necessary which is impossible. If I can have no belief in that of which I have no idea, then the pretension of a leap outwardly is all chimerical. Either the me is an idea, or it is not: if it is not, there is no possibility for a belief: if it is, where did I get it? The Regulative Faculty is *de trop* in either event. If I have no idea, it has no province. If I have an idea, it has no necessity. This is the grand argument. I can get my belief where I got my ideas. If I have ideas, I know whence I believe them. If I have no ideas, I am fighting about English words, and cause and substance are only alphabet.

(2) In the second place, that plea of necessity is the feeblest of all which pretends to be wholly philosophical. It is the old scholastic mark. Original truths are said to be universal and necessary, and the necessity, when it comes to be described, is that which is so much insisted upon by Hamilton, viz. that of which the opposite is unthinkable. Every effect must have a cause. Why? Because the opposite cannot be conceived.

Now what do we mean by that?

That the whole is greater than a part is an original truth. That I admit. The opposite of it is inconceivable, and therefore it is necessary. That every effect must have a cause is also an original truth if we begin by the definition of effect itself as having a cause. So of substance. If quality is quality of substance, and that is the definition, the inference is plain. All quality requires substance; and we may go on to build up aphorisms at pleasure. But what does it all amount to? Each one on the list is a truism; and the whole and its part, and the cause and its effect, are similarly related, the aphorism being stamped as true by the force of definition.

But if, as Sir William does, we go boldly to sea; if, as an actually aggressive argument, we say, Yon ship must have had a cause for the fact that the opposite is altogether inconceivable; or, again, that rock must have been created because its flashing out just so upon the field is beyond our thoughts,—we are giving in to proof which will establish altogether too much. What do we mean by conceivable? Do we mean that the phenomenon cannot be conceived? How then do we describe it? Do you say, it is past your consciousness that a rock should flash up without there having been any rock before? It is not past mine. Moreover, it is not past yours. Pardon me such an assertion. But I deny that it is possible to talk on that of which I have no idea. If then I can think of a ship flushing out without a creator upon the main, you are driven to another position, viz. that it is the *how* that is unthinkable, and then you are in a most atheistic attitude, for the *how* is unthinkable as to its having any creator at all. You prove too much, therefore. Either it is not fair to argue by the amount of what I can conceive, or you sweep everything:—the rock itself; the ship; the Deity on high. To think the rock without a creator is no whit harder than to think it with a creator; nay, to my thinking, not so hard. I can conceive of neither. A lazier thought will reveal to me the widow's cruse flooding over as by itself, than that farther thinking of a mystic hand to achieve the feat by an inconceivable creation.

Returning to reality, therefore, do we dispense

with God? By no means. We prove Him empirically. And there are our next reasonings. Intuitive Beliefs are not necessary; for the I and the not-I can both be reached in other ways which we have already considered.

(3) As the next step, therefore, conceive of being *analytically*. What do you find in it? Look over your whole Ontology, and tell me, What do you see in self or not-self that could not be put there by the facts of consciousness? The red color? That is sense. The order of shapes and color? That is consciousness. The images that are built up by the past? That is all recurrence. Permanence? That is all perceived. And so is power. Tell me anything in the whole range of fact that is not consciousness or its shadowy likeness. And as I pile these things in, and surely there is a vast accumulation of them, do not say that I have done nothing toward being until you at least have described something that you have done, or something in part at least that you have put into the significance of an Intuitive Belief. I tell you actual thoughts. I depict to you obvious images. I show you how they grow out of my sense. Do not say I must superadd a Regulative Faculty, when you admit that it gives no actual ideas, and only avers what in the very necessity of the case must be conceived of in some other way.

(4) And then, *synthetically*. How do you put your world together? I have shown you how I do mine. I have been free with all my material. I have shown you its grand variety. Outness, for example, and otherness; things that seem mental; things that look difficult, unless they can be catered after by an Intuitive Belief; I have shown you how they are actually conscious; how they come up into the sense; and

now match them, and, what is more, give *conceptions* of the things that you believe, or else admit that you have been adding what is supposititious, and impairing the honor of God in the alphabet He has fixed in the mind of His creature.

We spell out the universe.

That is not a good figure you say, for thought is one thing, and being is another. The mind may be full of thought, but that is not being. That is the eternal argument. We use it for purposes of recapitulation.

(1) In the first place, shame on *you* for using it,—you confess that you give us no idea.

(2) In the second place, if you give us no idea, the mind has to depend upon what it has at any rate; and how can it employ your mere idealess belief?

(3) In the third place, it does not stop at thought, but by thought as a great projectile it can assert its likenesses.

(4) Fourth, it does not stop at likeness: but

(5) Fifth, it is made aware of difference; and going to the verge of the dissimilar, it reports exactly what you say, viz. that there is something different from thought. And it reports about it all that you pretend; for you pretend to give no additional ideas, but only to assert a *something*, which is exactly what empiricism does, a something more and different beyond the sphere of a naked consciousness.

## CHAPTER XLIV.

### "PERCEPTION" IN ITS MODERN SENSE A FIGMENT, BEING BUT AN INSTANCE OF INTUITIVE BELIEF, SO CALLED.

THE world has accepted with a wonderful degree of unanimity the attempt to turn aside the old meaning of *perception*, and to install a different one. The old meaning was ours, and may be described as a general term for cognition or thought, and included sensation. But as Ontology wrestled with itself there came a change. Perception was made to mean a discerning of matter, and sense the mere occasion for it. For example, fragrance; it is a mere brutish sensibility; or taste; it was plausibly argued, it is possessed by animals; or sight, it is a mere color upon the eye. The doctrine was, that these were to be called sensations; but following them as the intellectual part, came a different power, viz. the perception of matter.

I need not say that this is our old friend of the previous chapter. Every one can recognize it at once. It is the old bridge as between the me and the not-me.

And, therefore, three remarks are sufficient. First, it cannot do the duty assigned to it. We cannot have a perception where we have no idea. Second, if we consult our consciousness, we will find that all that we directly cognize of the external world is sensation and its recurrences. And, thirdly, we shall discover that sensation is not brutish but intelligent; nay, is a pure mental act; and this we shall particularly advert to in the chapter that follows.

## CHAPTER XLV.

### SENSATION AS KNOWLEDGE.

IN denouncing "*Perception*" in its modern sense we have revivified sensation, and thrown upon it all the weight of our knowledge of the universe. What is sensation? It is the slender report of five bodily tissues. Consciousness reveals to us a smell, and a taste, an effusion of color, a sound, and a cutaneous feeling, and that, with a still more brutish sensibility of pain or appetite, is all our avenue to the world beyond us.

But then superb things can be stated of each.

1. First, these are not bodily phenomena at all. Whatever else we conclude, they are purely mental. And what I mean by this is, that the smell that comes from carrion is not material in any sense of consciousness. It may have a material origin. That is, it may take a dead carcass ever to send it to the mind. But this is a matter of discovery afterward. *Genetically* it may be as material as you please. But consciously, that is to say as a mental fact, the smell is pure intelligence; and helps by its intelligence afterward to find out the matter and its outward state that helped to bring it to the mind.

Nay, not even the nostril and its agency in it, nor the nerve which is the carrier of the actual sense, nor the brain which may be the seat of all of it, makes it the least material. The smell proper, as a thing looked at by itself, is a matter of mere consciousness. If I had not learned science, yet it would seem, as indeed it really is, a matter entirely within the mind.

But if this is true of smell, then how of taste? and how of color? Sensation is a form of consciousness; and as that idea is singularly complete, we must never forget it in all our unravellings of the mind.

2. But if sensation be a form of consciousness, then all sensation is intelligent. Sensation is a macrocosm. It is endless like the universe. No two sensations are alike. And, what must be uttered with the most emphatic eagerness,—no one sensation but has almost endless capabilities of thought and reasoning.

For example, what I see! Let me mention some of the things that I am conscious of in every vision.

First, I am conscious of color. That color is red or blue. If red, it may be any of a thousand shades. Second, those shades have shapes. Those shapes are literally endless. Third, those endless shapes may vary in size and number. Again, number and size may be abstracted, and viewed apart. It is impossible to enumerate all the consciousnesses. But I may pile in touch and odor, and recollect that these are equally intelligent, and, without going further into the crowd, I reach this general reality :—that if sensations are in harmony at all, there are enough of them, and they are enough significantly varied, and they are enough consciously intelligent, to build *something* up, whatever that something may intelligently appear.

Let us state that under the two forms of Being.

## CHAPTER XLVI.

### SENSATION AS KNOWLEDGE OF THE NOT-SELF.

SENSATION does very little, intelligent as it is, without the help of Recurrence. Stop any picture in the train. Stop a dozen of them. How very little in the current is absolute sensation.

I look upon a house. Recurrence almost builds the whole of it. And what it does not build, or rather what it does not seem to put together, it colors with all the past.

Let us think of that.

My mere sense-consciousness is a superficies of light. That it does not lie lazily within, and stands out a distant image of conception, is a tribute from the past. Understand me distinctly, I see simply what I see, but that conscious seeing is a mere surface, and (confining myself of course to sense) it contributes only that to my thought of Being.

Let us have no mysteries therefore. Recurrence; how shall we call it? It certainly is not Sensation, and yet it plays the larger part in the game of knowledge. The reality is this:—Sensation and recurrent sensation,—they are the things to speak of. I cannot say they are the whole of knowledge. We will speak of that presently. I cannot say, Sensations when they recur are still sensations. They are not. They are quite different consciousnesses. I can only say, Sensations and recurrent sensations are pure intelligences, and as such are largely concerned in my ideas of Being.

Now what else is concerned in them?

We have seen that sensation is conscious of its likenesses. Recurrence is but a bringer up of things like. No two sensations are anything but like. If sensation is never the same, recurrence does not even seem the same. And we have explained the slow receding of likeness till power and substance and God are slowly made to emerge, retaining scarce a patch of original likeness as means to recall my senses.

We will return to this point. For the present we will *assert* the truth, that Sensation and recurrent Sensation, though not our whole thought of the Not-Self, are nevertheless the foundation consciousnesses.

Whether there be more, we will state presently.

## CHAPTER XLVII.

### SENSATION AS KNOWLEDGE OF SELF.

Self without perception could of course never be discovered. No school is so bent on first truths as to affirm that a man could be conscious of self without ideas. There must be ideas coursing through his mind. And the second great fact we have already treated, viz. that he could never begin ideas without sensation. Sensation, therefore, must at least originate before he could have any ideas of self. And yet sensation never could give any idea of self. We have established this sufficiently. A flash without order, a sense without continuance, could give no dual notion. And we must have in effect a twin notion, viz. the me and the not-me, as well as the perceiving consciousness, before we can assert intelligently either being. That brings in recurrence. Sensation and recurrent sensation, as in the instance of matter, must both be possessed, before we can build the idea of spirit.

Keeping purely to these two however; I mean by that, excluding any other imagined consciousness,—how entire a self can we build up? Sensation as merely nervous, or (to revive the list) a sound, or a scent, or a light, or a taste, or a still coarser feeling, is all that starts thought; and now a recurrent sense, or nerve-feelings brought shadowily back, these are the self-builders. They could build a very decent self if there were nothing direct besides. They could build it as they build matter, partly (that I may show respect to usage) out of consciousness itself, but partly as a metaphysic *ens*, outness and power and permanence and otherness and number being seen in recurrences themselves, and then analogy and difference being also seen, and taking the leap that carries us to metaphysic being.

Yet if any one asks us, Is the self simply framed by these two? Must sensation and the recurrent sensation be regarded as the sum of knowledge? Nay, adding the increment of what is like, or plying the empiricism of what is different, must sense and recurred sense be all the base for projecting analogies toward the thought of being, we answer, No: but we postpone the secret for another chapter. We answer, No: as in the instance of matter. All being is perception and its analogues. Perception, therefore, plays the heroic part. But then, what perception? Perception must be all sensation; or perception rather must be sense or sense recurrences, or else there is a *tertium quid* that must be looked after as being directly conscious.

## CHAPTER XLVIII.

### IS ALL PERCEPTION SENSATION?

Perception might be separated from belief. I see the blue. That is sense perception. I see the likeness of the blue. That is also direct. But I assert the equality of the blueness; that is a belief. It looks ever so much equal. I cannot consciously assert it, but it passes into the other region of empirical uncertainty. So I hear a bell. I have heard it for a score of years. I have never known it to be silent. So, when the time comes, I perceive that it will ring again. But that perception is a spurious appellative. I do not really perceive. I perceive when there is a ringing now, but I perceive nothing of the future. That perceiving is really believing. It is an accommodated use, and means simply that I expect a ringing from analogies that have been experienced.

So the *ego*. What is conscious of it I perceive. And if that is a fair vocabulary that makes the me and the not-me take-in a patch of consciousness, so that far and no farther I may be said to be conscious of self.

But if there be a metaphysic *ens*, which *wears* the red color or *has* the thought which marks the outward and the inward, that *ens* is like the ringing of the bell. It is bred of analogy. It is believed in, and not perceived. And it is believed in not from a Regulative Faculty, but as with the being of a God, because we are driven to it by analogy and difference.

Perception, therefore, might be bounded consciously, and limited only to a metaphysical sense. And in this limit we do not say that we perceive the Deity, and we do not say that we perceive our spirits. We limit the vision to our consciousness. And there, as we have long ago explained, every atom of the thought is entered into and possessed as conscious.

Now, is every atom of this thought, sensation? Or, as that of course must be negatived, is every atom of that thought, sense or sense-recurrence?

We might come much nearer saying, Yes, than many would dream. What else is there beside these two? Number,—that is a sensation. Outness and inness and permanence and power,—those are all sensations. I mean literally what I say. These all may be dressed up by recurrence, but the base feature in each is imbedded in sensation. Recollect, each sense is all intelligence. That fact is not sufficiently remembered. Sensation of two ducks!—fancy that, void of number; or the blue sky without space; or two bell-notes without duration. These are all discoveries of sense. And if you yearn back after something intellectual, why not ask it in hue or pitch or beauty? Sensation is either all of sense, or else it is none of it. Either it fails at the delicate colors of the sea, or else it takes in all it sees, or else it staggers at the universal fact that it shows to us; and, therefore, time and space and permanence and outness and number are all a part of the actual facts of sense that come up by sensation and recurrence.

Now are these two all of consciousness?

Let us be very careful here.

I think of other selves. They are bred of a free empiricism. They are analogues, therefore, and not a consciousness. I think of them as I do of the future bell-ringing of which I am never conscious, but in which I only believe.

Nevertheless my mind is so constituted that I have certain emotions even when I do not conceive a thing but only believe. I do not conceive another, but only believe him. That is, I do not perceive my neighbor, but only put him together. I perceive his color, and loose talk may make that a part of him, but otherwise he is not a consciousness. Of all things he is an empirical conceit, and yet with this fact about him to which I wish to draw particular regard, viz. that as I build up the analogue,—his sense from my sense,—his thought from my thought,—his power from my power,—his joy from my joy,—*the emotion that his imagined happiness creates is totally different from that created by my own.* A mere analogy of consciousnesses that builds up a neighbor spirit, evokes an entirely new consciousness, not an analogue, but a novelty, not a mere inferred thing, but an original; that is, though the quiddity, my neighbor, is a mere inferred thing through an empiricism, my emotion thereanent is an original; and a different pleasure is awakened by his happiness from that which is awakened by what is consciously my own. This will be understood under Pathics. It is not true, therefore, that all perception is Sensation; for not only are many perceptions a recurrent sense; but these Pathic ones are quite original.

We could show the same in the realm of Taste.

Indeed, as another thing;—there are emotions which are upon emotions.

Let me explain.

I believe in others. I frame them as an empirical conceit. I do not squarely look at them, for they are matters of analogy. But I do squarely look at my emotion. They waken in me a species of perception, which, in the Pathic aspect, is absolutely new. This is a perfect consciousness, as much so as sense or memory. But then, this joy itself can in turn be looked at. It awakens another joy: this joy, in turn, is itself original. And now, multiply results. This joy is a matter of recurrence. Sense, therefore, and sense recurrences are not enough. The nobility of these moral joys is itself a consciousness. Perception, and the analogies of perception, are all we wot of; but perceptions are not all sensations. Perceptions are not all sensations and recurrences; but consciousnesses can spring out of conceits. That is to say, My neighbor, who is not a certainty, can breed in me consciousnesses that are, and that not mere belief-consciousnesses as of a future bell, but first-hand emotions that can spring on no other ground.

# BOOK IV.

# PATHICS;

OR, THE

# SCIENCE OF PERCEPTION AS EMOTION.

---

## INTRODUCTORY CHAPTERS.

## CHAPTER I.

### AN ATTEMPT TO INVENT ADEQUATE NAMES.

THE Science of Perception as Emotion has no name such as we have laid our hands on in all the other branches of our subject. To change an old name is awkward; and old names are very likely to straggle back to old meanings. To invent a new name is bold, but is very certain to end happily, if the speculation does to which it is attached. If the speculation fails, of course all will, that is launched with it. If the task succeeds, the names' being quite new is all the better, as they will not shift through some older signification.

The names we invent are Pathics, Eudemonics, and Agathology.

Emotion is perception in the aspect of pleasure or pain. Pleasure or pain are not the only aspects of emotion. If they were, our course would be much simpler. Emotions are pleasures or pains, but emotions are very different. Emotions are sensuous or poetic or moral; nay, just as different as perceptions;—I mean by that, with precisely the same differences as the perceptions of which they are but aspects. But more than that,—as emotions they are not merely pleasurable. They may be *right*, or they may be *heroic*, or they may be *tasteful*, as we shall hereafter see. If not, *Eudemonics* is the only word we would have had to invent. But emotion has other aspects beside the eudemonic, viz. the ethical aspect, and also the æsthetical;—moreover, not necessarily coterminous. Though they be all eudemonic; that is, emotions always of either pleasure or pain,—they are not all ethical; and they are not all æsthetical; and, therefore, we need a wider term. And accordingly, we have chosen Pathics, as of the same form with Ethics, and as embracing all of them. Pathics is the Science of Perception as Emotion. We still retain Eudemonics, and use it for that branch of Pathics which treats of emotion as simply pleasurable or simply painful. Then we have this division,—Pathics, including (1) Eudemonics, (2) Æsthetics, and (3) Ethics. This is the whole of the subject. And we know no better way to bring out all the facts that it can be made to exhibit.

And now, as coining is unpopular, let us finish that part of the business.

Eudemonics would save us from another term if the *good* of emotion lay only in its pleasurableness; but it does not. We delay the proof of this. All good lies in emotion; but, strange to say, all not in its pleasurableness. Pathics is the whole field of good. Pathics has all divine good. Emotion is all the good of the universe. What a splendid department Pathics is! Thought—what would that be worth, or wisdom, or infinite power, or being, eternal in its years, but for emotion? We need a term, therefore,—*Agathology*, as the Science of Good. It lies in Pathics; but we give it no separate discussion. There is other good than pleasure; but there is no other good than emotion. If there be good in being, and good in power, and good in wisdom, and good in the divine existence, it is all ancillary. The real good, whether in God or man, is that aspect of perception in which it goes by the name of emotion.

## CHAPTER II.

### PATHICS UNDER THE LIGHT OF PSYCHOLOGY.

WE learned, under the head of Psychology, that the Law of the Strongest Emotion was that which made pictures for us, or called out of sensation, or out of memory, that thought which would be most interesting to each particular mind. We should mistake this doctrine though, if we should imagine that perception happens to be emotional simply because unemotional perceptions are not called out. The law of perception is simply the law of the *strongest* emotion; and *some* emotion is inseparable from the very idea of perceiving at all.

But Psychology would be still a mistake if its doctrine was, that perception had *some* emotion. The fact that we found out was, that perception *was* emotion, for that emotion was but perception under another aspect; and it will be remembered that we formulated Pathics (B. I. Chaps. X., XI.) by saying (1) that all perception was emotion, and (2) that all emotion was perception, so as to make the truth presented one of the most clear-put and comprehensive in all philosophy.

(1.) That all perception is emotion, will appear best

from the very thought of the current. If the current is entire, and all our perception fills it ;—that is, if the current is all our consciousness, and there is nothing consciously in it but perception,—then emotion is not consciously in the current, or it is perception. But when we come to think, emotion is not only consciously in the current, but it is consciously in it all the time. This consciousness we can arrive at any moment. If we look within, the whole current is emotional,—nay, think of it for a single instant, the whole current is an emotion : and now not because it has sensitive sides, so to speak, or sensitive points ; for it is emotional throughout. The whole current of perception is perceptive in an emotional way.

And not only so, but each part is. It is by these different views that we inspect our consciousness. Let us try the driest things. An angle ! I say I feel it, just as much as I see it. You may ask, Why do I not talk so then ? I do not say, I feel an angle ; first, because it would be ambiguous, feeling being an emblematic word, and being derived from another sense. Moreover, I do not say, I feel an angle, because it does not suit me : I choose my words according to the perceptive or emotional aspect, just as I need them in my speech. But I say enough, in cases that admit the indifference, to set forth all the reality. I say I see or I feel with a freedom absolutely total. I feel the truth or I see the truth, I feel His power or I see His power, I feel the reasonableness of an act or I see the reasonableness of an act ; and I will let you dismember the sentence, and put one indifferently for the other. My appeal is simply to consciousness. If I stand at any hour of the day and fish in the current, and take the fish that first cometh up, perception and emotion are perfectly commensurate. Perception is all emotional, and emotion is all perceptive. And I can see it best by just touching my thoughts. Try it as we read. Each one is not a hard concept, but a warm sense, pleasant or painful according to its nature.

(2.) The other thought, All emotion is perception, is singularly fertile. It settles many a question. If taste have but emotion, men are ready to say, Why do we speak of reason as concerned in Taste? Or, as a far weightier case, if conscience beget emotion, if holiness be only emotion, if the law be all that is right, and love be the fulfilling of the law, why is reason appealed to? Conscience itself is supposed to be intelligent; the truth an instrument upon it; light necessary to it; illumination the beginning of its reform; and the Holy Ghost needed to enlighten it, as well as to wrap its frame with warmer feeling.

All these things are explained when we remember that emotion is perception. When a man says, We must believe first, and feel afterward, we say, No: there is a Pathical unity. Nor is it so very hard to understand. Emotion is conscious. That much is as well settled as iron. Now if emotion is conscious, how much of it is conscious? And if emotion attaches to perception, can it be conscious of all of itself, without being conscious of all the perception? If I feel warmth, must I not have all the warm perception? If I love virtue, must I not know it? or God, must I not know all that I love? or sin, must I not enter into its delights? And by this I do not mean either as a prelude or a consequence, but must not love that goes feeling down to the very bottom of the emotion, feel all the perceptive facts, or have the love precisely as the same thing as the perceptive consciousness?

Emotion is not only perceptive in perceiving the perceptions that attend it, as for example, that it perceives the light before it feels it: on the contrary, emotion perceives itself. It perceives the sight in its own emotional aspect. It can abstract its own emotionalness. Emotion is that functionary word that notes perception in its pleasurableness; but as to its seeing less than perception, or being less than perception, or being in essence different, that has been the mistake that has tangled ethical beliefs. I see beauty when I feel it, and right when I dote upon it, and God when I bow down and love Him. And if any one says, Why say feel, instead of see? or why ever speak of feeling? why pile up words when one would answer even better? I say, One would not answer. Feeling and seeing are both needed, and present a different sense; and there now we come to the point. If any one exclaims, How can seeing and how can feeling present the one reality of perception? I say, How can blueness and how can brightness present the one reality of color? Here is the secret. A bright blueness and a blue brightness are identically the same. But if any one declares them philologically similar, we take issue at once. The brightness and the blueness are distinguishably significant; and yet they are numerically the same. And so perception and pleasure are distinguishable, but only as aspects of a thought. The pleasure sees all that is to be perceived, and the perception feels all by which we are pleased; and the phenomenal facts are open throughout all of either.

## CHAPTER III.

### PATHICS UNDER THE LIGHT OF LOGIC.

IF nothing is intuitively known but perception, emotion is perception or it is not intuitively known.

This is the glory of Ethics.

A way of speaking of it has been, that we reason out duties, and when chastity and truth and gratitude and self-love have been inspected by the reason, they are brought near to conscience, and become subjects of emotional regard.

How superficial this is!

There are but two ethical emotions. Both these will be treated in the sequel. All duties are but instances of these. Out in life reason may have a play, I mean in its discursive acts, to judge whether this thing or that thing can be prompted by the two ethical emotions; but this is all empirical. The whole conscience is intuitive. If any one asks, Is not Ethics reasonable? I say, Doubly. Not only does it appeal to reason in its discursive acts, but to reason as the mind's intelligence. All conscience is reason. And now the explanation:—All conscience is a region of emotion: all right is in emotion: but then, as we have just explained, all emotion is perception. Conscience, therefore, both perceives and feels; and hence the clearness of what many men blunder over, that conscience should both be an intelligence of the mind and a region of the heart,—the heart and the mind being in fact the same region of the spirit.

1. Hence the question, whether faith or repentance comes first, is ploughed under by this metaphysic. Both will come first. The conscience and the mind are not even twins, but one unitary spirit.

2. Hence the nobility of the word conscience. It meant consciousness in all the earlier period of men. Even in the New Testament it is misinterpreted. When Paul said, "I have lived in all good conscience" (Acts xxiii. 1) he meant consciousness. The word in the Greek had not lost its original meaning. "Curse not the king, no, not in thy conscience" (Ecclesias. x. 20 *marg.*) of course tells a similar history. "Their conscience also bearing witness" (Rom. ii. 15; see also ix. 1, Heb. x. 2). "The testimony of our conscience" (2 Cor. i. 12). We would not multiply instances. The grand fact is, that ethical truth is so under the eye of our consciousness that it at last monopolized the word. Glory to God, that which we are to give account for at last is not, like our substantive selves, or like a substantive not-self whether divine or human, a matter of proof, but an intuitive conscience. The nobility of right is consciously witnessed under the very eye of the mind.

3. Hence the strength of our polemic in defending Christianity. Holiness,—that we are conscious of:—and sin. The great facts of religion are matters of intuition. We are not emboldened enough by this reality. Protoplasm; that is a mere empirical conceit. There may be much truth in it. The Unknowable; we have too great a dread of it. Half of Spencer can be swept at once into the coffers of the Church. We have expounded God too much, and forgotten that most that we know of Him lies in the region of our conscience. When the Gibeonites come and pretend to be groping for the Almighty (Jos. ix. 3, 9), their "clouted shoes" and mouldy provisions, and their "old sacks upon their asses," ought not to deceive us, as though they had come a great way; for they are

neighbor sinners; and, poor imbeciles like us all! let us at least deal wilily if they come among us, and make them hewers of wood and drawers of water for the men of Israel.

A vast deal may be gotten out of a working infidel.

They scour the bottom of a filthy sailing vessel.

Hume did it; and so did Mill.

And while our cause is the better for their rude attacks, it is never wrecked. Religion lies in the region of our consciousness. And while in teleological argument we have all the advantage of the infidel, we have a region into which he can never enter,—the testimony of conscience;—and, therefore, ought to allow the widest liberty in the outer region of empirical results.

## CHAPTER IV.

### PATHICS UNDER THE LIGHT OF ONTOLOGY.

THE very idea of God we have admitted as empirical; how, therefore, can we speak of consciousness in matters of religion?

Let us explain this.

The very idea of self, so far as scientific men have pushed it out of the region of consciousness (see B. III. Chap. XXXVII.), is empirical also. Another man's self is just as empirical to me as the existence of the Almighty.

It will appear when we come to Ethics, that moral emotion begins with our relations to other beings. Let us anticipate a little. We love others, and then we love the love that we thus begin with. Moral emotion could not begin except with the exercise of benevolence. We will not particularize. The knowledge of right must begin with the knowledge of other beings.

But now a strange anomaly! My knowledge of other beings is empirical. My knowledge of the differences of right is conscious. What is the solution? I can never feel benevolence except in the thought of other beings. How then can it be possibly true that benevolence can be a consciousness, when the sole object of benevolence must be empirically discerned?

Let us take analogies.

Blue; is not that intuitive? and yet the very object that breeds it is quite empirical.

Moreover, blue; does not that awaken emotion? It is beautiful. Is the blue thing beautiful? Unquestionably not—in the sense in which that question would be pertinent. And yet it awakens the emotion. All my reasonings about it are decidedly empirical. I do not know the not-me; I do not know the me; I do not know the Almighty,—except empirically. And yet that which shines out through these empirical conceits, I mean beauty, and the emotion of right, are conscious intuitions, the latter so gloriously so as to have usurped towards it the name of conscience.

Nay more, remember:—All things breed emotion. All perceptions are emotions. There are no such things as empirical conceits, or else they are emotions. All things breed different emotions. Just as the ideas differ, so do the different emotions. It seems that empirical ideas breed all the highest emotions. That is not wonderful. Empirical ideas are beyond us. They border the invisible. Blue sky we see. That is, we see its blueness. That breeds a low emotion. My neighbor I do not see. He is empirical. He breeds a high emotion. The great God is utterly beyond me. The only great emotion is built upon what is empirical; and conscience, which is the power of that emotion, would lie utterly dead, unless empirical conceits rose by experience before my mind.

Still the question remains, why is religion so comfortable because it appeals to consciousness, when right, which is indeed an intuition, is predicated of emotional regards which are bent toward that which is empirical?

Let us look at this.

The being of my neighbor I am not conscious of. It is a dictate of experience. God I am not conscious of. He is a dictate of experience. Without such other beings I could know no morals. This will appear (see Ethics). Why am I so entrenched because virtue is a consciousness, when the very neighbor that makes it possible is only found out empirically before my mind?

Empiricism, let it be observed, is a combination of myriad experiences. The heavier the combination, the stronger the empirical conceit. If Herbert Spencer's God and my God compare favorably in all other proofs, and I add moral ones which his does not possess, I gain the victory, for induction is of all facts, and if there be a world of consciousness which he does not take in, he fails that much. Mere benevolence; I will not assert that that proves the existence of other beings that we may be benevolent to; or mere love of right; I will not say that that proves a great Embodiment of Right to whom we may worship and bow down. But this I do say, that if Darwin and I have equal teleological claims in all other respects; and his protoplasm-brute and my Jehovah-God are equal, *in foro rationis*, in all physical respects; and I take in the moral, and he cannot, but must leave it meaningless and dead; then I have beaten by his own organon. That is the best theory that takes in all the facts. And if he, beginning with the monad, has to leave out so conscious a fact as conscience, then he had better strain a little and bring in miracle, which is not so improbable a fact as that the Power that made me made me more and nobler than He.

But once admitted—my God once suffered to come in,—then what follows? Why, that the nobler fact of Him is a matter of my consciousness. This it is that entrenches us so. If there were no God, facts of virtue would still survive. Men make their polemic rudely. Atheism is right, that right is right independent of the Deity. But when Theism is forced-in as necessary to explain the facts, how gloriously is it suffused with virtue! How strong we become! Our very highest consciousness puts the finishing stroke to our Theology. Blueness in the sky shows to us the not-self. Consciousness in the current shows to us the self; and soon aggregates to us in ten thousand ways notitias of other selves. Then our conscious virtues, not laying perhaps the base of the Deity, are ready to put in the key-stone. After that, the arch should not be shaken. The whole string of the curve is necessary. Every fact helps. But emotions are conscious facts; and morals are the highest emotions. And, satisfied there, Christians should be less timid about the rest, and should leave more liberty in physics when the moral God is firmly and strongly in their hands.

The moral God;—what does that imply? The moral God must be personal. The personal God must be intelligent; and, if intelligent, then also emotional, and possessing will and happiness. Give me a moral God, and I ought to allow more liberty to the students of Ontology. And if you say, 'No: they may undermine our arch: you yourself say that its foundations are empirical: virtue is conscious, but the God who is to possess it, is an empirical conceit:' I say, Yes, but an empiricism so broad, so matted in its world of facts, so moulded in its ancient arguments, so attacked since the world began, and so defended under every argument, that when I see it walled around by the very darts and javelins that it has broken, I think a shame to be so timid for it ; and, when we possess the citadel of conscience, let the empirical Copernicus, or the adventurous Galileo, take time to show what they can produce before our eyes.

# PART I.

## EUDEMONICS; OR, THE SCIENCE OF PERCEPTION AS AN EMOTION OF PLEASURE OR OF PAIN.

### CHAPTER I.

#### EUDEMONICS IN ITS RELATION TO PATHICS.

PATHICS is the science of perception as a pleasure or a pain. Eudemonics is the science of emotion in its pleasurableness or painfulness. Where is the difference? All the emotion is a pleasure, and all the pleasure is an emotion. Where can Eudemonics find room to differ from Pathics, and, above all, in any discernible way to be embraced by it? The doctrines of Agathology, which we are next to consider, will begin the answer to this most radical question.

### CHAPTER II.

#### EUDEMONICS IN ITS RELATION TO AGATHOLOGY.

EMOTION is the only possible good. Let one consider. If man had nothing but knowledge and power: or, to go at once to the Almighty, if God knew everything, and did everything, and lived forever, and reached immensity, but had no feeling, where would be the good of the universe? It is a very neat and very admirable question. A cosmos may be all rocks, or still nebular mist, or better yet never have been created, and be just as well as a universe without emotion.

Now emotion is never anything else than a pleasure or a pain. If a pleasure were no good except merely in its pleasurableness, then Eudemonics would cover the whole ground of Agathology. But pleasures are different. Some pleasures are merely pleasurable, like the taste of honey. Some pleasures are also tasteful, like the sight of beauty. Some pleasures are heroical, like a glow of courage. And some, above all, are Ethical. Here is the great heart of Metaphysical Science. All are Eudemonic as far as they are pleasurable. But some are Æsthetic. Pleasures that are Æsthetic we shall find are good in other ways than as merely pleasurable. And when we come to the two Ethical emotions, we will find the highest conceivable good. These right emotions will some day be the highest pleasures; but as a thing that is to take rank of that, they are pleasures excellent in themselves, or in other words *emotions consciously conceived as having higher good than their simple pleasurableness.*

## CHAPTER III.

### EUDEMONICS IN ITS RELATION TO ETHICS.

PLEASURE,—and now I mean in its sense as pleasant,—has one dignity, and that is that it is the starting point of all the possibilities of morals. Sensation we have seen must begin consciousness. And so benevolence, which requires for its province other people's pleasure, is the first occasion of all things ethical.

1. Benevolence we shall find is not the highest virtue;

2. And pleasure we shall find is not virtuous simply as pleasurable;

3. And self-love we shall find is a truism, and is fiercely misconceived when we call it virtue;

These are great facts of Eudemonics; and they leave for Ethics this great reality, viz. that there is that in two simple pleasures (Ethics, D. II. Chap. VI.) which lifts them above everything in the universe besides, and that this quality is not their pleasurableness, but a conscious excellence, not accepted through an Intuitive Belief (B. II. Chap. XVI), but actually seen in the heart's emotion.

---

# PART II.

## ÆSTHETICS; OR, THE SCIENCE OF PERCEPTION AS AN EMOTION OF TASTE.

### CHAPTER I.

#### DEFINITION.

Sir William Hamilton defines pleasure to be unrestrictedness of energy (Metaphysics, p. 577). Pain is obstruction of some energy. And to defend so bizarre a statement, he calls in Plato and Aristotle, and, to our amazement, those fathers of the human mind are guilty of such notions as this,—Plato, that pleasure is reaction from pain, and Aristotle, that it is a concomitant of energy. That is, I hang a flower before the eye of a child, and the pleasure of the child is a mere reaction from pain. So says Plato. Or I stick a pin into the flesh of a child, and his shriek of dismay is from mere impeded energy. Old monks getting hold of the manuscripts of these men could hardly make them seem more crazy by stuffing them with dreams. And yet these were deliberate arguings; and Sir William Hamilton, with his splendid gifts, lays claim to Aristotle, and argues at length for the "unimpeded" theory.

Now, how are we to account for these things?

If a house does not get down to the hard-pan for its base, it crazes and goes awry.

The doctrine of perception is the hard-pan of Pathics. As long as emotion floats as something separate, it is a Will-o'-the-Wisp. Men will make fools of themselves chasing it. But when it appears that emotion is but an aspect of perception, it is marvellously cleared. It does not need a definition. It cannot have one. We cannot define blue color (except perhaps spectrally); and so we cannot define pleasure, except in discourses about it as in these chapters. Pleasure is an aspect of consciousness. Consciousness is a definition to itself. Pleasure is down at the very hard-pan; and we cannot dig lower. And the jingle, Pleasure is pleasure, is a far better definition, and will be a better enlightenment even to a child, than all the mixed thoughts about energy,—empirical, and, therefore, of no kinship to the whole class that is to be defined.

So, eminently, certain definitions about taste.

I hang a lily before a child, and it gives him pleasure. Long ago it has been noticed that this is not a pleasure like that which is given to him by its smell; and yet it is a mere consciousness. The child, if idiotic, might clap its hands, and glare its eyes, at the lily.

How foolish to give any definition other than one that merely bounds and separates. To attempt to give all of beauty, and to make it all up artificially and of extraneous things, is the wildest dream possible; and yet precisely this has been done by Alison and other annotators.

Beauty is an affair of consciousness. If you do not see it, I cannot show it to you. It is like warmth from fire, or light from torch, or scent from the breath of flowers. It is a consciousness in a mind's emotion.* And when Alison says, it is Association, and thus builds it bodily; and when Plotinus says, it is Sympathy,—we always think of little seraphs, with wings, but with nothing to sit down on.† There is a *differentia* of beauty, and no doubt it will be difficult to fix, and there will be our labor. But we can start to build from the hard-pan. Beauty is an affair of consciousness. And by *differentia* we mean, that we can cut it daintily from all things else. But when we come to make it in the rough, we shall find, as in Alison's case, that it is an utter craziness.

* We are speaking here of course, seminally. There are three meanings of the word, beauty. We are pestered by these dictionary differences. If anybody says, there are but two, we shall not stop to differ with him. If any one says, No; only one,—we will have our agreements with him even there. The three we meant are, first, a consciousness; second, a consciousness thrown like paint upon the object; and, third, a power in the object, that is the empiric trait, by which the æsthetic consciousness is supposed to be aroused. Some may say, Not the first at all. The word beauty is always used objectwise. Some may say, Not the last at all. The conscious beauty is always felt to be suffused. We make little cavil. Abstractly, we triplify as we have done. Concretely, the three grow into a point. Self includes consciousness: and why should we wonder that the dry quality of reflecting beauty should keep itself suffused, first, with the objectwise charm, and second, with the charmed sense; *this last of course being the whole genetic reality?* (see Ethics, Introd. Ch. IV.).

† Of a like baselessness is "the old definition in the Roman school, that beauty is 'multitude in unity,'" of which Coleridge says, that "no doubt such is the principle of beauty."

## CHAPTER II.

### THE DIFFERENTIA OF BEAUTY.

THE *differentia* of beauty is hard to give, for three reasons.

1. First, it is a term *widely* generalized.

Perception is immense; and no two perceptions are ever alike. Perception of sound, perception of scent, perception of power, perception of heat, perception of time—there is no end of difference; and the difference of taste is almost as various as the difference of perception. To crowd under one word all varied beauties—such as of sound, such as of light, of music, of poetry, of a woman's face, of a bridge's curvilineal outline, is to insure a difficult *differentia*. A logarithm is very far from a harp-note as having the one element of the beautiful. In Ethics it is not so. There there are but two emotions. At least that is what we shall propound. This gives amazing simpleness, and just where man needs it. But in beauty, a *differentia* would seem a myth, so varied are the forms of it, and so many.

2. And further, secondly, there is so *bad* a generalization. Smell; has not that its beauties as well as color? The exquisite fragrance of the Jasmine,—is not that beautiful as well as flowers or birds? To me it seems so. And when we get among tastes of the higher flavor, there is a delicacy among its daintiest feasts that to my consciousness at least is strictly beautiful. Of course this breeds delay. For if, in defining beauty, I find it break over the very bounds it has, there seems no end to the investigation.

3. Thirdly, what we are to look for must be definite.

Is beauty mere pleasurableness? When I speak of delicacy, is it a mere quainter form of the pleasure? When I say, that to me the taste of a vanilla bean seems beautiful, do I merely describe a phase of the pleasure's pleasurableness? Here is a vital question. We insist on it for its light on Ethics: and we shall go forward for it to another chapter, viz. to Beauty as a Good. For here now is the vital question. Is a harp-note only beautiful as a higher dainty for my sense? or is it a good *per se?*—rather is the emotion a good, apart from its good as merely pleasurable?

If this last can be affirmed, *a fortiori* will it give strength to Ethical positions.

## CHAPTER III.

### ÆSTHETICS UNDER THE LIGHT OF AGATHOLOGY.

ALL good is of the nature of emotion. If all emotion is only pleasurable, then all good consists in being happy. This is the shirt of Nessus that has clung fast to the morals of the world.

But now, very discriminatingly, All emotion is a pleasure. That is beyond a doubt. Moreover all the emotion is a pleasure, and it is nothing else (unless it be a pain). And yet all the emotion is a perception. We say this to show that things may be numerically the same, and yet have very different aspects. Pleasure may be the whole emotion, and yet may have different aspects.

The question arises whether pleasure has but one aspect, viz. its being pleasurable, or whether it has other aspects, these other aspects being other goods beside its mere pleasurableness.

If pleasure has but one aspect, viz. its pleasurableness, this book of ours could be shut up like a telescope. Eudemonics could take the whole place instead of Pathics, and Agathology would only include Eudemonics, pleasure being the only good and the single pivot for revolving histories.

But, now, pleasure is not the only good. The emotion otherwise may have a conscious excellence. The splendors of art,—a man may actually worship them. He may say, I actually dote upon these pictures. If we ask him, Do they give you pleasure? He may say, Yes. If we ask him, Do they give you more pleasure than your food and banquetings? They may or may not. After a moment's hesitation he may refuse to say. But this he will say, that they give him a better sort of pleasure. And the more we investigate, the more we will come to the conclusions, that men see good in emotions besides their pleasurableness. And this not for their hygiene, and not for their pomps, and not for their results, and not for their reputes, but purely. There is a conscious good in taste above and beyond its being simply pleasurable.

And among plainer people, why do we say that cleanliness is next to godliness? Is it that it is healthy? Is it that by a roundabout reasoning we have found out that purity of body is favorable to purity of mind? And even then, why is it favorable? If a man were to confess, A good plum-pudding would give me more pleasure than a clean room, but yet the clean room would give me the higher form of pleasure, would we think him crazy? or would we think that he was conscious of a good in certain emotions of pleasure other than their mere pleasurableness before his mind?

We have hints of the truth here by what comes floating in our speech. Like when we come near to England the sea-weed begins to float, so, in this neighborhood of Ethics, the word *ought* begins to color our vocabulary. If a man says that for his part he likes roast beef; he does not care for pictures,—a man would not be thought senseless who should tell him, he *ought* to care for pictures. And when we float into the region of Heroics, a man *ought* to be brave even outside of a question of morals. We *ought* to be cleanly. A man *ought* to enjoy Niagara. And if it give him more pleasure to eat his dinner than to go to see it, he *ought* to see it, for the mere superiority of the taste, beyond its measured pleasurableness.

And men act upon this—miscreants who have no morality. Servetus will die at the stake. The devil will storm heaven if it sinks him leagues deeper into misery. All men smart for their heroics. And it is not a question of right, nor a question at all of happiness, nor a question of ultimate results, but a present heroism. All men will bend to their taste in sacrifice of that which has superior pleasurableness.

# PART III.

## ETHICS; OR, THE SCIENCE OF PERCEPTION AS AN EMOTION OF CONSCIENCE.

---

## INTRODUCTORY CHAPTERS.

### CHAPTER I.

#### EMOTION AT EMOTION.

CONSCIOUSNESS is the perception of our perception, or the awareness that each perception has of all of its own perceiving. Emotion is also perception, and is also self-conscious; and it can abstract. And emotion itself being an aspect of perception, it can abstract that aspect; that is, emotion can be conscious of itself in the mere aspect of being a perceptive pleasure. Now, in the instance of Æsthetics, there is a duplicity in this abstraction: that is, I can feel a pleasurableness in a pleasure, and I can feel a dignity apart from what is merely eudemonic. A blue sky, for example; it is not only a delight, but it is beautiful. It is a delight because it is beautiful; but it is beautiful more and better than simply as being a delight. This is not an Intuitive Belief; it is directly a consciousness. I see a thing blue. I see a thing round or square. That is not an Intuitive Belief. So I see a thing beautiful. The emotion of beauty is just as conscious as the emotion of warmth. I cannot define it, except as beauty is the chosen name for the power that a sky has to look beautiful, or to give that species of pleasure which is not a good simply for its pleasurableness.

So now of conscience. *There* is something still rarer. Emotions of taste abstract and separate their own especial dignity. But emotions of conscience do more than this. There are emotions at emotions. Let me define carefully. All emotions breed emotions. That is, all emotions are self-conscious, and all self-conscious things, when we turn to look at them, are again emotional, simply on the ground that all perception is itself emotion.

When I think of the sky, therefore, the emotion of beauty that it excites I can think of afterward ; and when I think of it afterward, it is again emotional, that is, the emotion of beauty, when it recurs, is beautiful again before my mind.

But Ethics goes a story higher. A first sight actually bequeaths a second sight, and that nobler and most discrepant. I see a beautiful cloud, and that is the end of the reality. But I see my friend's prosperity, and I rejoice in it, and that is a pleasure, like the pleasure for the blue cloud, dignified beyond its mere pleasurableness. But I think of this pleasure, and there is now a new pleasure again ; but not as in the instance of beauty a mere reduplication of the other, but quite a different one, not like the second rainbow fainter than the first, but more dignified and more imperative. In other words there emerge two excellences, one an excellence of my pleasure in the prosperity of my friend, and the other in my pleasure at that excellence, the germs as we shall hereafter see of our two sole virtues, one my virtue at being pleased for my friend, and the other the vastly higher one of being pleased for that pleasure, that is to say, the dignified emotion of being pleased at a pleasure simply for its excellence.

## CHAPTER II.

### EMOTION AS IT WIDENS ITS VOCABULARY.

LOVE is mere pleasure with a new name to make it fit better in the uses of our literature. So with a host of other words that confuse from not being kept unitary. I love a tune, simply as meaning that I see its beauty. I love to think, I love to pray, I love my neighbor, I love my Maker, partly let me here say as meaning a habit, viz. the fact that I could love if the occasion offered; but, as a conscious exercise at the time, it simply means pleasure; viz., thought pleases me, and prayer pleases me, and my neighbor pleases me when he continues prosperous, and God pleases me; that is, perception is emotion, and the perception of these things is emotional pleasantly before my mind.

So of desire. Digging down to its root in pleasure and in the opposite pain is mere dictionary work.

And so of will. These are all moral terms; but how they are bred of emotion has already appeared. There is nothing moral but emotion, and there is no emotion that is moral but two, as will hereafter appear; and will, as has already been seen, is a highly artificial vocable, bedded in emotion, with two narrow offices to meet, one in the play of the muscles, and the other in the mere phenomenon of detained perception.

## CHAPTER III.

### EMOTION AS IT LEADS TO ACTION.

AS *Not-I* can only be known through the five senses, so *I* can only act through my bare volition. If volition is that narrow thing (B. I. Chap. XXX.), moving my muscles, and fixing my attention, it is easier to trace to pleasure or the want of it all my personal responsibility. Will is a pleasure pained and straitened if it does not reach certain expectations. Killing a man, therefore, is not wicked till we have cut down past all the vile accessories. The knife; and, just as much, the arm; and, of the arm, the muscle; and, down the arm, the nerve; and, through the nerve, the brain; and, in the brain, the motions, whatever they chance to be,—these are all innocent. The whole guilt is in the pleasure, that is, the pleased emotion which begot the force which swept mysteriously down to the nervous agency.

We shall see hereafter what sin is. It is negative. It is a want of two emotions. If action is called sin, it is by accommodation. If positives are called sin, like loving wine, or like loving gain, it is as a sign or a sin-bearer. There is nothing primarily sinful but a want. And as the muscles of the neck pull it all awry when those are dead on the side opposite, so sin is really sin in its positive lusts, because they are not restrained and balanced in an opposite affection.

## CHAPTER IV.

### EQUIVOCALS.

If any one will try the phrase upon his lips,—'Beauty is an emotion,' he will find that it does not agree with general usage. If he will try it, however, in his consciousness, he will find that it might be the usage, for that beauty is an emotion turned objectwise; for that the joy is a consciousness; and that out of the habit of empirical reference it is painted on the object;

just as color is a pure consciousness, but, out of the same habit, we paint it on the sky; and paint it at a distance, though distance all now agree is an empirical conceit, found out, beyond all manner of question, after empirical delays. Now, beauty is also *equivocal;* for it may be put for that weird power which the sky has to produce the consciousness, or to give the inexplainable idea of beauty.

Precisely so virtuousness can be discoursed about. If we try the phrase, 'Virtuousness is a consciousness,' we will find it is not usage. But if we try the thought, Virtuousness *is* a consciousness, for we have no manner of thought of it but as it is revealed as an aspect of an emotion,—we find ourselves stating all the cognizable truth. Beauty is painted outwardly; but yet it is an emotion inwardly. Color is painted outwardly; and yet it is a bare sensation. Virtuousness is affirmed *of* the emotion; and yet what constitutes it, and makes it cognizable, is the emotion itself; just as the sensation *is* the color. The only confusion is, that we don't speak that way. We take an aspect of consciousness; in the instance of sight, *all* the aspect, viz, color, and color it upon the sky itself; and so when the sight is beautiful, we turn that objectwise also; though the beauty is all in the sight. And so, virtuousness, though really a consciousness, is turned objectwise also; though nothing can be more purely emotional than that tang of taste that belongs to the delights of conscience.

Where do we stand, therefore?

What is emotional is of the essence of virtuousness; just as what is sensational is of the essence of blue color. Nevertheless, as dictionary talk, the virtuousness is painted as a quality, just as blueness is painted on the sky. And now, to add also the *équivoque*, the word is made to apply to a drier quality, that is to say *that trait that starts the emotion*, just as color occasionally goes to that fancied power that projects the blue light upon the mind.

We can *imagine* virtuousness, therefore, with three meanings;—first, as a conscious emotion, just as beauty might be called a conscious emotion, if language worked that way; second, as a consciousness in the emotion looked at objectwise, just as beauty is all of consciousness, but painted outwardly on the sky; and third, a dry quality. This last is a mere empirical conceit; and is the made-up thought of something to produce the consciousness, or to warrant the emotion bred inwardly in the mind.*

Now, carefully hide these three distinct meanings. We wish to bring in for immediate use three totally distinct from them.

Let us take the word *virtue*. This word babbles like a brook. But, out of its dozen meanings, let us take centrally three. It means, first, the *virtuousness* which we have just dissected. This is the prolific meaning. We speak, for example, of the virtue of a certain emotion. It means, second, the virtuous emotion itself. It means, thirdly, the character that has the habit of such emotions.† Please divide our Ethics

* I need not say that this last requires Abstraction carefully to separate it. Practically, it mixes with the others, just as self takes-in the present consciousness. When I say, 'The coloring on that fence,'—it is very hard to keep out the conscious blue, and to think only of the chemical trait by which that projection can be made upon the eye.

† Here we must erect again the same guard. Self includes consciousness. The not-self includes the instant color. Men cannot keep such things separate. And hence these ethical meanings get mixed. The (1) quality of the emotion sinks into the (2) emotion; for there is nothing numerically but the emotion. And, again; the (3) character of

with these three; first, Virtue, or the Moral Quality; second, Virtues, or Moral Duties; and third, Virtue, or Moral Character. These will be the headings of our three principal Divisions; and, springing, as they all do, out of the first, they will keep in view our main idea; that it is on the Quality of Virtuousness that the whole Science is made to depend.

---

Here we mean to print a manuscript of twenty years' standing. We print it unchanged. We alter no word up to page 339 where it ends.

We wrote it as Ethics long before other metaphysical investigations. We were enamored of its analytical truth. We are so still. We have pursued all subsequent search that we might confirm or explode it. We have not been able to explode it. We have drifted in some of the detail, but in the direction of plus rather than of minus. Where we need it we will supply a foot note.* But we will retain all the text; first, because we could but little change it; and second, to show that we have not changed: that here has been a system, conceived in an earlier period, held steady for twenty years; that here has been a system that other metaphysical study has not modified; that here has been a system in the very centre of the interests of men, not bent to other systems, but itself enthroned first, and finding through a quarter of a century mere mental facts wonderfully assimilated to its understood moralities.

the man seems nothing but the (1) character of his act, from the reason above given, that self includes our present consciousness. These things are different, however; and can be kept apart by a discreet abstraction.

* Marked (1875), to distinguish it from old foot-notes.

## DIVISION I.

## THE MORAL QUALITY.

### CHAPTER I.

#### OF MORAL SCIENCE.

MORAL Science treats of that *quality* of certain conscious exercises which we call moral. Conscience is the mind in its power to discern this quality. Duties are those exercises of mind which possess this quality. Obligation is that aspect of this quality in which those exercises that possess it become our duty. Law is that formulary, written or unwritten, expressed or implied, in which those exercises that possess this quality are commanded. Moral Science, therefore, turns in no direction, and uses no language, in which this quality in its various connections and relations is not its sole subject. Moral Science, therefore, has this element of simplicity, that its subject is one idea.

### CHAPTER II.

#### OF THE MORAL QUALITY.

BUT the moral quality as the subject of Moral Science is not only one idea, but, what is more important, it is a simple idea. You can perceive it but cannot define it.* It is like beauty. Beauty is a simple

* This is all sufficiently true, though written obviously under the conception of simple ideas technically so called. There are no such simple ideas (see B. I. Chap. XV). Ideas are *more* or *less* simple. No

idea. You can perceive it, but cannot define it. And Æsthetics, which is the science of beauty, would be a fine illustration of Ethics or Moral Science, which is the science of the quality we are considering, if beauty were not so varied. It is, in fact, a congeries of simple ideas. For the beauty of a poem, and the beauty of a sunset, and the beauty of a chorus, and the beauty of a logarithm, are certainly not all one object of thought; nay, they are not all one simple idea. But the quality we are considering has no variety except it be in its negative or opposite. For except we make a second simple idea of sin, the moral quality all over the world is single: it admits of no definition; and Moral Science would have nothing to show for itself in the way of an analysis, if it depended upon resolving that most unique and indivisible idea or quality into anything like distinct or essentially different appearances or natures.

## CHAPTER III.

### OF WHAT THINGS ARE MORAL.

BUT though we cannot define the moral quality, yet we can tell what things *are* moral. This is a very different question. I cannot define beauty; but I can tell what things are beautiful. And it will be observed that a quality and the thing by which it is possessed can be looked at as different ideas. I cannot define color; but I can say what things are red and purple. And if it should be found that the moral quality belongs to a very few of the objects of our conscious-

absolute definition is possible. The simpler the idea, the less possible its definition. But no idea, however complex, is capable of precise definition; but only can have suggested its closest analogies in our consciousness (1875).

ness, and these few can be put into a catalogue, the doing so would be a beautiful analysis. For, once having settled that the quality is an indefinable idea, and that the things by which it is possessed can be all marked down and numbered, and the science is complete. No practical detail can afterward give us serious anxiety.

## CHAPTER IV.

### WHAT THE MORAL QUALITY SHALL BE CALLED.

WE might be satisfied with this very expression,—the Moral Quality: and indeed there would be some serious advantages gained; for it would oblige us always to consider that it is a mere quality, and nothing else. But then sin is a moral quality, as well as its opposite. It is important to keep these simple ideas more separable.

We had thought of *right;* that Moral Science was that branch of human philosophy that was concerned in right; that right was a simple idea; that being on that account incapable of being defined, we could only ask, What things are right? and so go on in our path of investigation. This would be very simple. But then, unfortunately, right means not wrong, as well as that which is positively virtuous.

And so *holiness, and righteousness*, and many other ethical expressions. Holiness, for example, is the moral quality; and that in no other than its absolute idea; there could be no other; but then, the moral quality in a certain restricted application. Holiness, moreover, is applied to character; and, moreover, it is applied to conduct; so that it is endlessly ambiguous.

We have determined, all things considered, to go

back to an old word, and call the moral quality *Virtue.*

Our objections to this are that virtue is really a name for eight or nine different ideas. We need not mention all of them. Some of them will never be confounded with any philosophical expression. We shall mention three of them. And these are so constantly important that we must keep them in our view. One is the moral quality; as for example where we say, The virtue of certain exercised affections. The second is the things that are moral; in which case the word is used in the plural, meaning those virtues or exercised affections themselves. Thirdly, it is applied to character. These uses are really the divisions of our subject as we intend to consider it. And we might have employed the word in the titles of our different books, and called them,

I. VIRTUE, OR THE MORAL QUALITY;
II. VIRTUES, OR THE MORAL DUTIES; AND
III. VIRTUE, OR MORAL CHARACTER.

This distinct discrimination will at least keep us from being confused by the word itself. For let us remember that virtue means, either rightness, or the things that are right, or the character in which these right things are found.

They are, in fact, altogether different ideas.

## DIVISION II.

## THE MORAL DUTIES.

### CHAPTER I.

#### OF WHAT THINGS ARE MORAL.

THERE are but two things that have virtue, or that possess the moral quality, and that become on that account virtues * or Moral Duties; and besides these there are no virtues in the universe. One of these is Benevolence, or a love of the welfare of other beings; and the other is a love of the Moral Quality itself.

We do not mean that all other virtues are implied in these, or that if these are observed all other duties are equally brought to pass, but that all moral duties *are* these, and that virtue is not a quality of anything beside, any more than taste or fragrance is a quality of anything else than matter.

### CHAPTER II.

#### OF BENEVOLENCE.

FOR one of these in which the moral quality is found we have a word which, for one derived from popular language, is remarkably philosophical. Love of others is a far more ambiguous expression. Love to others may arise from esteem as well as from Benev-

* The reader will mark the different uses of the word.

olence. Indeed, the love that arises from esteem, is much more properly expressed by the word, than the love which arises from Benevolence. The love by which we pray for them that despitefully use us and persecute us, is only a love for their welfare.* And I am no more bound to love those that are not lovable or worthy of my affection, than I am bound to love a spider or poisonous capello which nevertheless I am bound to regard and treat with a suitable compassion.

Benevolence, therefore, is a universal principle. "Do not I hate them that hate thee?" says the Psalmist; and yet we are commanded to "bless them that curse us." It is rare that in popular language a word is found so perfect in its meaning as this word *Benevolence* for the simple affection of wishing well to all others than ourselves.

## CHAPTER III.

### WHETHER BENEVOLENCE IS A VIRTUE.

NO man, perhaps, ever denied that Benevolence in any case had the moral quality; but there are men so inconsistent as to declare, that Benevolence is not moral unless it is indulged in from a sense of obligation. If they denied that benevolence had a moral quality in any case, it would be impossible to answer them; for, except by appeal to Scripture, which commands us to love even our enemies, whether benevolence be a virtue or no, is an affair of consciousness. If a man cannot feel that benevolent affection is moral, it cannot be proved to him.

To those, however, that imagine that benevolence

* (*Bene-volo*) benevolence.

becomes moral only when we conceive that it is right, there are three considerations to be presented. (1.) If a thing is not moral until we feel it to be so, then it is not moral at all; for how can we feel a thing to be moral, if it be not moral in itself? (2.) Again, if a thing is not moral until we feel it to be so, then we must make our election between the two ideas that are here stated. Here is the feeling of benevolence, and the feeling of duty. The two are not even coincident. We must first have a feeling of benevolence; and then a regard for it as our obligation. Wherein is the moral quality contained? If in the feeling of benevolence, that is the very thing for which we are contending. If in the sense of obligation, that is altogether a different idea. (3.) Then a practical difficulty;—If the thing be not moral until we feel it to be so, then a man who is so engrossingly benevolent that he does not stay to consider its obligation, may be more of a benevolent man but less of a moral one. In other words, his love is not moral at all unless he delays it long enough to think of its obligation.

These things are not all very consistent.

Benevolence is either a virtue or not. If it be not a virtue, then its opposite is not a vice, and I may be as hard-hearted as I please, without any dereliction of moral obligation. If it *be* a virtue, then it is possessed of the virtuous quality itself, for if we attempt to trace it and say, Benevolence is our duty because God has commanded it, the question returns, Why God has commanded it, and the answer, Because it is our duty. And if it be said, It promotes the general welfare, it may be asked, And why am I bound to promote the general welfare? and then it may be answered, Because it is benevolent.

Benevolence, therefore, is a simple and original virtue.

## CHAPTER IV.

### IS BENEVOLENCE THE ONLY VIRTUE?

BUT if it be asked, Is Benevolence the only virtue? I answer, No; and I prove it merely by finding another. That, after all, is the simplest argumentation. If the question arises, Are there only four senses? any arguments I might build up on the evil of having only four, would be far less potent than the proof that there are five.

Now I might stay to show the inconsistency of a certain mode of stating a certain doctrine,—*That all virtue consists in benevolence.* I might show that virtue is a quality, and benevolence the thing in which it inheres; and that unless virtue is used in a very narrow and uncommon sense, it would be just as awkward to say that all virtue consists in benevolence, as that all beauty consists in singing, or that all power consists in a steam engine. Virtue and benevolence are entirely different ideas. Or, returning to what is evidently implied, I might deny that benevolence is the only virtue,* because God has far higher aims, and man far higher obligations, than the happiness of others. And we might produce the *consequences* of holding that benevolence is the only thing that is possessed of a moral quality.

But a far simpler way is just to show that there is some other virtuous affection; and that that affection is primordial like benevolence itself, and cannot be confounded with it, but is a different idea; that benevo-

* In the second sense of that term; see Ethics, D. I. Chap. IV. (1875.)

lence and that other affection are reduced to an ultimate analysis, and are both separate possessors of the idea or quality of virtue.

## CHAPTER V.

### OF A LOVE TO THE MORAL QUALITY ITSELF.

NOW to find out what that other affection is, let us imagine a great instance of benevolence exhibited. Let us suppose a horse dashing along the public street, and some person periling his life to save a child that is playing upon the pavement. Suppose this to be an instance of pure benevolence. Suppose another man standing at his door, and the tears of a generous admiration starting to his eyes on seeing the benevolent act. Suppose this to be an instance of pure admiration of benevolence. Here then are two things, benevolence and admiration of benevolence, things unquestionably different, but both with the appearance of virtue; and, at first sight, these two might be imagined as at least worthy of being looked at as to whether they are not the only possible virtues.

Presently, however, a third person is seen eagerly watching the second. A love of benevolence has become in its turn an object of admiration, like benevolence itself. And so, a fourth person might express his approval of the third; and a fifth, of the fourth; and a sixth, of the fifth; and a seventh, of the sixth; and so on indefinitely; benevolence, and the love of benevolence, and the love of the love of benevolence, and so on, burdening our catalogue, until it might be thought to be impossible to have any more convenient statement.

And yet immediately we are reminded of the fact,

that what each man loves in his neighbor is the moral quality. The first man saves the child out of a simple feeling of benevolence. The second man loves the first out of a regard to that moral quality of which the act of his benevolence is possessed. And so on in the other cases. It is the moral quality in each. And if I say, BENEVOLENCE AND A LOVE OF THE MORAL QUALITY, I shall have described all the feelings of the case. The first man loves the child from benevolence. The second man loves the first because he loves the moral quality of his benevolent self-sacrifice. The third man loves the second because he admires the moral quality of the admiration which the second feels for the first. And the fourth man loves the third because he admires the moral quality of this previous admiration. And so on indefinitely. There is no difficulty in the further statement. Benevolence and the love of the moral quality are therefore all that appear in this whole concatenation of experiences.

Now, that this second is a virtue I need hardly stop to demonstrate: or that it should be the only virtue I need hardly stop to prove impossible. It is entirely distinct from benevolence. The two are reduced to their last analysis. And if any man imagines that what have been reduced to two, might, on a closer inspection, result in unity, he must remember that the two are simple ideas; that they are incapable of any further simplicity of sense; benevolence and admiration for the virtuous quality being emotions of the soul which can only be *felt*, and which cannot be conceived by any description of their meaning.*

* There have been two general theories of morals; one, that all virtue consists in benevolence; the other, that all virtue consists in a

## CHAPTER VI.

### PROOF THAT THERE ARE BUT TWO VIRTUES.

BENEVOLENCE and a love of the moral quality can be proved to be the only virtues in the same way that five of our physical gifts can be proved to be our only senses. No man would attempt to decide it by looking at any of the five, but at a sixth or seventh that might claim to belong to the catalogue. We mean to pass in review several of our common affections, namely, Love to God, Love to Self, Gratitude, and Natural Affection; and having exhausted the possibilities in the case, appeal finally to Scripture, which declares that there are but two virtues.

## CHAPTER VII.

### OF LOVE TO GOD.

GOD, though the most simple of all existences, is the most compound of all ideas. We put together all that is excellent in ourselves; and, making it infinite, attach it to the Supreme Being; and that is every idea of Him. A love of the Supreme Being is, therefore, a

love of right on its own account. The argument against the first has been, that then God has no real hatred of sin, and only opposes it because of its effects. The argument against the second has been,* that then there is no such thing as right; for that if all virtue consists in the love of right on its own account, where do we get the first right to love?

The theory we are introducing provides for both these difficulties. Benevolence is 'the first right we get to love'; and then love to right itself is the second right thing; benevolence playing the same rôle in Ethics that Locke said sensation did in Logic; *starting* us, so to speak, in our conceptions, or giving us the possibilities of thought in the case.

* Or, may be (1875.)

love of wisdom and power and justice and goodness and truth; and, so far as it is a moral feeling, it is a love of His moral character. For, except so far as it is gratitude, of which we shall afterwards speak, or benevolence, if any one chooses to assert that we are benevolent to the Almighty, it is a love of His moral attributes, and, therefore, nothing more than a love of the moral quality as it is embodied in the holiness of God.

In either case, therefore, benevolence and a love of the moral quality cover all the experiences in its history.

## CHAPTER VIII.

### OF LOVE TO SELF.

SELF-LOVE is neither a virtue nor a vice. It is constitutional. If we are made capable of happiness, being happy, which is very little removed from delighting or loving to be so, is as innocent as existence itself. Desiring to be what we are constituted happy in being is neither right nor wrong. The opposite of it is as inherently impossible as grieving when we are not sad, or joying when we are not happy. Self-Love, therefore, is not a virtue.

## CHAPTER IX.

### WHY SELF-LOVE HAS BEEN THOUGHT A VIRTUE.

PRUDENCE was one of the four cardinal virtues of the ancients; and, therefore, Self-Love has, almost by common consent, assumed to itself a virtuous character.

But then Self-Love, it must be duly considered, is

only one of the motives of prudence. I am bound to be benevolent. A care of myself is necessary to the welfare of others. Again, I am bound to love duty. The care of myself is necessary to the enjoyment of duty. I am bound to obey God. There are *many* motives for prudence. And Self-Love, on its own account, is not the virtuous motive. Nor has it on its own account a virtuous character.

Why some men have thought it a sin, we shall afterwards explain. But Self-Love is not a sin in itself. It becomes mixed with sin only through the want of benevolence. Self-Love is like the ball of the eye, which anatomists tell us is totally without feeling. It has neither one character nor the other, but is indifferent as to the quality of virtue.

## CHAPTER X.

### OF NATURAL AFFECTION.

KEEPING our eye, however, upon obvious differences, we must not say the same in respect to *Natural Affection*. The idea so often broached, that Natural Affection is not of a virtuous character, labors with many difficulties; for, in the first place, it is contradicted by conscience. If a man disregard his offspring, we pronounce it a sin. Moreover it is contradicted by Scripture; for the *astorgoi*, or, as the word is translated, those "without natural affection," are mentioned by the Apostle Paul in the list of the most outrageous sinners. The love of a husband for a wife, or of a father for a son, or of a niece for her uncle, are certainly virtues; and yet it would be impossible to believe, that each of these inaugurates a separate moral distinction, or, in fact, that there are as many virtues as there are relations among men.

The light that is to be shed upon these difficulties depends upon the fact that benevolence is regulated by circumstances. I cannot love a being till I know something of him. A stranger on a distant planet is out of the reach of my benevolence. I cannot love a being so much as when I know more about him, or he is living near me. And, therefore, the Bible commands me to love my *neighbor*. I cannot love a being so much who is of another nation, or of another race; and these differences are in the nature of the case. Benevolence remains the same, a simple and unchangeable virtue; but it is constitutionally affected by circumstances; and Natural Affection is, therefore, a compound. It is partly an instinct, and that far has no virtue; but it is also benevolence, and benevolence kindled by the most favoring appeal. If a man has no benevolence when the objects of it are placed at his fireside, and when the warmth of it is increased by an instinct, he must be singularly low down in his benevolent susceptibility. And, therefore, the Bible gives us little credit for this sort of benevolence, for it says, "If ye then, being evil, know how to give good gifts unto your children, how much more shall your Father which is in heaven give good things to them that ask him!"

Natural affection, therefore, is a compound phenomenon, made up partly of benevolence, in which respect it is moral, but partly also of an instinct which constitutes a favoring circumstance (along with others) for benevolence itself.

## CHAPTER XI.

### OF THE LOVE OF GOOD MEN.

THE like may be said of the Love of Good Men. The Love of Good Men is a compound phenomenon, made up of common benevolence, heightened and made warmer by a love of the Moral Quality.*

## CHAPTER XII.

### OF GRATITUDE.

AND the like may be said of *Gratitude*. It is an instance of common benevolence, heightened and made warmer by a love to benevolence itself; and that benevolence particularly attracting our attention, because it was a benevolence exercised toward us.†

I am not saying that I have given all the phenomena connected with these different affections; particularly all the phenomena of the different duties that flow from them. For example, love to God is immediately followed by the duty of unreserved obedience. But then obedience to God flows also from the duty of benevolence, as well as from the obligation to love

* Here it will be observed, both are virtues. But yet so much lower is benevolence when assisted by these favoring circumstances, that the Bible recommends it when it stands unaided by any; for "for a good man some would even dare to die. But God commendeth his love toward us, in that, while we were yet sinners, Christ died for us" (Rom. v. 7, 8).

† Where also the Bible testifies that it is benevolence, and not the favoring circumstances, that constitute the virtue; but that, on the contrary, benevolence is the more praiseworthy, the less it is assisted. For "if ye do good to them which do good to you, what thank have ye? for sinners also do even the same" (Luke vi. 33).

Him; because the duty of obedience is necessary to the general welfare. So also of the exercise of gratitude; it is for the general good. We have not exhausted our analysis, but sufficiently indicated that all may be included in fewer and more original affections.

## CHAPTER XIII.

### OF JUSTICE.

THE same may be said of Justice.

Justice is a name for a great many different things.

It has three meanings, like those that may be found in Virtue. That is, it means first the quality of which we speak when we speak of the justice of certain feelings. It means, secondly, the feelings in which this just quality is found; and it means, thirdly, the character of the persons to whom the feelings that possess this just quality belong. It is in the second of these three senses that we wish to speak of justice when we ask if we are obliged to consider it as a separate and independent virtue.

Justice, moreover, has a great many different meanings in each of the three senses in which we have considered it. It means virtue in the general. It means honesty. It means strictness in governing, including, on the one hand, strictness in rewards, and on the other, strictness in punishment. It has been divided into *general*, *commutative*, *distributive*, and *vindicatory* justice; a division, however, which can be of but small philosophical account, because it is all an illogical jumble; *general* justice including all the rest, and *distributive*, which is defined to be "the giving of every one his due," being much the same as *general*, or, at least, certainly including *vindicatory*, and, in this way, overleaping all the bounds of a metaphysical division. To follow justice, therefore, into all the windings of popular speech, would be utterly impossible. And we have thought that we would take two great instances of it, which, if they are not the great meanings of the word, are nevertheless sufficient as examples of how entirely it may be included under the forms of our original virtues. *Honesty*, which is one of the two, is to be considered in the present connection; and *rectitude*, as it is applied to *government*, that is, strictness in rewarding, and strictness in punishing, will be taken up when rewards and punishments come to be the subject of inquiry.

## CHAPTER XIV.

### OF HONESTY.

If a poor widow, living alone, and with no one to depend upon but herself, has scraped together through the toils of a laborious life a poor pittance against the infirmities of age, and some man with no shadow of a right robs her and takes all that she possesses, it would seem to be an imperfect statement of the moralities of the case to say that *benevolence* had been grossly violated. Is there not such a thing as an original justice? Or is it true that a regard for the welfare of others, followed of course by its obligation as virtuous, and by the command of the Almighty, is all that is to restrain us from robbery and fraud?

Holding that there is nothing else than this, we challenge the party that may differ to tell us what that other thing is. What is it? Is it a love for others' rights? What we call for is a distinct expression that may serve to be an account of an original virtue.

I. It cannot be a love for others' rights, because, under that word is included an endless variety of meanings. There are rights that come to us by war and accident. Indeed there are all possible varieties; rights of law, and rights of equity; and these opposite oftentimes; rights that cannot be maintained in the forum of conscience, and yet that cannot be denied in the forum of human adjudication: rights of discovery and rights of possession, and rights of whimsical technicality, that nevertheless are held sacred by men. How can that be an original affection that has for its object a vast multiplicity of things?

II. Again; justice has exceptions. The poor widow would be sacrificed for the benefit of the state. A cargo would be thrown overboard for the safety of a vessel. Fortunes would be squandered, or houses blown up, for the gaining of a battle; and property might be seized upon in cases of starvation. We hold everything at the call of a higher principle. And how can that be a primordial right which becomes wrong or the opposite according to our need?

III. Observe, this is not the case with benevolence. Benevolence has no exception. We are to love even our enemies. Nor is there any exception in the love of virtue. Benevolence, therefore, and the love of the moral quality might be proved to be the only virtues by this fact, that they are the only forms of obligation that admit of no exception.

IV. And moreover, fourthly, when we come to consider what the exceptions are, they are all on the one principle of the general welfare.

V. And, therefore, I say, fifthly, that as the one principle of the general welfare accounts for the exceptions of justice, so, *a fortiori*, may it account for justice itself; for if a regard for the general good is so potent as to put away the equities of ordinary administration, then benevolence must be higher than justice; that is, it must stand higher in logic; that is, it must go nearer to the origin of right; I mean by that, justice must be derived from benevolence, because, in the last appeal, it yields to the consideration of the public good.

Now let me not be mistaken. I do not mean that a care for that poor widow is all that should restrain the man from defrauding her of property: but that the general welfare makes necessary a general law, and that that law must be very exact, and that that exactness must reach even to the slenderest obligations; and that when that law is set up, then duty comes in to press it; because benevolence is followed by a recognition of duty, and that duty becomes interlocked by all species of confirmation; by the command of God; by the need of example; by a respect for ourselves; and by all the forms of the interlacing of duty by which two simple virtues can combine in all the forms of obligation for men.

It is not, therefore, benevolence *in this simple case* that keeps the man's hand off the property of his neighbor; but benevolence grown into an intelligent system, and that system enjoined by the authority of the Almighty, and recognized by its wisdom as essential in the very constitution of affairs.

## CHAPTER XV.

### OF TRUTHFULNESS.

THE same wisdom makes it necessary that one man should tell the truth to his neighbor.

But if truthfulness aspire to be itself an original virtue, we have of course a right to inquire what it defines itself distinctly to be.

Truthfulness is not a love of truth on our own account; for then it would run into all the departments of philosophy and science. Truthfulness, therefore, is more properly a love of the possession of truth by others; or to put others in possession of the truth; or, if we might make the matter somewhat more complicated, perhaps, it is a principle such that if we intimate anything in the presence of others, we ought not to deceive them. Truthfulness, therefore, is the attribute which refuses to deceive.

I. Now, that it is not an original attribute we argue, first, because it has many exceptions. God tells Joshua to set an ambush behind the City of Ai, and thus he deceives and defeats them. He tells Samuel when he fears to go up to anoint David king over Israel, Take a heifer with thee and say, I am come to sacrifice. And though it may. be said, '*Benevolence* has certain practical exceptions: we refrain to do good to others in certain cases of practical necessity:' yet, when we come to consider it, it is at the call of benevolence itself. We refrain to do good to others for the sake of some higher design of benevolence. But who can say that we fail to tell the truth for the sake of some higher design of truthfulness?

II. No; and, therefore, truthfulness finds its exceptions outside of itself.

III. And, thirdly, truthfulness, being controlled by benevolence in such a way that when its exceptions come up we find them dictated by the public good, the only question that remains is, whether the public good may not account for truthfulness. *A fortiori*, if the public good may impair and make exceptions to truthfulness, may it not be the occasion of truthfulness itself? In other words, if truthfulness be a great and important blessing, and in its highest exactness fully accounted for by benevolence, and yet sometimes subject to exceptions, and those exceptions prompted by benevolence itself, is not the demonstration complete that benevolence is the origin of truthfulness, and that except so far as it is enjoined by the authority of God, or laid on us by other obligations *because* it is benevolent, benevolence is the only source of the obligation of truthfulness?

## CHAPTER XVI.

### OF CHASTITY.

In chastity we find the peculiar illustration of a virtue in which exceptions are made by the very ordinance of God. Chastity in any way that *we* can define it forbids things that were the law in the family of Adam, and that were announced in statutes by God on Sinai. Truthfulness may have exceptions in cases of necessity; or honesty, in cases of starvation; but chastity has had exceptions for a whole age together. And when it is said, "Moses for the hardness of your hearts" allowed you certain liberal concessions, that does not mean that it was not lawful, but that chastity was a dictate of benevolence, and that where polygamy, for example (to take one instance out of the many), became a less evil than its inexorable prohibition, "for the hardness of their hearts" God adjusted his commandent, making it lawful to marry many wives, not that it was not a prodigious evil, but that the mischiefs in the case were less than of its rigid prohibition.

Now this does not prove that polygamy in our day is right; for God has again prohibited it; but it proves that it is subject to His ordinance, and that it is not in this respect like benevolence, which is always an obligation; but that it is, like the aberrations of justice, to be directed by the law of the Most High.

## CHAPTER XVII.

### PROOF FROM SCRIPTURE.

WE come next to Scripture.

In the 13th chapter of the Romans we have a passage which in a remarkably accurate way states all that we have said in respect to benevolence. Indeed, it would be hard to imagine how language could be more philosophical. The Apostle is saying, "Render to all what is owing (τὰς ὀφειλάς); tribute to whom tribute; custom to whom custom; fear to whom fear; honor to whom honor": and then, for the manifest purpose of showing how reasonable these exactions were, he says, "*You do not owe any man anything* (μηδενὶ μηδὲν ὀφείλετε) *but to love one another.*" And though, by an unfortunate translation, the imperative* has been put for the indicative—"Owe no man anything"—yet the context sufficiently corrects it. The indicative and the imperative are of course the same in the original, and it is left to the reader entirely to decide in the case.

* Perhaps, however, the imperative must stand on account of the peculiar negative (though eminent scholars, Reiche, Koppe, Rosenmüller, Böhme, Flatt, Erasmus, do not think so), but we must count it an indicative-imperative such as was of usage in the East; as, for example, where Christ says, "What thou doest do quickly," or where the prophet says, "Make the heart of this people gross"; which we are never to understand as a usual imperative, but as a more than usually asseverating indicative (1875).

But the Apostle goes on. He not only tells the Romans that it was interesting to perform our obligations because all were a part of the duty of mutual benevolence, but he tells this more plainly,—"He that loveth another hath fulfilled the law." And then he goes on to particularize. "For, Thou shalt not commit adultery, Thou shalt not kill, Thou shalt not steal, Thou shalt not bear false witness, Thou shalt not covet; and if there be any other commandment,—it is briefly comprehended in this saying, namely, Thou shalt love thy neighbor as thyself." These, you perceive, are the very obligations we have been considering. And the duty not to steal and not to commit adultery; that is, the duties of honesty and chastity, and the duty not to lie, and not to kill, and, as the Apostle says, "if there be any other" duty,—they are summarily comprehended in this,—which is nothing more than the duty of common benevolence. "Love worketh no ill to his neighbor; therefore," says the Apostle, proving his seriousness by the philosophy of an abundant explanation,—"therefore, love is the fulfilling of the law."

Now the other important Scripture that I will bring into notice is where Christ tells an insidious questioner that on two commandments, namely, "Thou shalt love the Lord thy God," and, "Thou shalt love thy neighbor,"—are summed up all the law and the prophets.

He is no longer speaking of mere obligations to others (τὰς ὀφειλάς), but is speaking of the whole law, and we might imagine that he would divest it of all metaphysical abstraction, and speak in the common language of secular men. He does not, therefore, say, Thou shalt love other beings; though the command, Love thy neighbor, includes, of course, duty to animals and all the objects of compassion. Nor does he say, Thou shalt love the moral principle; though the command, Love thy Maker, is formed, as we have shown, upon the basis of our obligation to holiness, but he says, "Love the Lord thy God," as a far more useful way of commanding our affection for holiness, and "Love thy neighbor," as a far more popular style of enforcing benevolence among men.

But, strictly, the passage says, that there are but two commandments; certainly it says, that on these two commandments hang all the law and the prophets; and unquestionably, if these two commandments are not adoringly to honor holiness and warmly to love our fellows, it lies with a different exposition to explain to us their original meaning.

## CHAPTER XVIII.

### WHETHER ONE OF THE TWO VIRTUES IS EQUAL TO THE OTHER.

ONE of the two virtues is undoubtedly equal to the other in its claim of being original; but whether equal in degree will best appear by asking whether their objects are equal. Holiness on its own account is the object of the one, and we are to compare it with the object of the other; and though no reason can be given, yet our own consciousness declares, that holiness is in itself the higher object. Benevolence, therefore, yields to its sister virtue, not in the sense of being dependent or derived, but in the sense of being feebler; the welfare of others being a poorer object of desire than the no more original desideratum, the quality of virtue.

## CHAPTER XIX.

### WHETHER BENEVOLENCE IS ALWAYS EQUAL TO ITSELF.

THE welfare of others is not only a poorer object of desire than the no more original object, the quality of virtue, but it is also a poorer object of desire in one instance of benevolence than another. I cannot love an animal with the same earnestness that I do an intelligent being; and, therefore, I sacrifice animals. I cannot love an individual neighbor more, other things being equal, than I love myself; and, therefore, the Bible commands me to love my neighbor *as* myself. I cannot love an individual neighbor as much, other things being equal, as I can a million; and, therefore, I am to sacrifice one to many. I am to love a world of mankind more than I do any single individual. And, therefore, I am to love a world more than I do myself.

Accordingly Paul says, "I could wish myself accursed from Christ for my brethren my kinsmen according to the flesh;" and though this passage has been the ground of error, yet never in respect to benevolence. Till we come to speak of holiness it is clear enough. Paul loves the happiness of Israel, as he necessarily must, more, whether temporally or eternally, than his own felicity.

"Hereby know we love," says the Apostle John, discoursing on the very evidence of our own conversion; (and we regret that just at this point our translators should have clouded the sense by inserting Italics,—"Hereby perceive we the love *of God;*") "Hereby know we love;" (just as on other occasions he has said, "Hereby know we the spirit of truth," or, "Hereby know we that He abideth in us;") "Hereby know we love, that He laid down His life for us, and we ought to lay down our lives for the brethren."

Moses, when he cried, "If not, then blot me out of thy book," may be a subject of criticism in respect to its bearing upon his holiness; but in respect to its bearing upon his happiness, he had a right,—nay, it was his duty, to prefer all to one; and, therefore, to desire the salvation of his race in a style that would be fatal to his own inheritance.

## CHAPTER XX.

### WHETHER THE OTHER VIRTUE IS ALWAYS EQUAL TO ITSELF.

BUT whether the other virtue is always equal to itself; depending, of course, upon the question whether the moral quality is always equal to itself,—is a much more delicate subject of inquiry. Happiness we must put far off at the very opening of our investigation. The love of happiness must not only yield to the love of holiness, and that whether it be for ourselves or others, but must never come into the account. The moral quality is so superior to others' welfare that they can never come into comparison. The highest measure of one can never match the lowest farthing of the other; because virtue is perfectly imperative. God's infinite felicity could not be a match for the slightest betrayal into the smallest crime.

Virtue, however, having this sort of imperativeness, has it only in the form that I have described. Its imperativeness does not consist in its being infinite; for then all forms of virtue would be precisely on a par. It matters not who should be the being, whether saint or angel, nor would it matter what should be the action. The making of a world, and the sparing of an ant or caterpillar, would be precisely on a level.

The measure of virtue, therefore, is not always alike; and whether the love of it is so, is an easy question. If the measure of virtue is not always alike, the love of it is similar. The love to God must be greater than the love to man; the love of one action greater than of one confessedly lower, even when both actions are perfect; Gabriel, a higher object of affection than inferior excellences. And even when we understand objects better, that is a valid ground for a higher exercise of virtue.

As God, therefore, is infinitely excellent, God, under the eye of a Divine Nature, should be infinitely approved. God, under the eye of God, appearing in His excellence, becomes, so, an object of infinite affection; but God to man is not infinite; God to man grows, and, therefore, there is but one instance of infinite affection. God to man changes, and, therefore, our love to Him is not infinite; nor does He claim that it should be. All that He desires of us is, that we should love the Lord our God with all our soul and strength.

But if the love of man to the Almighty is not infinite, much less is his love to any inferior degree of moral elevation. Our love of virtue, therefore, is of all degrees. And taking care only to keep up that fact of its imperativeness, and to make virtue prevalent over all measures of felicity, we can reason about holiness, and prefer it, the one case over the other, just as as we did the object of benevolence.

The holiness of God is more important than any other reality. This is the end of the universe. We have reached a point that is the highest in the affections of man..

And if the holiness of God is the greatest end of the universe, of course I am to desire it more even than my own holiness. I cannot be a sinner. I cannot transgress a precept even though it be for the honor of God. I cannot sin to uphold the universe, or to uphold the Almighty. The thing is preposterous; for sin admits of no license. But I can coolly think, that my holiness is less than the holiness of God, and I can cooly say, "Let God be true," and, as a mere comparison of relative desires, all the world may sink into apostasy. The Apostle, we deliberately believe, meant that.

So now in respect to his wishing himself accursed from Christ;—If God's holiness is more important than the holiness of man, the holiness of man is more important than the holiness of one; and I can throw that fact into an expressive proposition. I cannot consent to sin; and it would be infamous in me to be willing to be eternally a sinner. And it would be infamous in me to be eternally a sinner even for the salvation of humanity. But then we are immediately to consider, What is being a sinner? Being a sinner is the opposite of being holy. Being holy is to possess two positive affections. To possess two positive affections is to be holy in all the sense in which being holy can possibly be conceived. Now these affections are love of other beings, which of course permits us to love others more than we do ourselves, and (as the only remaining virtue) love of holiness.

Now the difficulty seems to be that Paul could not say, I could wish myself accursed from Christ, without compromitting this last affection. And we are willing to admit that if Paul had said, · I could sin for my brethren, my kindred according to the flesh,' it would be inconsistent. But what is sin? It is, *not* loving others, and *not* having an affection for holiness. Now, if Paul had said, 'I could be unbenevolent,' or, 'I could be unregardful of holiness, for my brethren according to the flesh,' that would be preposterous and wicked. But what does he say? 'I am so withered by the idea of a whole nation being given up to sin, that is, I love holiness so much, that I make the obvious comparison of one man's holiness as compared with many; and, as every ideal comparison is capable of being translated into speech, I merely utter it:—that, out of regard to that higher excellency the love of which is the first and great commandment, I would rather see that excellency spread over the world than to see it possessed by *any* individual believer.'

Nor are we saying here more than what every one believes. What every one believes is, that a thousand sinners are more to be mourned over than the existence of one. If that one happens to be I myself, that does not alter a certain form of the proposition when we come to a comparison. And what I mean is, that that form of the proposition is the one intended by Paul. When he says, "I could wish myself accursed from Christ," he means, that the high character of millions was more important than the guarding of his own, and that he had rather those millions should be saved than that he himself should be kept from eternal undoing.

If any one says, This means that he would be willing to sin, I retract so much as by any possibility could mean that,—and I keep his mind undividedly to this proposition, that Paul meant, only what he himself must believe to be true,—that the holiness and happiness of a nation were more to be desired, than the holiness and happiness of any conceivable believer.

This much we suppose every one will admit.

## CHAPTER XXI.

### OF WHAT THINGS ARE MORAL IN GOD.

THOSE things that are moral themselves are moral also in the Almighty.

The doctrine that no things are moral in themselves, but are made moral by the will of the Almighty, is the only doctrine that can oppose this simple proposition.

That no things are moral in themselves, would make no things moral in the Almighty; for I take it that it is an easy reasoning, that if God makes things moral, there can be nothing moral to Him. Moreover, if He makes things moral, He might make immoral things moral; that is, originally He might make benevolence and love of virtue, which are confessedly right, shamefully and universally wrong; and destroy altogether the present system.

If it be said, 'He is too wise for this,' then there is an original virtue; for if originally what is indiscriminately right, is made wrong by the will of the Almighty,—then it is evident He has no liberty of will, or things are made wrong or right according to His pleasure. And, moreover, having no principle for Himself, but being obliged to make one by the freedom of His will, His holiness is only to be adored for being the object of His choice, and not on the principle of having any peculiar excellency.

These postulates are so absurd that we mean to pass on as though no such things were ever entertained; and those things that are moral in themselves being moral also in the Almighty, we return to that region of thought where we discover that benevolence and the love of virtue are the only things that are themselves virtuous.

Benevolence and the love of virtue being the only things that are themselves virtuous, benevolence and the love of virtue are the only virtues in the Almighty. And so, John, speaking of the virtue of benevolence, descants upon it in this wise, "Which thing is true in Him and in you;" meaning that its eternal obligation belongs as well to God as to man. We are created in His image, as the Bible repeatedly declares. And our Saviour, when He wishes to press in the furthest climax, a love of enemies, says, "Pray for them which despitefully use you, that ye may be the children of your Father which is in Heaven"; and then explains this reference to their relation, by saying, "For He maketh his sun to rise on the evil and on the good, and sendeth rain on the just and on the unjust."

Benevolence and the love of virtue, therefore, are the only virtues in the Almighty.

## CHAPTER XXII.

### OF GOD'S LOVE TO HIS OWN HAPPINESS.

HAPPINESS being an object which it is no virtue to pursue, but yet which it is right to pursue if we pursue it no farther than its own importance, it is right in man to pursue his own happiness as far as he does his neighbor's: and it would be right in God to pursue *His* by a corresponding measure of relation.

As therefore the happiness of God is more important than the happiness of the universe, it would be right in God to pursue His own happiness more than the happiness of the universe. But as the happiness of the universe can never interfere with the happiness of God, the happiness of God being infinite, and the very infinitude that makes it infinite being independent of the happiness of men, the two things can never come into competition. The happiness of God, therefore, can never interfere with the happiness of the universe.

## CHAPTER XXIII.

### OF GOD'S LOVE TO HIS OWN HOLINESS.

THE holiness of God is not very different in respect to its bearing upon others.

The holiness of God is the greatest object of His nature. Holiness, being most excellent in itself, is infinite in case of the Almighty. His desire for it, therefore, is boundless. Having no object above it in the scale, there is nothing beyond it in the region of his pursuits. The holiness of God, therefore, is the highest object in the universe.

The holiness of God being the highest object in the universe, it is the כָּבוֹד,* or excellence, that is generally translated glory. The glory of God, being the great end of His being, means his holiness. The idea that has conferred this honor upon the *display* of it, is a singular mistake. If the display of His glory be the great end of the excellence of God, then what is the great end of that? We may reduce it to absurdity by going behind it. But if the holiness of God be the great end itself, there our inquiry must pause. The display of His holiness centres His object upon man.

* Literally, *weight.*

And how absurd it is, that, for centuries together, an object that centres in the creature should have been thought the highest object of our Great Creator!

If, therefore, the holiness of God is the great object of all His being, the question arises whether it ever interferes with the holiness of man; for as all things else must yield to it, if the holiness of God ever interferes with the holiness of man, the universe is less holy than if there had been no such interference. We want to see whether this *supreme desire*, namely, for His own holiness, could ever interfere with the holiness of His creation; because we would like to show that if it does not, then the next most supreme desire, viz. for the holiness of all beyond Him, has an undivided and unmitigated sway in His soul.

Now, what is the love of His own holiness? The love of His own holiness, in God, is the love of His own benevolence toward other beings, and the love of His own regard for moral excellence. The love of His own benevolenee for other beings cannot make Him less benevolent toward them, or do them less good; and the love of His own regard for moral excellence cannot make Him care less for the moral excellence of all His creatures. Though the love of His own moral excellence, therefore, is supreme, it cannot hinder that the love of others' moral excellence should appear as though it were supreme; and therefore the love of God for the moral excellence of all the universe, is just the same as though it were the leading feature of His excellence.

## CHAPTER XXIV.

### OF GOD'S LOVE TO THE HOLINESS OF OTHERS.

GOD'S love to the holiness of others, is, therefore, as great as it could be, having no possible impediment. And as He is an omnipotent God, and has no other impediment in His nature, and this is His leading desire,* there is no reason why it should not have been granted. God's universe, therefore, is as holy as it could possibly have been made.

As each part of the universe is dear to Him in its relative part, each part of the universe is as holy as was consistent with the whole; and each part of the universe, in the ages to come, will be as holy as this supreme affection of the Almighty, combined with His omniscience, can possibly cause it to be.

The Christian, therefore, who has fallen under no ban of the Empire, and who has been left in no state demanding his eternal confusion, will be lifted all lengths, and will be carried all heights of perfection, and will be raised as near to the Almighty, as the plan of the universe will possibly devise.

The lost would be made holy, if it were not for invincible demurs.

And insects would be lifted into men, and the universe incredibly enlarged and promoted, if it had not received, each moment, the highest promotions of the Almighty.

These are some consequences of God's love to the holiness of others.

* Next to His own holiness, which we have seen does not interfere with it.

## CHAPTER XXV.

### OF GOD'S LOVE TO THE HAPPINESS OF OTHERS.

God's love to the happiness of others is of course altogether secondary. The slightest consideration of holiness would at once command it all away. Yet God's love, like the atmosphere, presses upon all His works. Like the atmosphere, it presses everywhere; and steals into every crevice that holiness (which is weightier) will allow.

Hence, benevolence is unlimited. And we make a distinction here between unlimited, and infinite. Benevolence is not infinite, because it is greater or less; but benevolence is unlimited, because it clamors endlessly. It has no limit in benevolence itself. It has no limit, except in some higher principle, why it should not make an angel of a man, or why it should not lift the wicked to the highest or holiest felicity. It taketh no pleasure in the death of him that dieth, but that all should repent and live. It so loved the world as to give the Only Begotten Son. And it has this glorious reality for the Christian, that he may know that God will do all for His vineyard that can possibly be done; that He doth not afflict willingly; that He is kind to the unthankful; and that, even in respect to the depraved, His tender mercies are over all His works.

Yet though benevolence is so great; for the simple reason that holiness is greater, men are punished, and millions sink into eternal ruin. Wherever holiness comes into collision with happiness, happiness must yield; and therefore we are back at our premise, that God will make this the holiest possible universe even at the expense of wickedness and misery.

The only question is, whether the holiest possible universe must not necessarily be the happiest possible; and as it would be utterly preposterous that the opposite of this could be maintained, we believe we have arrived at both the propositions,—that, while this universe is the holiest possible in spite of its being tinctured by the presence of sin, it is on this very account the happiest possible in spite of its being afflicted by being an abode of misery.

This universe, therefore, is the best possible universe.

## CHAPTER XXVI.

### OF SIN.

POSTPONING all consequences till a time when we have more thoroughly brought out the features of our system, we go next to what stands opposite to virtue, I mean, the evil of sin.

We had supposed that the expression, sin, would be found to agree in the number of its meanings, with the expression, virtue; and accordingly had determined to say that sin means the quality of wickedness, or secondly, what is wicked itself, or, thirdly, the character of him who does the wickedness. It was much to our surprise that we remembered that it means only the second.

We hear, indeed, of the sin of a certain action; and, in a still more restricted instance, of the sin of a certain character; but, on examining the sense, we find that it means the sinning, or actual transgression. It does not mean the quality of the act, or the character of the person, but the sin that is committed; and we have only to prove this by substituting the word sinfulness, when a nice ear will detect, that the sin of an act and the sinfulness of an act are not entirely synonymous; but that one means the sin which the act is understood to commit, and the other the quality of sinfulness that belongs to the commission.

Accordingly, the term "Original Sin" is perhaps not well chosen for the fact that is intended. The transgression of Adam, or our share of it, or our original trespass, if any such thing were intended in the view of theology, might be called original sin; but original character, which is the idea intended to be conveyed, ought only to be called original sinfulness.

At any rate, in this treatise, sin will be only those things that possess the moral quality, and sinfulness (1) the character, and (2) the moral quality itself.

## CHAPTER XXVII.

### OF THE QUALITY OF SINFULNESS.

THE quality of sinfulness is a simple idea. It is the opposite of virtue, but cannot be defined by it. It can be understood only by being conceived by the conscience. It cannot be analyzed; and, therefore, cannot be discussed as an object of philosophy.

## CHAPTER XXVIII.

### OF WHAT THINGS ARE SINFUL.

BUT though the quality of sinfulness cannot be defined (though we have a very clear conception of it from the disapprobation of conscience), yet we can tell what things are sinful.

There are but two sinful things, want of benevolence, and want of love to the moral quality. These two make up all the iniquity that exists in the creation.

The evil that falls upon the universe, falls upon it for these two sins. And Hell has eternal punishment for nothing but want of benevolence and want of love to the moral quality.

## CHAPTER XXIX.

### PROOF THAT THERE ARE BUT TWO SINS.

IT might seem that the proof that there are but two sins, is contained in the proof that there are but two virtues,—that we have but to consider what are the opposites of benevolence and the love of virtue, to be able to infer, with a good degree of probability, our only sins; but, now, in the first place, not only is this a thing not altogether to be taken for granted, but, in the second, the opposites of virtue are not altogether so easy to be declared.

For example, there are three sets of opposite affections, either of which might be possessed of the attribute of sinfulness. The love of others and the love of virtue may be opposed, in the first place, to the love of self and the love of wickedness. Again, the love of others and the love of virtue may be opposed, in the second place, to what may be equally regarded their opposites, viz. the hatred of others and the hatred of virtue; and, then, in the third place, benevolence and the love of virtue may be opposed to the want of benevolence and to the want of the love of the moral quality.

These six phenomena of mind are all in their nature sinful, except self-love, which becomes sinful when it degenerates into selfishness; and the only way in which we can prove that they are not all six equally original, is to look at them one by one, and to show that all but two are forms or instances of the two that we have already suggested.

We shall alter the order a little; and as the love of wickedness can be best considered when we have a better idea of wickedness itself, we will put that the last of the four, and show that they are, all alike, derivative or else complex iniquities.

## CHAPTER XXX.

### OF SELF-LOVE.

Self-love, in itself considered, is, in a moral point, entirely indifferent. Benevolence being a great primary virtue, self-love, in itself considered, may be conspicuously right, and yet may afford the exercise in which the want of benevolence may be found to appear. For example, it is right to love my neighbor no better than I do myself, where circumstances make the comparison a fair one. If, therefore, I love my neighbor less than I do myself, self-love becomes, so to speak, the *kakophoron*, or sin-bearing exercise of mind. Benevolence, in that case, being a negative quantity, the want of it shows itself in the overgrowth of principles otherwise indifferent. And covetousness and selfishness (which, by the way, may be defined to be that measure of self-love which exceeds our love to our neighbor) and theft and any principle that sacrifices others to ourselves become wrong, not because self-love is itself a principle of evil, but because it manifests the other. The want of benevolence, being a negative, and therefore unable to exhibit itself, it is a parasite, and grows upon its neighbors, and therefore all exercises become equally depraved in which there is manifested a want of this original benevolence.

And so of the love of virtue. Selfishness is also manifested where self-love has outgrown an affection for holiness. It is not that self-love is wicked, but that the man is not willing to mortify himself or crucify himself at the call of virtue.

And now to *prove* that self-love is not wicked in itself, we have only to remember that the wicked have no more self-love than the righteous (except in proportion). God has more self-love than His creatures. Angels have more self-love than we have, and probably to a wonderful degree. Heaven has more self-love than the earth. And as men grow old in wickedness, self-love crumbles away. And it is the keen, exquisite, enlivened ideas of the saint, that open before him the highest conceptions of happiness, and therefore the highest appreciation of his own felicity.

Self-love, therefore, is not the measure of selfishness; but selfishness is to be measured by the disparity. A man is selfish to the degree that he loves self more than he loves others, or to the degree that he loves happiness more than he loves holiness; and the sin, in either example of the two, lies, not in his affection for self, but in his want of affection for the other objects.

## CHAPTER XXXI.

### OF MALEVOLENCE.

MALEVOLENCE, on the contrary, is not an original trespass, not because it is morally indifferent, but because originally and on its own account it does not exist. We love our own happiness by an original and necessary principle of our humanity. We love the *un*happiness of other beings not at all as an original principle, but on account of other affections, which are themselves the original transgressions.

Benevolence and malevolence are so much alike in their appearance, that we would fancy they were equally at the fountain-head in respect to order, were it not that we can prove in respect to the latter, first, that originally there is no such thing, and, second, that derivatively or in respect to its origin we can mark it out and show how it is awakened and continued in the mind.

Originally there is no such thing, because unhappiness in others is not agreeable in itself, nor is it conceivable how it can become so except from some other inducement that may exist at the time; moreover, we are conscious that, unswayed by self-love, and uninduced by some other object than itself, man's unhappiness is not a thing that we desire, and not a thing that is desirable in any conceivable way on its own account.

But when we are seeking our own happiness, and others thwart us; or when we are seeking our own honor, and others stand in our place; and when we are seeking the luxury of power, and others rebel; then we hate and envy them; but this, you see, falls in with the idea, that self-love is at the bottom of malevolence, and self-love, itself made wicked by a want of benevolence and of true regard to the principle of virtue.

For example, we are so constituted as to love our own happiness. An instance arises where another man diminishes it. As an obvious consequence we hate him; not because his happiness is undesirable in itself; but because he has diminished ours; and because a want of benevolence and a want of the existence of its sister grace give us up to ourselves, and leave us to the influence of our own resentment.

The self-love is not the cause of the disease; nor especially is it the feeling of malevolence; but, instead of "being angry and sinning not," or, as the Bible intends it, feeling our injuries and being held in place by benevolence and the love of the moral principle, it is the want of these principles of government that are the sum and centre of our whole malevolence.

## CHAPTER XXXII.

### OF HATRED OF VIRTUE.

THIS will appear still more strongly of our hatred of virtue. The hatred of virtue is not a thing that can exist directly and on its own account; for virtue is the love of the happiness of others, and the love of a pure benevolence itself, and a love of this very affection, and so on, presenting an order of feelings creditable to the race of man, which our own consciousness declares never could become objects of hostility; and which, like the azure heavens, or like the starry firmament, can become invisible on account of the blindness of the eye, but never can become repulsive. Holiness, therefore, on its own account, as the impenitent declare, never can become an object of hostility.

But when it defrauds us of our pleasures; when it interferes with self-love; when it condemns us for what we have committed; when it erects a strong barrier against pride, and other engagements of the wicked,—virtue becomes an enemy, from its opposition. "He that doeth evil," says our Saviour, "hateth the light;" and here he gives us all the doctrine that we are propounding; for he declares, that "he hateth the light, neither cometh to the light, *lest his deeds should be reproved.*"

Give a man no true benevolence, which is the idea we have offered for his original iniquity; and give him no true affection for the quality of virtuous excellence; and give him up to self-love, even though that self-love be blunted by the effects of wickedness; and the opposition that he meets, will turn him against virtue with the bitterest malignity.

The hatred of virtue, therefore, is derived from the opposition that it gives to our natural appetites; and the sin consequently consists in a want of original love to it; a love that would have sanctified its restraints, and made them happy and delightful to the mind.

## CHAPTER XXXIII.

### OF ENMITY TO GOD.

Now, if moral excellence, viewed abstractly and in itself considered, is not the object of the sinner's hatred, neither can it be when it comes to be embodied in an Infinite Divinity.

"The carnal mind is enmity against God;" and some have carried that text so far as to say, that enmity to God is of the very essence of iniquity. But what is it in God that we oppose? Is it His immensity? Is it His infinity? Is it that He is all wise, or all powerful? Is it supposable that we could be His enemies because He is infinitely lovely in any mere grandeur or might of His omnipotence? Or is it the fact, that it is His holiness that is the object of hostility? And if so, must it not observe the rule that we have given; that is, that it is not His holiness itself, but that cross upon the sinner that is imposed by His punishment of wickedness?

"The carnal mind is enmity against God;" but

then, as a great proof text, we quote the last part of the passage,—"*because it is not subject to the law of God, neither indeed can be.*"

It is not the loveliness of God that the sinner despises;—His long suffering to us ward, not willing that any should perish; but His tyranny over the wicked, as it appears to the man who has no true love to holiness; and this our Saviour declares when He says, "Me it hateth, *because I testify of [the world] that the works thereof are evil.*" *

## CHAPTER XXXIV.

### OF LOVE TO WICKEDNESS.

SO, it is an entire perversion that men love wickedness on its own account. They love those things that possess the wicked quality; that is, they love sinful indulgence;—nay, they love that lenity that wickedness observes toward their sins, as compared with the rebukes and the comparisons of virtue; but no infamous quality itself, or hardness of the feeling of benevolence, or crookedness of spirit, can intrinsically be felt as agreeable, or a pleasure to the sinner.

A sinner can love sin because it permits him to be sinful; but that he can love sin by any direct appreciation of enjoyment in the quality itself, or of lovableness either in the want of benevolence or in the want of love to the principle of virtue, is an idea incapable of proof, and utterly at variance with an understanding of the Scripture.

Our inference, therefore, from all these chapters is, that sinfulness is an indefinable quality; that it is found

* John vii. 7.

in two negative conditions, a want of benevolence and a want of love to the moral quality; and that these two can turn into sin self-love or any affection in which they can appear.

## CHAPTER XXXV.

### OF WHAT THINGS WOULD BE SINFUL IN GOD.

God, having, out of the superiority of His nature, a benevolence unequalled in its strength, and a love of virtue infinite when His own virtue is the object of His affection, would be sinful, not only if He wanted these, but if He wanted either in that immeasurable degree in which they belong to Him as an infinite Creator. If He were not more benevolent than Gabriel, He would be more sinful than Satan. And as the universe is the dictate of His character, it would be sinful in Him not to have created it; and it would be sinful not to have created it in that form or order in which His benevolence and love of virtue have brought it into being. "The Lord is righteous in all His ways, and holy in all His works." And though it would be irreverent to suppose Him sinful; yet it would not be, to say, "All thy works are done in truth;" and to argue, that a hand-breadth of departure in all the myriads of them since the universe began, would be aside from truth, and, therefore, opposite to His eternal obligation.

## CHAPTER XXXVI.

### OF GOD'S CHIEF END.

God's chief end in His own infinite existence is that in His own infinite existence which is the highest and the best. That in His own infinite existence which is the highest and the best, is His own infinite holiness. The infinite holiness of God is therefore His chief end in His own infinite existence.

But if the infinite holiness of God is His chief end in His own infinite existence, then the *display* of His own infinite holiness is not the chief end; and this we prove from four considerations :—

First, if the display of His own infinite holiness be the chief end of the Almighty, it is either at the call of holiness or not: if it be not, then we have such a thing as the chief end of the Almighty unprompted by His holy character: if it be, then we have a chief end of the Almighty which is prompted by something else.

Secondly, if the display of His own infinite holiness be the chief end of the Almighty, then we have the chief end of such a being as the Almighty terminating on the creature.

Again, if the display of His own infinite holiness be the chief end of the Almighty, then the question may be asked, What is the chief end of that? but no one can ask the question, What is the chief end of holiness? seeing that it carries in itself its own infinite claim upon the mind.

Lastly; if the display of His own infinite holiness is the chief end of the Almighty, then He had no chief end in the ages that preceded the creation.

Now we do not deny that the display of God's holiness is an *important* end; for he says of Pharaoh, "For for this cause have I raised thee up, that I might shew in thee my power, and that my name might be declared in all the earth;" but it is at the call of benevolence, and the love of virtue: and therefore the *ulterior* end is the glory,* or supreme excel-

* *Kabhodh.*

lence itself; and not the glory in the other sense, i. e. the instrumental display which is so often spoken of as a high end in Scripture.

## CHAPTER XXXVII.

### OF GOD'S CHIEF END IN CREATION AND PROVIDENCE.

God's chief end in His own solitary existence would be that holiness which, in that case, would be a love of other beings that were yet to be, and a love of that holiness that would exist at any rate in His exalted character. The invisible things of Him *before* the foundation of the world would be all determined by benevolence and love of virtue.

But when the universe began, His chief end would come more distinctly into notice. And His benevolence being, as we have seen, undiminished by His love of virtue, and His love of virtue untarnished by the utmost display of His benevolence, His universe would be the result of both. God's chief end, therefore, in Creation and Providence, is His own infinite holiness; and holiness demands the highest results of benevolence, and the highest diffusion of holiness, all over the worlds that He shall have brought into being.

To give happiness, therefore, to the greatest number of intelligent and immortal creatures, to raise it highest, to keep it longest, and to occasion it to grow with the highest conceivable celerity; to diffuse holiness all over His works, and to make it the highest possible in all periods of time,—that is what is dictated by benevolence and love of virtue; and these being the divisions of His holiness, are that in which He consults it to the very highest degree.

## CHAPTER XXXVIII.

### OF OPTIMISM.

GOD, therefore, is either incapable or weak, or that which He aims after with the highest desire is that which He attains in the very highest degree. Holiness is something that He does not value more than anything else; or else there is something weak or imperfect in His nature; or else there is something in His own holiness which impedes the holiness of others; or else He uprears the holiness of others to the very highest possible degree. And happiness, is either impaired by holiness; or man's happiness is inconsistent with the happiness of God; or God's happiness makes Him indifferent to the happiness of man; or else the happiness of the universe will be extended to the utmost possible extent.

We are not afraid, therefore, of being accused of optimism, if optimism were only these extreme ideas,—that God's universe is the happiest possible, and that God's universe is the holiest possible, making the holiest possible that (as the superior in its excellence) in which the beltistic reality most gloriously consists. We have no fear to enlarge upon these points, and most thoughtfully to affirm them, that God could not have made a better,—that he could not have made a holier, and that He could not have made a happier; and that this universe is the most complete, not only as possible with God, but as conceivable in the very nature of affairs.

But when the optimist comes in and teaches, that all virtue consists in benevolence, or that all virtue consists in utility, and so builds up a universe, the best only because it is the happiest, making the beltistic property to consist in its ability to make its inhabitants enjoy life, then we demur,—not because of an inferior beltistic conviction, but of a better, and because our optimism, though establishing a maximum felicity, has piled up above that a holiness that is superior to all.

## CHAPTER XXXIX.

### OF OBJECTIONS TO GOD'S NOT BEING ABLE TO CREATE A BETTER UNIVERSE FOUNDED UPON HIS OMNIPOTENCE.

BUT then it may be argued, If God is not able to create a better universe, then we have an argument that throws us all into confusion at once, founded upon God's omnipotence. Let the beltistic property be what we please; yet if it be finite; if it be a finite holiness, and a finite happiness; or a finite excellence in which holiness and happiness are blended, or in which one is the superior, but both the extremest possible; then, when that property is reached, God's mightiness is brought to a pause. The little increment beyond is as impossible as the creation of Divinity. And God is limited; that is, the infinitesimal fraction of a line cannot be passed, when what is called the highest possible condition has been reached in a finite creation. Now, to all this we answer, God *is* limited. It may be said, He could throw out other worlds, and create, this very morning, higher and holier abodes than He has ever brought into being. Suppose it done. Then, of course, He can create others. And suppose it done. Then of course there can be multitudes of others. And when the last sentence had been uttered, announcing the possibility of constellations happier than the rest, some one could take his stand and say, He could create a thousand more. Now of two things one;—either God *could not if He desired* create the noblest possible universe, or, if He did, it must still be finite. There is no limit to the talk of casting out other worlds; and yet there must be some limit to the execution. If God desired ever so much to make the holiest possible universe, it must still be finite; and that is all that can be asserted of the universe that His hand has made.

Now, I know, that it is hard to imagine what that could be that could make Him stop, if He really desired to go on and on to the very acme; but this we know, that He must somewhere stop; and, after creating a universe that is nameless in extent, He must somewhere set a horizon to His work, and must somewhere stop short of its being as immense as His Divinity.

Now, if this be the case, where is the unreasonableness of taking advantage of it in our belief? And as, if God *did* wish to make the holiest possible creation, He must still stop somewhere for its boundary, where is the sin of thinking that He has chosen the wisest and the best? and though He still means immeasurably to expand its excellence, yet He pauses at each bestowal that He makes, out of the necessities of its finite nature?

## CHAPTER XL.

### OF OBJECTIONS TO GOD'S NOT BEING ABLE TO CREATE A BETTER UNIVERSE FOUNDED UPON THE EXISTENCE OF EVIL.

BUT it may be asked, How does this agree with the existence of evil? Could not God create a universe as holy and as happy as the best, and yet leave out of it those parts that are beset with evil? And is it possible that God is limited in such a sense that He cannot work out the highest purposes of good without admixture of eternal evil?

Now, we dare not talk of these things without talking in the clearest and most intelligible way. When we say that God is limited, we mean that He is limited in a way that all will admit,—in the power to make creatures *un*limited, or to raise a nation to an equality or likeness to Himself. If, therefore, it *were* His wish to make all sentient and intelligent existence the highest and happiest that He could, there must be a pause, from this very confessed and necessary imperfectness. He could raise a universe so high, and no higher. For if any one should take His stand and say, 'He could, a little higher,' this sort of speech might be perpetual. There is evidently a point at every stage of what is finite, where Omnipotence must pause, out of the very necessities of its * finite nature.

Now if it be the will of the Almighty to make this the best possible universe, He would set that point the highest possible at each stage of His duration. Whatever circumstances would do this, those circumstances He would embrace. And if evil were such a circumstance, the very holiness of God's character, which binds Him to the best possible creation, would lead Him to the existence of evil; and, therefore, eternal truth, which is that which His holiness obeys, would sanction the employment of a power thus known to be for the advancement of the universe.

Now, in respect to evil as a means of benefit, we utter two truths. We challenge any one to doubt them:—

First, it *may* be the fact that evil is a circumstance

* That is, the creation's (1875).

in the arrangement of the universe, connected with the highest good ; and,

Secondly, there is much to convince us in the arrangements of the universe that such *is* the fact.

Natural evil would give us no difficulty. Moral evil, which absolutely requires the other, is the sum of the objection. And now let any one ask, how much of the glories of Providence is connected with the existence of evil, and he will be staggered, at least, with the idea, that it *may* be necessary to the design that has been made.

## CHATER XLI.

### OF MAN'S CHIEF END.

GOD'S chief end being His own infinite holiness, man's chief end can be neither higher nor lower. It cannot be higher; because that which is highest to God must be highest also to the creature. And it cannot be lower; because that which is highest in itself, if discerned, must be highest to all that discern it. Man's chief end, therefore, is the holiness of God.

But, as the holiness of God is not an object actively to pursue, except by desiring it, or praying for it, which seems to be our duty, man's chief end of a more practical kind is the holiness of others. If any man say, No; man's iron obligation is to be holy himself,—I answer, That is the very question. The very question is, What is man's highest holiness? If any one say, Man's highest holiness is man's highest holiness, I agree, but doubt the *progress* of such a proposition. Man's highest holiness, next to the holiness of God, is to promote the holiness of the world around him.

## CHAPTER XLII.

### OF THE PRACTICAL CONSEQUENCES OF THE FOREGOING SYSTEM.

I. A system that makes all virtue an indefinable quality, must shorten debate, because it precludes the questions on the nature of virtue.

II. A system that makes all virtue belong to two definite affections, must assist our theology, because theology, though the science of God, is the science of God chiefly in His moral relations.

III. A system that makes all virtue belong to two definite affections, must assist us in duty, for duty is the creature of light, and light could hardly be shed more expressly upon the boundaries of obligation.

IV. A system that makes all virtue belong to benevolence and a love of virtue, must be a basis for happiness, because it shows that this universe is not a failure, but is the noblest possible that even God could have prepared.

V. A system that makes all virtue belong to benevolence and a love of virtue, should aid us in worship, because it makes God not a mysterious Sovereign, but a glorious Creator, managing the best for the lands that he has made.

VI. A system that makes all sin, want of benevolence and want of love to the virtuous principle, must aid us in piety, because it simplifies our penitence, and shows us but two evils that it is needful to restrain.

VII. A system that makes this universe the best possible universe, must include the existence of evil, and take away the appearance of arbitrariness of what we are accustomed to contemplate as the naked sovereignty of God.

# DIVISION III.

# THE MORAL CHARACTER.

## CHAPTER I.

### THE MORAL QUALITY A QUALITY ONLY OF SINGLE FEELINGS.

THE first Division being on the subject of the Moral Quality, and the second, on the subject of the Moral Duties or those things in which the quality is found, it follows that we have gone no further than the consideration of single feelings; for benevolence and love of virtue being our only duties, we have only to remember that benevolence and love of virtue are transitory feelings, to see that transitory feelings are all the length we have yet gone in the phenomena of the mind.

Now, the question arises, Do these transitory feelings come up in any order as to their goodness or their badness? or is there an entire uncertainty? Can I only say, This feeling is a good feeling, and this feeling is a bad feeling? or can I also say, This man is likely to feel what is right, and this man is accustomed to feel what is wrong? Can I only pronounce upon feelings when I see them? or can I also say what feelings they are likely to be? for if the first of these statements is the fact, we have finished our work; but if the second, we have another entire department, and that department is the department of *Character*.

## CHAPTER II.

### OF CHARACTER.

CHARACTER (χαρακτὴρ) is derived from the Greek word χαράσσω, which means to cut or engrave.

I. Character, therefore, in its first sense, meant a cut or engraving, such as was used for a hieroglyph or letter. And letters under the name of characters are spoken of up to the present day.

II. Characters, however, being made in a particular way, and every man's characters having something peculiar in them to mark them as his own, a man's character came to mean the letter he was accustomed to form, or, more comprehensively speaking, his handwriting.

III. This, which was only used by the Greeks and Romans, gave place in a later period of the world to another meaning; for a man's writing being seen to resemble conduct (that is, as he fell into one, so he was found to fall into the other), a man's character came to mean the conduct that he shewed, or his prevalent behavior.

IV. This, being supposed to arise within him, gave the name of character to nature or inward disposition of heart:

V. And, afterward, to the man himself, as possessed of such a nature: in which case we say a man is a shocking character.

VI. Finally, it came to mean character as ascribed or imputed to a man, and which might be ascribed or imputed to him justly or unjustly; in which sense a man might be said to be better than his character.

Now of all these senses, the third is the more philosophical, but the fourth is perhaps the common one. We need not, however, be particular. Our work, as it proceeds, will sufficiently distinguish our own immediate meaning.

## CHAPTER III.

### OF CHARACTER IN ITS CONNECTION WITH GOD.

GOD being Creator only in such a sense as to give being to an object for the instant while He is engaged in creating it, it follows that Providence is a new creation every moment. Accordingly, a horse might be one moment a horse, and the next might be nothing. In the nature of finite things it is *better* that it should continue a horse; but this is only the *reason*. The efficient *cause* of its continuing so, is solely the will of God. It might be one moment a horse, and the next moment a wall, and the next moment a college. Its continuing a horse is solely because God considers it better to create it the same; although, if He had created it an elephant, it would be as simple to create as though He had created it just continuously a horse.

Now, in respect to mind, the continuance is no different from the continuance of matter. It might be one moment mind, and the next moment it might be created a vapor. It has in it only at the time what God puts into it by the act of creation. And as the rules and the reasons of its being are no part of that which God puts into it at its creation, it may be said that what He put into it yesterday has passed away, and that it is a different creation at each act of His continuing of it in its being.* Now, if it be a new

* We ought to have had some reserves for ignorance. We do not know all that God might create. We should not be too positive. But, from the Law of Parcimony, we have no reason to posit atoms; and, therefore, the *like*lihood at least, or what we have traced as the empirical probability, is that each creature is continuously brought into being (1875).

creation by each act of God by which He continues it in its being, then it is evident that it might be man or devil according to His will. There is nothing in the arm of God to forbid Him to make a new creature just what He may please. And if the upholding of a spirit is a new creation, there is nothing in the universe of God that would make the new being like the old, except the mere good pleasure of a will that has to select its pattern as though no old one had ever been created.

Now, if the new mind and the old mind might have been entirely different, it is evident that they might have been different morally. Yesterday, I might be a saint; to-day, I might be a sinner. If God new-creates my whole existence, surely He new-creates my character. And it is just as impossible to believe that He must make me all new because what He made me yesterday perished at the moment He was making it, and yet that he must not make my character, as it would be to believe that He must make a star all over again every moment, and yet not make the greenish or the yellow light that twinkles from it in its passage through the heavens.

What we teach, therefore, is, that character, as a thing to-day, is revived by the Almighty from the character yesterday. He gave me my character this morning when I waked. And this He does, not arbitrarily, but under the direction of reasons.

There are, therefore, two things, the power and the eternal reasons. The power we have found to be from God. We are to consider next the reasons that direct it.

Our next subject therefore is the reasons of God in the direction of character.

## CHAPTER IV.

### OF CHARACTER IN ITS CONNECTION WITH HAPPINESS.

IT has been remarked upon as an interesting fact, that God takes care of a man in the exercise of virtue; that is, that as virtues are a disinterested exercise, God takes care of our happiness. Now this statement is not adequately profound.

God does not make benevolence and love of virtue a source of happiness by arranging our nature so as to make us happy in the exercise of these affections; but (what will be instantly perceived) these virtues are happinesses themselves. God could not make virtue any different. And virtue belonging to benevolence and the love of excellence, it will be seen that virtue belongs to two pleasures: for pleasure at holiness and pleasure at others' welfare are the only things that are actually virtuous.

It is not profound, therefore, to say, that God arranges our being so as to make virtuousness happy; for virtuousness belongs to happiness; happiness at the welfare of others and happiness at the excellence of virtue being the only possible forms in which God even is a possessor of excellence.

These pleasures also are the highest. There are none which have more to do with heavenly felicity. It is a truth, therefore, that happiness *is* holiness * in the highest forms in which the idea of happiness can possibly exist.

* By holiness, of course, is here meant, that which possesses holiness, or holiness in its second meaning. By happiness is meant, those two forms of happiness which a man feels at virtue and the welfare of

But though being happy in the two highest possible forms in which happiness ever exists, is the only possible form of the possession of virtue, yet happiness, notwithstanding that, is a high inducement to virtue itself. I am made more virtuous because happiness is virtue. And not only in the nature of things does happiness, where it is itself a virtue, serve as an inducement to virtue itself, but God uses other happinesses. He not only elicits virtue by help of the happiness of holiness itself, but also by superintending other happinesses; that is, by a system of rewards that is made as general as Providence itself.

## CHAPTER V.

### OF REWARDS.

NOW, these rewards need only be described by saying, that happiness has an intrinsic tendency to be an inducement for virtue. No man will have a doubt of this. Happiness may have an intrinsic tendency as an inducement to wickedness, in those cases, for example, where chastisement is better. But happiness offered to the innocent, and having an influence not only upon

others. The proposition less briefly stated is, that two of our highest happinesses are our only virtues.

This shows what those ethical philosophers were in search of who were betrayed into the very erroneous doctrine, that "virtue was only the highest form of seeking our own happiness;" a proposition that would be entirely true if rectified in two ways, first, by taking virtue in its meaning as that which possesses virtue, or as virtuous affection, and second, by striking out the idea of "seeking." Virtuous affection is no doubt the highest form of personal happiness (1855).

We have already shown, however (Pathics, Introd.), that happiness, in the instance of holiness, is good distinctly from its being happy; that is, possesses an ethical excellence which is a consciousness in the happiness itself (1875).

them but upon the public that witness it, must be an encouragement to virtue; otherwise, where is the principle of reward? Without being particular, therefore;—happiness, as a gift to the innocent, is a high inducement to character.

But now, happiness largely consists in holiness. Not only are the two holy affections the highest possible happiness; but happiness, as we have just been declaring, is accorded to holiness. For God to keep a character holy therefore, is the highest possible reward.

We see, hence, one great reason for character. My being holy to-day is the chief of my recompense for holiness yesterday. And so, holiness is made to continue. I retire to my bed with no hold upon character but as a reward of the Almighty.*

## CHAPTER VI.

### SUMMARY OF THE PRECEDING.

IT becomes us, however, to make all these things somewhat more distinct.

I. Affection, in each separate case, is comparatively simple. It glows in the mind, and passes off and has ended forever.

II. The question is, whether, ending forever, it leaves behind it no influence, or no ground for knowing whether the affection that comes after will be virtuous or sinful; or whether the hundreds that come after it will be all tinged with a prevailing quality.

III. This we have answered by saying, that all that comes after it is with God. He only can decide, for

* Man, however, has really no holiness, and no proper reward. The reward that he meets with, is really the reward of the Redeemer.

He only sustains our existence. If, therefore, the existence of the future borrows anything from the existence of the past, it is God that carries it over, and, therefore, it is God preëminently that is the connecter of character.

IV. Yet God's having the power, does not prevent His acting under the authority of reasons. On the contrary He has the strictest reasons for the bestowment of character; and these reasons are chiefly * the need of reward.

V. Reward is all forms of happinesses, used in their influence to encourage virtue. Virtue being a happiness itself, and, moreover, being the thing that calls for a reward, it becomes therefore, immediately and mediately a reward itself. The continuance of virtue is, therefore, that it may serve as a reward.

Now in saying this we mean to say, that this is all the principle on which reward is based. Righteousness does not deserve a reward in any sense of immediate connection. But it deserves a reward in a roundabout way, and that roundabout path is this:—First, happiness, in the nature of things, is an eternal incentive to virtue. Here lies the principle of reward in the nature of things.† Second; being an eternal incentive, God must notice it, and use it as such. Third; if He use it at all, He must use it accurately. God, therefore, having a high affection for holiness, will

* I mean reasons for the discriminations of character. The bestowment of good character, other things being equal, is a main governmental desire of the Almighty (1875).

† For a man to say that we see by conscience directly that virtue deserves a reward, as though desert were a simple and separate idea, or even part of the idea of virtue, is simply absurd. We see that virtue deserves a reward in no other sense than gangrene requires a knife, or drought requires rain.

reward its possessor from the intrinsic nature of reward to be an incentive to holiness.

But it will be asked, How can three things agree? I. God is the Creator of character, that is, restores it again from night to morning. II. Reward is a promoter of character; and III. Character is itself a reward. Now here seems a harmful jumble, that keeps anything clear from being appreciated. So let us treat these matters very plainly.

God is the Preserver of character, and yet helps it by rewards, in just as plain a sense as God is the improver of character, and yet advances it by the gospel. Where had I my character this morning when I slept? Certainly where I had my being. And if God is charged with one just as much as He is charged with the other, certainly the fact of His agency cannot be one moment denied. But power is one thing, and instruments another. Without instruments I cannot have any benevolence at all. Unless God shows me virtue, I cannot have any love of it. And, therefore, the sight of the truth is necessary to the exercise of character, even though the whole of the power should come entirely from God.

Now take reward in, in the horizon of truth, and we have but another instrument. I cannot love others unless I see them; and it seems I cannot love others as much, as if I am rewarded for it. Both then are instruments.

Now, that character itself should become a reward for character, is not so unnatural, seeing it is the nearest to us. That fishing itself should become a reward for fishing, is not so unnatural, seeing that it gives me pleasure. I open my eyes and see virtue all bathed in happiness. I take in, therefore, two sights; the excellence of virtue, and the happiness with which it is attended. Both these apparitions help it; and not singularly : the happiness of virtue is the nearest pleasure at the time.

## CHAPTER VII.

### OF COVENANTED REWARDS.

Now, it being possible to state all these things so clearly, we might fancy some *measure* of reward. Certain it is that reward must be perfectly accurate. Yet though the principles of it are so entirely simple, yet the statutes of it are entirely unknown.

Indeed, we are troubled by dangerous exceptions. Satan, after obedience to the right, was afterwards forsaken, and abandoned to the wrong. So was Adam. Adam's children never knew anything of right.* It would exhaust any man's intelligence, if he spent his life in laboring for a law that would comprehend the administrations of God. It was necessary, therefore, that He should reveal Himself; and, therefore, all the rewards of which we know anything very clearly, are *covenanted rewards.*

All these are founded in nature ; and yet some of them are very peculiar. For example, God promised to Adam that he would bless all his race perpetually for his temporary and single obedience. This, in so artificial a connection as birth, of which Adam knew nothing, and which psychologically seems no connection at all, was a promise to millions for the labor of one ; and yet, *quoad* Adam,† it served all the uses of a reward. It was an inducement of the highest kind ; and

* Of a perfect kind.

† And so it should be treated. It was not our reward, but Adam's ; though the guilt, as a mere matter of philology, is both ours and his.

moreover, a lesson to the universe that will last forever and forever. So Jesus Christ was promised the salvation of his people. We must not, however, dwell upon these things. The simplest rewards are those that were promised to Adam, and to the angels.

## CHAPTER VIII.

### OF MERIT.

MERIT is only a convenient word for expressing all that we have been saying. It is the suitedness of a mind to be blessed with happiness according to those principles of inducement and encouragement which we have just been stating. A man merits either, when, in view of his own past character, the highest interests of holiness and happiness would be promoted by giving him either. Christ merits the salvation of His people; and so do we, in a modified use of that term, merit through Him our own deliverance. We shall return to these subjects. The difficulty of ourselves having been guilty, need give us no uneasiness; for reward, though founded in nature, is only for the end of the highest inducement of virtue.

## CHAPTER IX.

### OF PUNISHMENT.*

LOVE of others and love to the quality of virtue being the only virtues, of course a disposition to punish must be an instance under one or both of them. It is an instance under both. Punishment, therefore, is not a virtue, original on the part of God, and the fruit of a primordial desire; but an instrument. It is

* With this caption written down, the old manuscript ceases (1875).

not moral, any more than a plough or a flail. If any one dreams that it is, consciously so, and that we think of its desert intuitively, and as of the very nature of sin, we have but to point him to the idea of distance. The two ideas are similar. Distance seems so evident when we look at a star, that it seems a consciousness, like the very light that twinkles. And yet it was long ago found to be the fact that distance was empirical. So of punishment: it is so fixed an instrument; so bred in the very nature of things; and has been used so long, and borne so often,—that it seems one with trespass. We hardly separate them. And yet, beyond all manner of doubt, it is a mere instrument, demanded by nature, and which it would turn everything awry not to threaten and to employ.

Punishment is of two kinds, suffering and sin. The former is what is usually conceived. But if suffering were the whole of punishment, there would be no hell; * for sin is not an infinite evil such that if it were not punished by apostasy, a single sin would merit an eternity of punishment. It pleases justice that sin should corrupt us; that is, that it should defile our nature. That is a part of its punishment (Rom. i. 26). That is the serious part. I sin, and I am given up to sin. I sin more, and it becomes more. It grows. Sin, therefore, is a part of the punishment of sin. And it adds to suffering, because, first, it is a suffering in itself, and, second, it deserves more suffering; it is the great prolific centre from which the hell of the soul must emanate.

One word more. Punishment is an instrument. Now an instrument for what? If sin more and greater goes on as the punishment of sin, how can punishment

* Prov. xix. 19. See Author's Commentary.

be an instrument for repressing sin and advancing holiness? This it emphatically is. Not singly for the greatest happiness, but for the greatest good, moral and mental; and, as moral good can never interfere with happiness, then for both objects. Punishment we define as an instrument for increasing the holiness, and so the happiness, of the widest universe.

Punishment employs sin. Punishment (for the widest part of it) consists in sin. Punishment entails sin; and, for men and angels, makes it perpetual. But none the less on that account can we see that it is a moral engine. (1) To the few that escape, and (2) to the wide universe that were never implicated, it is the deepest teaching; far deeper than reward; far deeper than a simple suffering; opening the huge proportions of guilt; stamping the hateful lineaments of sin; and building a wider monument out of its infernal growth than could at all be reached by pain as penalty.

## CHAPTER X.

### OF COVENANTED PUNISHMENT.

PUNISHMENT, therefore, not being as of an original taste, we are prepared to hear that, as an instrument, it can be shifted; that is, where no oath is violated, and where the end can be maintained, some other punishment might be substituted than that which is straightforward to the sinner.

1. Adam, for example, was punished twice; once in himself, and once in his offspring. All men are punished similarly. If I sin, it strikes other parties. But, in Adam's case, it had a plighted definiteness. He lived under its shadows. He may not have known what offspring was, or understood all that was to follow.

But he understood more than the one blighted life. He knew that he was under bonds for others. And, therefore, that breadth of penalty increased his caution about the Fall, and increased immeasurably the monumental testimony.

2. The second Adam was a still different case. Here the punishment was not multiplied, but narrowed in. Here the penalty was shifted. Here the punishment was shown artificially to be an instrument, and the punishment of one was made to answer by covenant for many. Here the penalty was lifted off where it was shockingly deserved, and freighted down on Him who was entirely innocent. It is not vengeance, therefore. It is not the greed of an original taste, or the fire of a self-justified anger. But it is a government expedient, sworn to by solemn oaths, and required by the very nature of our spirits, not to produce happiness alone, but to produce the widest holiness among all the creatures.

## CHAPTER XI.

### OF VINDICATORY JUSTICE.

PUNISHMENT having been carefully defined, our true policy is to lay justice side by side with that, and let them define each other. We shall do the same with guilt; and we shall do the same with forgiveness and atonement. If punishment is a mere expedient, Vindicatory Justice is a form of words to tell that whole story. It is not a primordial trait. The two primordial traits are benevolence and the love of virtue; and we have but to look at these to see how simple they are, compared with anything we can think of in the forms of justice. Given a creature, no matter what the form of its thinking or sentient life, and man and God and devil are bound to love him. There is no exception. Given a right thought, no matter who has it, or what the form in which it may appear, and men and angels are bound to reverence it, and with no reserve of which we can conceive.

But how different justice! There are cases when it does not overtake the guilty. There are cases where it does overtake the innocent. There are cases where two parties have been guilty for the same offence. All these things have been illustrated in the sacrifice of Christ. The guilty have been glorified, and the glorified have been made guilty; and both have been followed by Vindicatory Justice according as the good of holiness has demanded this or that. Christ has been punished that the guilty might escape, and the guilty have ceased to be so by the mere award of a divinely accepted covenant. Vindicatory Justice was the appropriate term in each of these changes. Did it follow Christ, it was equally in place. And, therefore, I say, that this alone puts vengeance just where it ought to stand. That vengeance upon Christ and vengeance upon the lost are the one form of a primordial trait, is dangerous and absurd; and, therefore, there is no such virtue. Vindicatory Justice is but a convenient speech of that story of God which tells of Him how He discourages iniquity.

## CHAPTER XII.

### OF GUILT.

AND so of Guilt.

We are really most pronounced and most elaborate where we are most brief, and where we go to the mark in the very shortest period of time. Guilt is the converse ot punishment. Tell me where anybody ought to be punished, and I will tell you where he is guilty. And even here that word *ought*, must be distinguished. It is used sometimes in the instance of desert. But tell me where a man ought to be punished for the advancement of holiness, and I will tell you where he is guilty. So Christ, He became an object of wrath. So Cain, in his unconscious infancy. So all the world, upon the sin of Adam. These were all innocent; though innocent in different ways. And yet they were all guilty. And so guilt is a like term with wrath and vindicatory justice, variant in its case, and anything in the world but a primordial idea.

## CHAPTER XIII.

### OF ATONEMENT.

KEEPING close to the ideas thus defined, we get the best conception of the Lord's Atonement. It was a punishment. It was a punishment of the covenanted sort. It was a punishment in the shape of vengeance,—vengeance however never being primordial. It was at the call of Vindicatory Justice ; this, as best seen in Christ's case, being secondary, and never primary. It, therefore, implied guilt ; but showing more imperatively on that very account that guilt was a whole bundle of speech, telling the whole story of punishment, and meaning that Christ could be punished for men with the same plighted results in the advancement of holiness.

## CHAPTER XIV.

### OF FORGIVENESS.

THERE are but two virtues, a love for the welfare of others, and a love for the quality of virtue. Neither of these must eventuate upon forgiveness. In the first place, not the first; for we must love the welfare of others, even if we do not forgive them: and in the second place, not the second; for we must not esteem others, even if we do forgive them, except as they become worthy of this species of love.

There has been infinite error about this matter of forgiveness.

When I forgive a man, I lift away punishment. When God forgives him, He does precisely the same thing.

Let us keep among these words. They wonderfully clarify each other. Guilt,—that is the correlative of forgiveness.

When a man says, I hate him, and can't forgive him, and means by that, he wishes him evil, he has a mongrel idea of the duty of forgiveness. So ought he never to have hated him.

When a man says, I hate him, and can't esteem him, and mourn my hardness of heart that I cannot forgive, he is mistaken again. He *ought* not to forgive. At least he ought not to forgive in that sense in which he understands forgiveness. Men are tormented by these mistakes; and alas! die hard, because they cannot think well of their enemies. It was never intended. We are bound to *wish* well even to the devil. We are bound to *think* well only of the estimable. Forgiveness lies in another beat. Even God forgives only upon an atonement; and so it is with men. We punish for morals' sake. We punish for defensive purposes. We punish as a remedial act. Now satisfy these ends, and it is time to forgive. When will men understand these facts? The Bible says,—Upon an offence rebuke; upon repentance forgive (Lu. xvii. 3). We scatter all this to the winds. We have a notion that there must be a universal forgiveness. We get it all mixed. (1) We think we ought to forgive and cease resentment. We ought never to have begun resentment. (2) We think we ought to soften and think well of the base. We ought never to do it, whatever their courteous amendment. (3) We think we ought to shake hands with them whether they apologize or no. This whole thing is wonderfully mistaken. The Bible says,—"If thou bring thy gift to the altar, and there rememberest THAT THY BROTHER HATH AUGHT AGAINST THEE, leave there thy gift before the altar, and go thy way; first be reconciled to thy brother, and then come and offer thy gift" (Matt. v. 23, 24). This shows what I am to do when I am the transgressor. But now again,—"IF THY BROTHER TRESPASS AGAINST THEE," (Matt. xviii. 15). Here is something that will shed its light upon the whole subject of forgiveness. There are to be conditions. I am never to need to forgive as ceasing to resent; for I am never to feel resentment. But I am never to dare to forgive as ceasing to inflict, till there has been the proper remedy. Our Saviour insists upon this. When justice is committed to the state, I am to depend upon its adjudications; but where it must be by private attitudes, I am instructed to a very hair. "IF HE REPENT, forgive him." I suppose that means, that if he does not repent, we are not to forgive him. The direction is yet more explicit. "If he trespass against thee seven times in a day, and seven times in a day turn again to thee saying, I repent, thou shalt forgive him" (Luke xvii. 4). And then, when all remedies fail, we are distinctly instructed (and how different is this from our goody-good conceits), "LET HIM BE UNTO THEE AS A HEATHEN MAN AND A PUBLICAN" (Matt. xviii. 17).

Like diatribes against hanging; like extreme views about temperance; like general-happiness schemes,—these softly notions about injuries breed injuries, as one might naturally expect. A Puritan mistake about offences breeds a Congress that can give the lie with no troublesome results. It breeds a manhood that can take an insult, and shake the hand that may administer it; that admires a Christian who can smile forgivingly under an affront; that can manage schools of learning by random imputations of deceit, when the scholar is nearly grown; that can bring Billingsgate up into the higher markets of exchange; and that can make it appear as of the teaching of Christ, to take lovingly, and with relations afterward, an unatoned assault upon honesty and honor.

## CHAPTER XV.

### OF JUSTICE.

THOUSANDS of persons will be sure that orthodoxy is put in peril, and will see no basis for the central doctrines of the cross, if justice is made not primordial, and is denied a place as an original attribute of God. Justice, of all moral traits, seems to demand a position at the side of mercy, and to claim to be first considered if there is to be any priority the one over the other.

But by all the rules of philosophy, to say nothing of Scripture, how can that be a primordial trait that refuses unity? We defy any one to tell us what justice is by a word. Benevolence is a perfect expression. It tells the story of an original virtue thoroughly and once for all. There is no vestige of an exception. I am to love my enemies. I am to love the wicked. In the sense of *bene-volens* I am to wish well to the devil, and have a pity for him, for so has the Almighty. I am down at the hard-pan of the absolute, just as with that other virtue. For God and man and devil and angel and all intelligences have two moralities with which there is no varying,—a love of others, which consists in desiring their welfare, and a love of virtue, virthe being a simple quality, and a love to it being of so plain a kind that an exception can no more occur than in the duty of God to keep Himself from palpable iniquity.

But how is it with justice? It begins to drop its meanings as a balloon parts with ballast. We get down to a forensic sense after endless distinctions. Honesty and things like that are crowded into it. And when we say, We will treat of rectoral justice, our difficulties have scarcely begun. Let any man declare a law of rectoral justice. Let him so much as declare a fragment of one. We defy him to attempt it. Suppose he says, The innocent may not suffer like the wicked. That is not so. Animals suffer. Some poor brutes are bred deformed, and do nothing but suffer to their dying day. Suppose another enouncement. Suppose he says, The wicked must suffer. That is not so. Vast multitudes of the wicked are to be gloriously lifted. Where shall justice appear? Are the righteous to be rewarded? Satan was righteous. Is every good work to be blessed? Adam had good works. It would puzzle any one to see where a line could be drawn that would take in justice in that well bounded way that marks all ideas that are truly primaries.

But when we resort to the two sole virtues, benevolence and the love of virtuousness, we can argue out from there with the utmost clearness. Justice becomes a bundle; a sort of huge store-house of proprieties and sequences under these. Punishment becomes an instrument; vindicatory justice, the norm that wields it; reward, the encouragement for virtue: covenant, the pre-promised scheme for making all recompenses more efficient; justice, therefore, not an unnatural trait; not one not based in the origin of things; not one not fortified by promise; not one not seated like the primaries from which it is derived; but not one itself primary, but, contrariwise, deriving from those that are; and on that very account hard to be defined, and bundled loosely like all other derivative ideas.

## CHAPTER XVI.

### OF RIGHTEOUSNESS.

INCIDENT to the derived nature of justice, is the looseness of all these attendant conceptions. Guilt coming as the counterpart of punishment, we might suppose that righteousness might fix its meaning as the opposite of guilt. But try that on an example. The guilty are certain to be punished; but are the righteous certain to be rewarded? No one can write a sentence or begin a paragraph on the general subject of righteousness without coming to the utmost difficulty. Disembarrassed of all equivocals, and not noticing that righteousness means holiness or goodness of heart; confining ourselves to what is strictly forensic,—who understands even that? and will come aboard and sail our craft through three leagues of sea without discomfiture? What is righteousness? Is it a merit that secures reward? Then what characterizes it? Give us a case of it in some noted instance. Is Gabriel righteous? Then how about Satan? Satan, exactly like Gabriel, up to a certain mark of time, deserved well of the Almighty. What is righteousness? Is it righteousness beyond a mark of time? Then it is not primary. What was the righteousness of Adam? Was it righteousness if it lasted a certain age? And what fixed that age? After all, is there any righteousness? Is it not a thing of covenant? And if it be so, that explains our Saviour,—After we have done all "we are unprofitable servants" (Lu. xvii. 10): and that explains Ezekiel,—"His righteousness which he hath done shall not be remembered," etc., etc., (Ez. iii. 20): and that enforces our facts,—that justice is no primary trait; for it is impossible to build difficulties like this around benevolence and the love of virtuousness.

## CHAPTER XVII.

### OF DESERT.

Righteousness being a merit of reward, and guilt an obligation to be punished, it might be supposed that desert corresponded to each of these, and it does correspond, perhaps, in the instance of reward. I do not deserve reward, unless I am entitled to it; and it appears I am not entitled to it, unless it is given me by covenant. I only deserve, therefore, covenanted rewards. It is different with punishment. I deserve punishment often when I am not guilty. My guilt may have been removed by the Gospel, but not my ill-desert.

And, again ; Christ may be guilty; and, indeed, an infant may be guilty; and, in a certain sense, the unborn world may be guilty,—but not ill-deserving.

These things are the mere usage of language.

Nevertheless this word desert has played an important part in arguments about the nature of justice.

It has been said, I am conscious of ill-desert.

Now, if there be no such thing as ill-desert, except as a convenient expression for saying that there is a certain use for punishment, and that I am a sinner, it is evident that this argument from consciousness is altogether beyond the facts. I am conscious of sin. I am conscious of its filth and shame. I am conscious of its pestiferousness as an evil. If that be ill-desert, then I have a sense of it. But that it deserves punishment as a thing consciously revealed, is about as true as that I am conscious of the distance of a house. I am conscious of the color of a house, just as I am of the odiousness of my sin ; but that it requires force to build it, or that it requires bricks to go into its wall, I am not conscious ; any more than I am conscious of desert, though I am conscious of the infamy of sin, and see men naturally benefited by pain and penalty.

Desert, therefore, like guilt, is an expression for describing the suitedness of recompense : only, unlike guilt, it sticks to the broader features of suitedness; while guilt, straying into theological speech, goes into all the niceties of award, where covenant and astounding grace transcend the bourne of any usual administration.

# BOOK V.

# THEOLOGY;

OR, THE

## SCIENCE OF PERCEPTION AS KNOWLEDGE OF THE BEING OF A GOD.

---

## CHAPTER I.

### THEOLOGY UNDER THE LIGHT OF PSYCHOLOGY.

IF there is nothing consciously in the mind but perception, God is perception, or He is not consciously in the mind.

We should like to see a professorship established in some great university, on Rudimental Thought as hinted at by Rudimental Language. We never hear of a man being conscious of himself, or of his being conscious of his own soul. We never hear of his being conscious of a rock, or of a tree. We never hear of his being conscious of God. We hear of his being conscious of pain, and conscious of sin, and conscious of joy, and perhaps conscious of the love of God in his own heart; but it makes us feel strong in our philosophy to remember, that we can be loyal to the most delicate hints of established idiom. If any one hears of being conscious of a peach, or conscious of the *me*, or of the spirit, it shall be in the writings of some philosopher who is placing himself in the wrong by unusual language.

We hear of the sun rising; but, then, justifiably;

for the sun does rise. Relatively, that is just the very appearance. And so we hear of a pain in the fingers; for that is the sensation; but when the fingers are cut off, and the pain keeps where it was, that does not falsify the fact. The language speaks the conscious seeming; and thus it becomes our appeal as to the conscious seeming among men when we say that it does not speak of our being conscious of our souls, or conscious of that loftier Soul, the Spirit that is declared invisible.

## CHAPTER II.

### THEOLOGY UNDER THE LIGHT OF LOGIC.

IF there is nothing intuitively known but perception, God is perception, or He is not intuitively known.

As God is not perception, and, therefore, not intuitively known, and as nothing is certain but what is intuitively known, it is not certain that there is any such being as God.

This reasoning we admit.

1. But then we insist upon a technical sense of certainty.

If nothing is certain but what is intuitively known, certainty must be confined to what is so *ex se*. Consciousness is consciousness. To deny the truth of consciousness, is to deny that we are conscious. There is nothing else that is certain in a similar way. Now unless we are conscious of God, He falls short of original certainty.

2. And why should we repine at this? because the most pious men are engaged in *proving* that there is such a being as the Almighty. Do they ever *prove* that there is such a thing as their being conscious?

3. The Bible speaks of "faith." Why not say certainty? It uses a word (πιστεύω) meaning trust or confidence. It applies this very word to our theosophy. It does indeed speak of our knowing God (1 Cor. xv. 34); but it is referring there to certain conscious qualities; as when I say, I am conscious of the goodness of my neighbor. In the great matter of the divine existence it says, "Ye believe in God" (Jo. xiv. 1); "Thou believest that there is one God" (Ja. ii. 19); or again, "By faith we understand that the worlds were framed by the word of God" (Heb. xi. 3).

4. Nor is there any hardship in this. The A B C of all knowledge is intuitive. Nothing else is. The City of London is an empirical percept. So is self.* So is the existence of every creature. If God can condemn me at the last as having had a like facility for discovering Him as for discovering my own existence, the lack of certainty of the conscious sort will not defraud Him of the right to punish me.

Beyond all question, however, there is nothing conscious but consciousness; and unless God is consciousness, I do not intuitively know any such existence.

## CHAPTER III.

### THEOLOGY UNDER THE LIGHT OF ONTOLOGY.

BEING is either Self or Not-Self. God is not Self: therefore He belongs to the great class of Not-Self. The class of Not-Self, more easily than the unit Self, is seen to be empirically discovered.

But the class of Not-Self, as well as the unit Self, with children, and with all peasant-men, and, therefore, with all men, for all men are partial children, never

* So far as it does not embrace consciousness (see Ontology).

divorce themselves from qualifying consciousness. Self is conscious self; and not-self is the red cherry, or the gray rock, or the High God; in which the redness or the height is not put apart, but is put in consciously. Let abstraction be complete, and let self and rock and the Almighty be thought of emptily, and they are all alike in Logic. They are inferred empirically. They subsist invisibly. They are known by likeness. And that likeness is not (1) Direct (B. II. Chap. X.); neither is it even (2) Partial; but it is of that (3) Intermediate sort, like *x*, *y*, *z*, in a lengthened arguing.

There is nothing intuitively known but perception. God is certainly unlike any perception. But we trusted ourselves to things that were like; and from those to other things; and from those to other things; each last thing, like the one before it; till, at last, the discrepance was so great, that the first likeness faded out; but we were carried by a bridge of analogies to results that were singularly different.

## CHAPTER IV.

### GOD AS LIKE OTHER BEINGS.

THERE is nothing consciously in the mind but perception. There is nothing intuitively known but consciousness. God, therefore, being not consciousness, is not intuitively known. But being invisible, as substance is, and as man is, and as the universe is, and, indeed, as I myself am, considered apart from qualities, His history genetically, that is, the genesis of the Idea,—is ontologically like all His creatures.

Here then is vast resemblance.

Hence (1) the teleological argument.

Precisely as I trace cause, so I trace the First Cause.

Hence (2) the *nature* of the teleological argument.

It is not,—I see works in man, and, therefore, I infer works in the Great Jehovah. The argument is the same for each. We neither see man nor the Almighty. We begin with consciousness. The beauty of Metaphysics is, that it deals with that which we intuitively know. I have neither seen God nor my neighbor. But beginning with that which I have seen, viz. my perceptions, I see two growing orders; and, in an inevitable way (immediate to a childish mind, and distant to one more abstract), I trace analogies. And whatever God is, man is. That is, I see neither in himself, but both as the result of an ontological experience.

3. Hence also the *consequences* of the teleological argument.

Man seems to be moving about. God is hidden. How mad I shall appear in saying, Both are similar! But when I come to weigh, it is clothes that are moving about, or at least flesh or body. It is certain appearances of sense. I grant you we come to man first, and reach him earliest in the train of analogy. But what do we really reach? We reach his works. We reach certain appearances in our inward consciousness. We see man mostly in ourselves. And hence, in going on to God, we can only say, Man came first. We saw in him the closest analogy. But the raiment of God; and the mark of His busy fingers; and His tokens (which were all that we saw of man),—were precisely similar as empirical beliefs.

Hence the consequences.

First, man is intelligent; therefore God must be intelligent. Second, man is powerful; therefore God must be powerful. Third, man is somewhere; therefore God must be somewhere. Fourth, man has virtue; therefore God must be virtuous. And, as virtuousness is a quality of emotion, and emotion has to do with happiness, (fifth) God must be happy. Teleologically we infer all this: loosely, at first; but endlessly confirmed by analogies of working.

And there is one great mercy in empiricism. The things that are most important, have the closest analogies. Power; that is a shadowy ghost: I dimly realize it. Being! who sees it? Place! it is half a figment. God's Person, I know is little like, and His mind nothing similar, to any of His creatures. But His morals are close up at once. What a mercy! The only thing we are to give account for: the only thing we are to win heaven by: the only thing we need Christ for: I mean the only region of thought in which guilt and the need of an atonement and the purchase of the Spirit, nay, the only field in which the worship of God at all, is obligatorily set forth, is the only field that comes closest to my consciousness. I am conscious of His goodness if there be a God: but I am not conscious of His wisdom; nor am I conscious of His power: I am not conscious of His being. His wisdom and His power must be other things than mine. But, given a God empirically discovered, and His goodness is my goodness. I see it in Him as I do beauty in a star; and I have, imbedded in my consciousness, the very thing I have to give an account of in the day of Heaven.

## CHAPTER V.

### GOD AS UNLIKE OTHER BEINGS.

BUT, though God is like man in holiness, He is variously unlike man under the light of Ontological analogies. We need more and other in God than what we need in man, as a theoretic percept.

Being slowly recedes in man, till it lies back of all consciousness. This is the triumph of scientific light. But the religious triumph is still greater than this. It carries the thought still further in its analogies. A group of order was the first non-ego. I carried it back. I conceived of something that *had* the order, and *gave* the impact! I conceded rock when I was not looking,—and spirit that had not (my) consciousness. But analogy travelled on, and I found SOMEBODY ELSE was working as I worked, and as my neighbor worked. I made a watch, but I found one in the sky. I made a pulley, but I found one in my cheeks. I made a telescope, but I found one in my eye. The analogies that would find man out, would be empirical of the Almighty; but now with this difference:—man would not now need so much efficiency. By the law of parcimony, much that we had conceived in man would be relegated to the Most High.

Exactly now what our idea of God would be I need not depict. The simplicities of the thing have been altered by revelation. What our idea without revelation would amount to I need not measure. The simplicity of that reckoning has been altered by the Fall.

Only this I say:—Travelling out from consciousness we would arrive first at the creature. And there, like an unfinished Road, there would be gathered much that would not be permanent at that terminus. When the road-building went on to God, much that had grown up by the way would be carried on to that abiding dépôt.

See then the difference. Man has being, and God has being. But man's being must be so different from

God's as scarcely to claim the right to a common vocable. So Power. God has it ; and man has it : but God's power is so much more archaic than man's, as to breed a right to say, that both are the power of the Almighty.

All is so shadowy that we forget that it is an empirical result, where we clamor so for unity. Morals! there we ought all to agree. Wisdom! there we ought to have but little difference. Infinity! in the like of that we should be at one. But being! as to what it is in essence; and power! as to what is mine and God's; there we are in the clouds. Only this I say, that the best intellects have thought that all power was of God; and that whatever we thought of ours, even our power was God's power in certain more important respects than it could possibly be our own efficiency.

And then another important difference! God is a Spirit. What is meant by that? It does not mean that He is a tenuous fluid, or any atomic ether, such as we are quite apt to imagine; but it means an emblem. It means that He is of that tenuous sort that penetrates every atom. It means that He is a breath (Job xxxiv. 14), and like a breath can raise the dead. It means that He is pervasive like an ether: and therefore, that His personality is in His traits, not as with us as persons; but, on the contrary, that He is entire everywhere; as pervasive as a mist, and yet as local as though He were all an atom.

These things we should keep in view.

They are not a whit more shadowy than our own spirits. For nothing is *seen* but consciousness. And he has taken a good step, who holds himself possessed of just so *little* about being, as to be unencumbered for a stand, when differences that he *does* know, and light that he *does* possess, are dangerously brought to be denied.

## CHAPTER VI.

### THE MISCHIEVOUS EFFECTS OF MAKING GOD RESEMBLE OTHER BEINGS WHERE HE DIFFERS FROM THEM.

WILL has two provinces, musculation and attention. Efficiency, as it belongs to man, is either brute efficiency, like the digestion of food or the nisus of a muscle, to which he contributes nothing consciously; or it is mere volition; volition being nothing but that complicated thought, which we have before described as being the whole of our imperial potency.

An efficiency so narrow in man, and in many particulars so helpless, we might be expected to transfer to God; and we do so in two ways, leading to the two extremes, either (1), on the one side, of Pantheism, or (2), on the other, of Arminian independency, or segregation of the divine and human.

(1.) God may be the Former of our bodies, and the Father of our spirits; and yet, if emblems, as those words undoubtedly are, are pushed too far, we attribute, in spite of ourselves, some of our impotency to the Almighty. We are the former of a body, simply by altering its positions. If it is a statue, we chip some of its mass. If it be a photograph, we array the chemicals; we have hardly a dream of the *modus quo;* we trust all to the actinic ray. If we are the father of a spirit, we are still darker. The Bushman has an immortal progeny, and hardly knows as much of what has come from him as the bee does of the wax upon his legs; and no wonder; for, what we call agency in man, is not even nisus. Musculation and attention are all that include the possible activities that are human. No wonder, therefore, that we should impair with them our conception of the divine.

Hence that strange phantasy, that God comes to consciousness only in His works. The rock is not conscious; and, therefore, God is not conscious in the formation of the rock. Man is conscious; and, therefore, God is conscious only in man. In our attempt to conceive of God as a pervasive spirit, philosophers are strangely warped. Evolution must be blind evolution. La Place's Theory must draw to it formative efficiences such as ours. Requiring a shrewder God than the older theories, it proclaims one less so; and driven from the narrower personality of man, we tumble into the opposite incompetency. We bury God in the nature of what He frames; and, as Father of spirits, make Him no more conscious of His work, than man is, of the child that he has begotten.

(2.) Driven from Pantheistic thought, the Church has gone stupidly to the opposite extreme. Man being a creator, God must be a Creator. Man creating mechanisms, God must; and must stand separate from what He makes, as man does from a ship or from a scythe. Man being the begetter of a son, God must be; and must stand separate from the son whom He begets, as man does from the children that are given to him.

See then the two extremes;—either, first, Herbert Spencer's Unknown, with all its blind obscurity, refusing to carry the analogy from man even as far as man's intelligence and man's conscious motive; or, second, a universe set sailing like a ship. In either case it is the curse of emblems: in the one case man's agency made to fix its obscurity upon God's; and, in the other case, the ship, for example, made to pattern the sun or the planet; the separateness of what we do, because really we do nothing very deep, made to separate God from His works; made to create an atomic theory, for example; and made to pronounce it heresy, unless some tertium quid separates God from the forces of the creature.

Let us not be misunderstood here. We travel out from consciousness to the self and the not-self. Our chariot is analogy. It fades as it travels farthest. The ulterior not-self is the Almighty. I say, *Hæret in cortice* when we force the emblem.

I mean that from the one analogy of man there spring two opposite Creators:—(1) One a Pantheistic one. The man on the locomotive has no efficiency but will. That is of the very narrowest. The muscle and the rude engine effect the balance. What is the result? We are steeped in such thoughts of God. He is the obscure will in the locomotive; and if we are scientific men, we make Him pervade the work, but with a poor thread of consciousness. We separate Him not a moment. We bury Him in the whole design. We tie Him fast in our idea. But He is the Grimy Engine-Driver. The great machine He drives is made to bury His obscure intelligence.

But men have rarely science. Therefore the opposite error:—(2) The engine stands clear of the driver,—nay of the builder. That is the nature of man's work. He finishes it, and it may stand loose upon the track. Hence another analogy for God. Venus stands clear of Him, and may whirl without Him in her orbit. And if men shape that a little, and admit that He sustains the creature, still they are horrified even by Bible notions that in (ἐν) Him all things consist (Col. i.

17). They must have some separate entity, such as man looks at when he completes a fabric.

And though it is beyond a doubt that God is responsible for His work, even though it stand aloof like a car upon the rail, yet there is this mixture in the thought. The way man puts out a work, and is done with it, and leaves it to itself, will taint with inevitable fault our thought of the Most High.

## CHAPTER VII.

### THE MISCHIEVOUS EFFECTS OF MAKING GOD DIFFER FROM OTHER BEINGS WHERE HE RESEMBLES THEM.

It is a kind provision of Providence ; or, perhaps, I should rather say, a glorious reality in the very nature of the case,—that God should be unlike us in secular traits, and like us in moral ones. He is omnipresent and local. We are only local. He is immense. We are limited. He is omniscient. We know nothing but our own consciousness. He is omnipotent. We have no power of a conscious sort; only volition. Unless we include the body, which is really a not-self, we have no conscious nisus, and no imperial realm save our willing. When we say, He wills and it is done, we describe man. Man wills and it is done, but God has to do it. God wills and it is not done, unless there follows a stricter Efficiency, which actually accomplishes the work which the Will designs to be done.

Now there is a vast perversity in man in that in these natural traits in which God does not resemble us we make Him resemble us, and in moral traits in which He does resemble us we make Him differ. We have seen the former of these in the previous chapter.

The latter we start into best, perhaps, by thinking

of this concept,—will. What is will? It is a narrow exercise that looks to the muscle and to the act of attention. We impute it to God. We speak of the will of the Supreme. We make it broad as His works: not foolishly, if we remember that it is an emblem, and not hurtfully, if we make it accord with the broad affections of the Most High.

But now notice. It illustrates both errors. We make it like, where it is unlike; and unlike, where it is like; and just as we have said. Where it is a secular trait, we make God's will like man's will; and where it is a moral exercise, we make them differ.

Let me explain.

(1) The will of man as a natural efficiency is an efficiency at all only in an imaginary way. We will, and there is motion. That is all our conscious knowledge. We are imperial because we are dependent. If we were omnipotent, we would have to make the motion ourselves; but, as we are dependent, God makes it; and, as the fruit of this dependence, we attribute to God the sort of will that we witness in ourselves.

How common the remark, that the universe survives by God's naked will.

Hence our delight in the rhetoric of the Bible. "He spake, and it was done. He commanded, and it stood fast."

And though, with God, there is no *logos* like this, but a patient travelling to results; and molecular work in every hand-breadth,—yet there is this strange perversity,—which makes the emotions of Heaven command as ours do, and makes Providence a law, as though there were something to obey it outside of Deity.

(2) But hugging the analogy where it fails, we cast loose from it in those higher particulars where it obtains and would bless us. The will of God is like the will of man in its moral attributes. Holiness is a quality. It belongs to two emotions (Ethics, D. I. Chap. VI.). One of these is benevolence. The other is a love to the holy or right quality itself. These are all that is worth living for in man; and these are all that is worth existing for in the Most High.

Dim in a conception of any *being*, it is a mercy that we know most of God just in the direction in which we have to worship Him; and, now, it is a strange perversity, that, having compared Him with man in all natural particulars, we begin to separate Him here, just in the point where we possess His image.

How we do this has appeared already under the head of Ethics. Suffice it to say, again, We make a different right for God than we do for His creatures. We give Him hard attributes. We make man all for duty. We make God all for Himself. We make man love right in itself considered. We make God make right; and we suffer its obligation to depend upon a decision of His will. We make God primordially revengeful; man not so; God aiming for display; man never; God not doing the best; man bound to; God not bound for the best possible work; man always (see Dr. Hodge's Systematic Theology, *passim*); in one word, the morals of man differing from the morals of God; impairing the rule, that we are to be holy as God is holy (1 Pet. i. 15).

And, now, the evils of this are immense. All entity being empirical, because arrived at, whether self or not-self, by shadowy analogies, it is an immense outfit to start in the search with the intuitions of virtue. God may be singularly Unknown ; yet, if we can put into Him the timbers of virtue,—make that the end,—make that also the root,—declare that God would not desire to be, nay, would not consent to act, but for the sake of holiness,—we make a queen-cell that will vastly centralize the hive. Then there may be many drones. Then there may be dreadful battles. Then there may be vast mistakes about the outworks of our theism. Then we can wait for science till she settles her shifting facts. That soul is wonderfully at peace that has its refuge in its conscious part, and in plenitude of hope as to what will turn up at last in empirical demonstration.

But the opposite, viz. an unmoral God ; that is, a being not humane, or with no intelligible excellency,—is just the idol to destroy the personality of Jehovah. It breeds the Pantheist. What care I for Pantheism, if it only transfuses God in His works? He has not a bald will; but, on the contrary, a diffused efficiency. He cannot stand off and order, but must go in and work; and, *being* in, all over the universe, I do not object to knowing that I live in Him, and have my being (Acts xvii. 28). But how can I get him back again, without His holiness? How can I get Him back out of myself, if you confuse me in my notion of His being a God of conscience? That monstrous dream of an unconscious Deity, with no light, and no separate thought, and no individual accountability for what He does, is most of all promoted by destroying conscience ; that is, by taking away from Him a virtuousness like man's, and causing us to merge His excellence into a dry Supremacy.

## CHAPTER VIII.

### PANTHEISM.

THE outer world reveals itself to us by our five senses. The revelation is said to be made to us in every instance by power. I do not mean by this that what I see is power. On the contrary, what I see is sense. If I smell a flower, the fragrance is an absolute consciousness. So of a note in music, or of the light, or of a hard surface, or of a taste: what I actually perceive, is a naked consciousness. But, without going back to bring up tediously the analogies, no one doubts that matter gets at sense by power. If I taste, or smell, or see visions, or feel warmth, or hear a bugle-note, the thing is done by impact. Force is used upon the nerve in every instance of sensational perceiving.

Then that is a plausible account of matter, that it consists in power. Other ingredients have dropped off. It began with order. But the grouping of harmonized sensations will not answer; for, after all, order is not being; and sensation itself is something different from metaphysical * existence. Body helped much at its birth; but body is one form of it: so did will; but will is itself perception. It helped as a shadow of power; but soon disappeared as not efficiency. Cause vanished also; not as a thing of no sense; but as the same as power. The best thinking that the world can give, is always bringing back this idea;—that there may be ten million things in the world beside power; nay, that there may be no power in the shadowy way in which we conceive it; but that the very best image

* I say, metaphysical, and the reader must notice such cautionary terms, or else excuse us for the tediousness of repeating, that, as a mere usage of speech, existence does include the instant sensation.

we can make of the world is power; and that, by the law of parcimony, we have no reason to posit substance, in the vulgar form in which it is asserted.

1. For, as the first step; if sound sense seems to be offended, let us treat her difficulties. If she says, Something is necessary that must *have* the power; or, with more particular plainness, something must resist it, and something must exert it,—let us look at this more narrowly. We are to acknowledge molecular atoms on the solitary plea that matter cannot act where it is not; or that force needs something actively to possess it, and forcibly to resist its onslaught.

But notice.

Where is the matter between the atoms? Air is infinitely compressible. That means, the learned tell us, that its atomic grains are each of them distant. What holds them? Force. What sort of force? Repulsion. What kindred force? Attraction: which keeps them reined in to their place, and keeps repulsion from repelling endlessly. Where is the matter between the atoms? for if it is ice or silver, there is an appreciable distance? How does atom get hold of atom? And if the very essence of the theory is, that matter must be there to hold the force, or to meet the wrestle, where is there any between the monads? and where is the good of substance if it fails to meet us at the very point desired?

2. But, secondly; if matter be nothing but power, self may be nothing but power, and for the same reasons.

This we admit

At the same time we claim, that we have gone farther on a most shadowy path, and where there is the largest room for the very utmost difference.

Power at all is a mere shadow,—a high empirical conceit. Power, as force, is a clearer notion; because analogous to the conscious nisus. But power as a power to think, is the dimmest of the dim. Still there is an analogy; and I admit that there is no substance in mind, that can be thought of as separate from power, unless it be a suppositional something, which we all along admitted, viz. a creature of our ignorance; that, whereas (1) we know nothing but power, and, again, (2) little of power and much of our ignorance about it, therefore, third, (3) there may be a vast deal else, and indeed must be a vast deal more, than we have ever brought to be intelligently considered.

But a posited something; made familiar to us, and given names to by us as a substantial ego,—that we are not convinced of. Power is by analogy. The first power was my muscle. Nay it was a complex thing, first my will, and then my nisus. It corrupted the notion. It carried it into matter. It tainted it with a gross duality. It carried it into mind. And I confess I am not prepared to say that there is a *brutum tertium*,—first a power to think, then a substance. I cannot fix polemically three quiddities as certain; first, thought; second, power to think; and third, substance,—this last separate from God, and looked at as isolated work like a car upon the rail.

But then why should I? Who cares for the mere hulk, if I keep the conscience? There is the difficulty. Men shudder when we throw man so closely upon God as to deny the molecules; because they shudder for God. They think man is bad company for Him. The *brutum ens* is necessary to give man a separate responsibility; otherwise bad acts are God's acts. This is the gist of the polemic. Men would not care what we did with an intervening hulk, if we did not throw man blasphemously upon God; and did not make the wickedness of man too much the part of the Almighty.

But now, notice. What defends God if we adopt the molecule? Did we make it? Are we responsible for it? Did we bring our wicked selves into being? Did we begin far back in eternity, and decree all our going? Do we uphold these lives of ours? and could we carry them without *concursus?* and could we possess them a single moment without the power of the Most High? Now, imperatively, where is the difference? If I live in Him and have my being (Acts xvii. 28), where is the responsibility of God greater if I live by the mere flow of His power, than if He has bred some substantial *ens*, and keeps it in being by the breath of His lips? It seduces men, to prate a difference. We have shown already what morals are. We have shown the likeness between God and His creature. And though it is beyond our ken how God could create such a wicked world; yet it is not beyond our ken that He does do it. "I form the light and create darkness. I make peace and create evil" (Is. xlv. 7). It is not beyond our ken that the potter has "power over the clay" (Rom. ix. 21), and that it is disgraceful to God to defend Him, as with the Ahriman of the East, by the shelter of intervening particles.

3. But the best men will say, You are mad. You are not seeing the vile consequence. You are sinking man into God. You are sinking matter into mind. If rock is nothing logically but power, then whose power? If man is nothing but a power to think, then whose power to think? and, logically, whose thought? Moreover, if power does not imply substance, how

God's power? And are we to have the madness over again of denying entity to the Great Almighty?

Now, with abundant caution:—

Note; here are five difficulties,—(1) If matter is only power, what holds the power or meets its pressure? (2) If matter is only power, mind is only power. (3) If matter and mind are only power,—whose power? or is there any room for maintaining a power of God separate and different from the power of either? (4) If, therefore, mind is only power, how do we teach a responsibility of God separate from the responsibility of His creature? And (5) if mind is only power, God is only power; for how can we argue substance in God, if we deny it as possible to be demonstrated in the instance of the creature?

Now, first; that matter is only power we have not taught. We have been infinitely far from teaching it. We have felt Herbert Spencer's reasonableness in much of his argument for the Unknowable. We do not know what matter is. The use of infidels is to scour the bottom of the faith. We scout his atheism; but it clears our theism. What we really teach is, that by the law of parcimony power covers all we know; that we have no right to imagine atoms; that they are bred of certain dualities of will; that they do not account for the results; that it is ours to seize power as the best residuary gleam; and to admit the possibility of more; nay, to assert that there must be much unknowable,—under the forms of matter.

Second, precisely the same of mind.

Third; precisely the same of sin. An appeal is to the law of parcimony. I do not deny that there are difficulties about power; but atoms do not help them. I do not deny there are difficulties about sin. But atoms do not help them. I prefer to mark down great facts about God, and imagine that something unknowable will come to reconcile them. It belittles Him to appeal to atoms. To say that He upholds me constantly, and so much that I vanish without Him, and then to make that less responsible than some more direct nakedness of Power, is to make an unworthy difference. Men see through such things. It is far better to speak like Paul (Rom. ix. 21). If I sin when upheld by God, it is explained just as little, considering all the circumstances of that upholding, as if I sinned if I live in God (Acts xvii. 28). It is better to imagine unknown circumstances of explanation. This usual defence does mischief by its clear impertinency.

So of the last point. If mind may be only power, God may be only power. That is, analogies, out from consciousness, leading us at last to power, if they teach nothing more in matter, and if they teach nothing more in mind, teach nothing more in God. Atoms, if not necessary to hold power, and not imaginable indeed, and therefore not noticeable, in mind;—I mean by that, mental atoms, or, more properly speaking, some mental substance,—the same argument would strip a substance away from the Almighty.

This is partly sound and partly unsound.

1. It is partly sound; because if we do not see a substance; if it is bred of human weakness; if it comes from muscular power; if it arises from where our thinking began, viz. from the muscular nisus, preceded by the desires of will,—then it is traceable how we got it into matter, and it is not traceable how we ought to get it into God. God has no nisus, and no muscular will. He has no duality of nature. He moves uniquely

and at a blow. Why He need to have substance to *hold* power is scarcely apparent; and the whole thing seems disreputable. In other words,—Power alone as being God is (a shockingly inadequate idea, but) just as adequate as a Powerful Substance, or Powerful Spirit, or Powerful Entity, distinct from power, which like the two lines in the vapor betoken the medium of human life through which we see it.

The Divine is "invisible." This is the doctrine of the Bible. Marking empirical boundaries is, therefore, dangerous work. Imputing brute atoms to man, reflectively bears upon God. Imputing stark substance to God, reflectively bears upon man. Both theories play into each other. But when we come to ask for proof, we are left with this idea,—God is a Power. Even that is a shadowy idea. And all beyond is the region of the Unknown. He is a false defender who binds himself with the small cords of his fancy when called upon for proof of what is essential to the Most High.

2. Nevertheless stripping substance away from God because we strip it away from man is partly unsound. Stripping it away from either is sensible enough if it rebuke the folly of theorizing and explaining substance as though it could be consciously conceived. Stripping it away from neither is sensible, too, if it simply mean that there is more in both than power can possibly contain. But stripping it away from God has a redundancy of fault in this last direction, because power could do better for man in its shadowy shape than it possibly could for God, as our whole idea. Man could live in God, but who could God live in? Empirically, and as a mere following of the *like*, we could dream of man as a mere immanence of power. But God is the great terminus. Analogy has reached its crest. There

cannot be anything beyond. And, therefore, the *conjecture* (that is a very good word), the *throwing together*, of analogies from self, dictates a terminal will, and therefore a something, if it is ever to be traced, an origin, if it is ever to be conceived, and Being in its most real sense, if it ever be needed to explain the order of the universe.

It is all empirical, and, therefore, all unconscious; but the LIKE, as it reaches out, speaks more for an *Ens*, when it comes to deal with the Almighty.

Anchorage in this tossed ocean can always be found in the region of Ethics. What would God be without it? What would creeds be? Theology would be a creeping dream.

Let us notice this point. The very gem of evidences is to be found in morals.

Ontology might be much more machine-like but for the phenomenon of conscience: and morals, whether in God or man, is the mother of all those proofs which are teleologically rich in shaping the Deity.

And blessed be God, it is a conscious thing that is essential!

And be careful here!

Let me not be misunderstood. Power is essential. Being is essential. Skill is essential. But what I mean is, essential in our knowlege of God. Power is of the most shadowy; Being, not less so; Skill, unsearchable. But Holiness is right under our eye. What a mercy this is! The great trait of God is conscious. Be very particular with this. That God has a conscience depends of course upon His having a being. That He had a being is empirical, and, therefore, metaphysically not intuitive, and, philosophically, never certain. Nay, that He has a conscience if He has a being, is empirical besides.

What we thank God for, therefore, may be easily misunderstood.

There is a great theory. The sum of it we call Theology. The pith of it is, that it takes all the facts. It pins itself together. Like a gallant arch, it holds by its mass. Morality is the key-stone. It could not get into its place without the others; but, being there, it is singularly defined and well shaped. Now, what I mean is, that everything else may lie in the haze. Power, what that may be, and substance, how that is to be fixed, and life, how that is to be supposed to live; atoms, how they are to be understood, and molecular physics, how that is to be fashioned forth,—lie in shadow; ought to do so, because they are uncertain; must do so, because they are empirical; and have done so in every period of the world.

But morality, once set in place, is evident. It belongs to consciousness. I know what right is. God, as powerful, is a mist. God, as conscious, is a riddle. God, as anything you think, is a wonder, and a maze. But God, as good, is all simplicity. I draw to Him at once. And it steadies all other thought. Here is where theologians ought to stand; and, like a captain on his deck, the watchful believer on this key-stone of the arch should govern all his theories.

(1) Matter, therefore, may be only power. Why? Because I see no ground for atoms. (2) Mind, therefore, may be only power. Why? By a kindred parcimony. (3) Power, too, may be all of God. Why? Because why the opposite? (4) God, then, must be responsible for sin. No: because God is holy. God does not sin the sin if man sins it; and God cannot sin in men if

He acts from the impulse of benevolence, and from the love of holiness in Himself and in the universe. (5) Still, He must be a Power, therefore? Not necessarily. That would limit God by our knowledge. He must be more than power; because, as Spencer establishes the fact, He must be much that is unknowable. But that He is specifically this or that, spirit or matter, being, as substantial *ens*,—all this, is mere insanity. He is Power. This Power is guided by conscience. This power is itself a shadow. We know nothing of His essence. And the man who insists that there are atoms, that he may insist that there is a God, is losing the whole logic that he seeks, and likening the Deity to a material image.

To what extent, then, may true philosophy be Pantheistic?

To this extent;—that it may deny to matter atoms in the more brutish sense. How far is that Pantheism? Not at all in that pestilent folly that makes God find His being in matter, and find His consciousness and His only personality in human minds. We not only execrate this, but we do not even understand how it could have arisen. If God's power is matter, and God's activity is the ceaseless producer of mind, He needs all the more on that account a mind of His own, and a separate personality, where thought and morals may hold their court. We do not so much as know why, when God emerged as always in the creature, producing him always, and never able to be rid of him by setting him apart, that therefore we should suppose that God is less personal, and must, therefore, bulk into the universe, and *be* the creature that He is perpetually issuing into being. We need, the rather, more of a Person on this account. And, moreover, to call us

Pantheists, you must satisfy another thought. We are merely negative. We merely deny brutish atoms. We merely say, They have no foundation. We merely see that power is the shadowy idea. We say that power itself is the flimsiest conceit. We are merely holding to parcimony. And instead of saying, There is nothing but this or that, we are distinctly advancing the Unknowable. It is not atoms; it is not entity; it is not a *brutum quid;* it is not intelligibly anything to mislead us by its imagined marks; but it is, what the Bible calls it, an "Invisible" (1 Tim. i. 17; Col. i. 15). We are only Pantheists in the privative refusal of its being known. We are anything you please as to a room for a Jehovah's being.

Going back, therefore, to Ontology with its distinct avowal that the not-self is either perception or else some fabrication from perception by analogy and difference, we give that as our account of God. He is not atoms, because we have no thought of atoms, and, therefore, among a thousand things we have no reason why that surd thing should be. He is not spirit, for a kindred reason, that when we come to speak with emphasis there is nothing inside the word that we distinctly mean. But He is a Spirit as a verisemblance to man. Spirit is nothing ontological. It is philological. It means a breath. It means that as a breath God pervades; that as a breath God acts; that as a breath He is invisible. And the very name betokens rather a blind something impossible to be conceived, than a bold-faced word attempting intelligence as to a style of being.

We believe in God, therefore, because we believe in man. We believe in God mainly as of the image He gave to man. We believe in God most of all as by our moral image. That thought of Him is best that comes under the eye of conscience. I am a theist, therefore, most and strongest in the realm of Ethics. When you drive me out of what is moral, I catch up but the dimmest shadows. I make no complaint of this. Worship involving morals, and law involving morals, and judgment only morals, it is to me an unspeakable relief that morals will bring me nearest to the Deity through all the period of my being. What He is in essence it concerns me less that I should conceive. To keep His morals right, I see no advantage in molecular atoms, or that I should be anything but an immanence from Him. Did I assert I do, I should equivocate ; for I see no superior responsibility in God did He continually create, than did He make me separate, and yet hold me up all the time. I see no *piety* in thinking that the *ego* is more than power. And if the *ego* is no more than power, then Pantheism is true in a certain Christian sense. But that the *ego* is only power would be a vague conceit if a man did not perceive how shadowy it is; if he did not remember how false it is; if he did not confess how certainly ten thousand other things are likely to be true; and if he did not pursue the negative plan of merely denying results. I will not believe in atoms, and I will not believe in mind, and I will not believe in God as an intelligible *ens*, for this is the hypocrisy of belief. Power is the shadow that He has given to bring us near to the conception of a being.

## CHAPTER IX.

### POLYTHEISM.

POLYTHEISM might be reached in two ways; either, first, by a highly polished people slowly declining; or, by a low, brutal people slowly climbing up.

1. Polytheism as a symbol of decay, is where a polished people, possessing the idea that God pervades all His works, choose an object indiscriminately, and take it as a reminder of the presence of the Deity. This, which, at first, might be thought innocent, becomes, as divine truth dies out, the origin of multitudes of idols.

2. The other is the opposite route: we doubt whether it has been ever travelled,—where a savage, seeing power in himself, imagines it in a tree and in a rock. This supposes the childhood of the race, and imagines thought actually travelling out to the Invisible. We doubt whether it ever made that journey. We believe in an original revelation, and doubt whether it was ever lost; that is, whether any tribe of men were so entirely embruted, that they had initially to think out the fact of a Divinity.

It makes little difference, however.

I mean in the view of Polytheism. It makes great difference in the respect of Archaic Science. But, in the respect of Polytheism, it would be reaching it, going up or coming down; and it would be reaching the same result. A man, seeing divinity in himself, I mean a certain image of what is divine, sees that things around him are like him, and is therefore very likely to put will and intelligence into the storm or into the plant that acts as he acts. This is done, therefore, by multitudes. Nevertheless, if we read Hindoo literature, or search deeply even into the fetich-worshipping as among the blacks, we will find that Polytheism is never a square thing among a people. The more brutish conceive of it in part, but their *gangas* explain it away. There is but one God among the more thinking class; and we can find Him with the Malay and the black as a unitary or Nzambi Deity.

## CHAPTER X.

### EVOLUTION.

EVOLUTION, as a doctrine of Ontology, is attracting more attention than perhaps any other of the beliefs of men. On this very account it is unsettled. We shall trace the most common doctrine; or rather, that thread of thought that runs through most of the systems. If any man believes in the eternity of matter, or some one else believes in the *interference* of God, or still another in Divine *support*, and yet still claims Evolution, we will not be able to give each all his theory: for, in the nature of things, we must choose one central stem, and, in this eclectic account, call that Evolution that lies nearest to the centre, and which takes in most of the thought of most of the promoters of this influential system.

Evolution shall be the doctrine of those who believe that matter, in its full quantum, was originally created with such gifts as would enable it to live apart from its Creator, and with such powers as would enable it gradually to evolve all specific changes, and all the developed facts of life and spirit. Matter, with this creed, is the origin of thought; but not with the absurd faith, that the weight-qualities, and the force-qualities, and the blue-qualities, of observed matter, are to be attached to its thought-results, but simply that there is one original *ens*, and that the greater *Ens*, in originally endowing it, gifted it with all that lives, and that the shooting of a ray, and the shooting of a sprout, and the shooting of a thought, unconscious as we are how they are arranged, are arranged in one; as, by the appearances of matter, there is the same exhaustion of power in producing one as in producing the other.

Evolution, therefore, is an eternal system, not eternal *a parte ante*, but eternal *a parte post*, by which a nebular mist, freighted for an eternal voyage, has, stored within it, all change, and by powers resident in its parts, and by powers acting back upon it from other parts, not even excepting the change (inexplicable) of thought and consciousness.

Let it be noticed, that this does not get rid of God; but rather makes Him great: neither indeed of Teleology, but rather enforces it; for it leaves all the existing marks of current design, and adds the unspeakable feat of providing it in the original creation.

How, therefore, could I reject the system? I could reject it, first, if it clashed with Ethics. There, on that account, will be our first inquiry. I could reject it, second, if it clashed with Scripture. There will be our second. I *do* reject it, thirdly, because it embroils Ontology. Such, therefore, will be our order of discourse. I. We do not object to Evolution as thwarting Ethics. II. We do not consider it as assailing Revelation. III. But we do consider it as no Ontology. Here, where the system claims the most, we regard it as unspeakably the weakest. Its development facts weave in better with better systems: and yet, ontologically tried, the man who reasons differently upon the material facts has a perfect right to his scheme; and, if he deal fair with Ethics, and allow A CERTAIN CORRECTIVE on the part of Christianity, we have no objections. A pious Evolutionist will be a constant phenomenon among future believers.

## CHAPTER XI.

### EVOLUTION UNDER THE LIGHT OF ETHICS.

ETHICS teaches the fact that God's highest motive is His holiness. Ethics, therefore, teaches the fact, that this universe is the holiest possible. For, either God's holiness, which is really His highest object, must diminish the holiness of His creature, or else the highest holiness of His creature is the object of God. Now of two things one, either God does not reach His highest object, or the holiness of His creature is the greatest possible.

There are great numbers of His creatures, and there is an eternity for them to live in. God, therefore, must strike a balance. If His object is the highest holiness of His creatures, He must prefer the greatest number and the longest time. It follows that He might sacrifice some of the number (Ethics, D. I. Chap. XL.), and some of the time.

We cannot tell *a priori* which must be the time. God, wishing to give the greatest holiness through the greatest time, might be thrown upon the earliest time. As with Satan, holiness might come first, and trespass, or even reduced holiness, from lesser light and less spiritual endowment, follow after. We cannot consciously decide. But the vast probabilities are, from mere passing analogy, that holiness must grow. I am speaking now ethically, without the Bible. The path of the just would naturally brighten. For though Adam did not grow, but fall, and righteousness has no merit without the fixedness of a covenant, yet, in its total sphere, morals has probabilities of advance, *and in that case it has its Evolution.* At any rate, God gives the highest holiness; and this involves the sum of the creature and the sum of its duration. And if the aggregate advances, then this follows,—viz. that each particular moment is holier than the last, and grows holy upon the last, and that there results a scheme of ethical Evolution. Each last moment is *for it* the holiest possible; yet the next is holier. And the Evolution goes on. If this is to be the rule for eternity, then there is an eternal Evolution. And when we remember what this involves; and that happiness is to keep pace with holiness; and that matter is to be the handmaid of either; we see the consequence, that Evolution, if the right Ontology, comes right in place. God must have had an original scheme. That scheme, if the holiest possible, must be necessarily one. God had no liberty: none in the vagrant sense. He preferred A BEST which was always mapping His work. And, therefore, if His course was fixed, and He had power to create a protoplasm, it is no contradiction of Ethics that He bred all change in the egg. *Credat Judæus.* With *a certain corrective* that Revelation gives, and with room for that corrective that even Darwin leaves, let these egg-builders go on.

Ethics *makes sure* to me a beltistic scheme. Ethics *makes probable*, at least, one that shall advance. Grant me this much, and I have an Evolution of my own; an Evolution that takes in miracle and every change; an Evolution that never flags; an Evolution set to a hair, because, on *its* base, it can never alter; an Evolution, therefore, built upon a original decree, that needs no retouching of the plan, and that would look smilingly upon a scheme (*if one corrective were allowed*) that would make a nebulous egg act, once it was laid, independently of the Most High.

*Our* Evolution no facts can oppose. There is pain in the world. Well, we have seen that even the innocent can suffer pain. There is death in the world! Well, even the innocent can suffer death. We have seen that death existed before apostasy. Shoals of mammals suffered death thousands of ages before there was sin. Justice I would like to look better at when I arrive at Heaven. But benevolence and the love of virtue,—these I can look clearly at now. They are conscious. These are by God's side, His Builders * (Prov. viii. 30). These know no exception. What they demand of animal pain,—that is Justice. What they give up,—that perishes. What, they build,—that stands. And as they are exquisitely precise, they have but one dictate. And all I mean to say is, that if Evolution has but one dictate, and that the wisest and the best, God might have put it in the egg, and shown only the more in that one respect His strange Omnipotence.

## CHAPTER XII.

### EVOLUTION UNDER THE LIGHT OF REVELATION.

EVOLUTION is thought to contradict the Mosaic Record. Certainly, under the hand of some expounders of it, it does do it. We do very wrong not to distinguish better than we do one field of Theology from

* See Commentary.

another. One field of Theology is Theism. Another field, requiring different proof, is Christianity. We do very wrong that we let both these fields get embroiled together. It ought to be remembered that Theism is much the less vulnerable. When we behave as though Theism were ceaselessly in danger, and let it share all the panics that belong to technical Christianity, we build with very unphilosophical haste. We should posit Theism, and get that well entrenched, and then proceed to what is Christian.

Let us do something of this logical sort.

Revelation is of two kinds, that which might be known without it, and that which might not be. The word *might* must be peculiarly handled. When I enter under the first head Theism, I must distinguish. It *might* be found out, considering man to be perfect, or it *might* be found out by perfect men in a long heredity, but this is doubtful. Let us define the *might* by saying that one class of revelations could be demonstrated after they were revealed, and one class could not be. In one class would be Theism, and in the other, for example, the Incarnation.

I. Now this first class is but little exposed by Ontology.

1. Take for illustration the fact of a Decree. If Darwin is right, all future is fixed in an original mist. How could he object to Predestination? Or bring, to test his theory, the ideas of Ethics. If God would have existed singly but for an Ethical taste; if that taste is a love of holiness; if that taste rules each successive act, and begets but one line by the possibilities of the case, and that the very holiest and the best,—Predestination is but another name. The dust that floats in the air is where it is by the Almighty; is where it is

as the very best; is where it is by a decree; and the three propositions are all blended into one; and take in kindly, too, the original egg, if that be the method that God originally fixed for the fulfilment of His will.

2. So of *miracle*. Darwin teaches the greatest miracle. I beg that this may be considered. We think of Darwin as putting an end to all miracles. But how unjustly. Darwin I do not speak of in his detail. I do not answer for him in his miscellaneous speech. He may say a thousand things that are profane. I only say that Evolution, as above declared, is very favorable to miracle. And I press home the proof. The greatest miracle on earth is Darwin's miracle. And after that there is room for all. Darwin is right in saying that miracle is a matter of faith. Having announced the loftiest miracle that we can conceive, viz. the creation of the mist,* he justly says that, after that, it must be *against nature*. What can be more reasonable? For, having transcended me in miracle, that is, having announced one that I cannot grapple, going beyond all other theists to speak of God as creating all things in a single egg, what can he deny afterward? This he distinctly notices. He does not deny miracle, but shuts it out into the region of faith. Well, is it not in the region of faith? He says it denies nature. Well, does it not deny nature? Nay, does it not suspend it, and bring it to an end? Does it not violate it? and cause it to take up its thread afterward, and begin anew? Is not this the very nature of mir-

* We are imputing here to Darwin the evolution not exactly in the shape in which he holds it. We have explained this already. He believes in protoplasm. We have chosen a main stem of theory, and treated it as representative of all. Darwin would doubtless posit many protoplasms. We mention one clear theory, and that is to be representative of all the rest.

acle? And though I carry science into the domain of faith, and speak of mental science, and of ethical science, and theological science, and though, therefore, science carries me to miracle, and carries me to the very throne of God, yet Darwin's Evolutionism is in a lower sphere. Darwin's Evolution must be violated by miracle. But the system does not forbid that it should be so violated: only it says, You must get your proof from a higher reasoning. Darwin has set the model of a most astounding act; and no act that can possibly follow can be half the miracle of the mist in its original creation.

3. And now of *prayer*.

It is a false argument that says that prayer is inconsistent with Darwinism, and that demands miracle, or demands extemporized Providences, in order to answer our requests. Of course I must insist that Darwinism must be what I have defined. To follow it into all its wanderings, or to believe this or that infidel speech, is another affair. That God built all things at a stroke, that is, created a mist, and endowed it to sail alone, is in our belief a mad Ontology, but it is not the death of prayer, and supplementary schemes are not what we might think them to be to afford hope for the answer of our supplications. For, think a moment. Suppose a miracle. Or suppose a chance for God to come in for extemporized acts. It might seem all simple. Elijah prays, and the heavens give rain. Or I pray, and God keeps me from death. It might easily seem that Evolution, settled from the egg, would leave no room for requests, and that miracle or extemporized relief were the only chance for the hopeful offering of supplication.

But look further.

Miracle or not, God fixes everything from the beginning. That is a thing forgotten. Darwin fixes everything in an iron frame, but so does Ethics. Miracle might offer a look of freedom, but there is but one system. If it admit miracle, it is broader than if it follow law; but the law of nature, if superseded and deposed, yields to a higher law. This universe is the holiest possible. To make it so, there must be a frame like iron. No two bests can exist. And, therefore, miracle or no, there is a path mapped out from the first, which has never been transcended. Pray, and there will be the same beltistic consequences. Entreat, and nothing alters. Tyndall can transfer all his scoff. For, if we held to the fixity of nature, it could not be more entire than the fixity of grace. God sees a certain plan. No other eye sees it. It is nevertheless fixed by law. And if miracle came, and God directly intervened at my request, that would not alter the iron of His will. In the ages of the past He fixed that miracle. And now we have only to choose between the iron of Darwin's scheme, and the iron of a higher one, both being equally unchanged, and both being impossible to alter by prayer or anything.

What is the solution, therefore? Why that the iron includes the prayer. In the observatory in my village, the seat moves round with the dome.

Tyndall argues, My daughter's malady is fixed by nature. Pray, if you like; but the result is settled. Nature will remain unchanged; and if matter moves finally to a relief, well. Prayer does nothing. Now, grant it. Give me Darwin's scheme, and will I surrender prayer? By no means. There was an original act. That act was Providence. Darwin's Providence was sealed up in an egg. Beautiful beyond my possibility to conceive, that Providence was finished at a stroke. God might have vanished, and the universe move on. Prayer, therefore, must be built into the system. Darwinism must take in all instruments ;—what seed is to crop, what steam is to travel, what heat is to life. In view of the provided prayer, God had arranged the provided healing. If Darwin says, 'This exacts too much ; '—behold the audacity of his system ! There being a world of act,—ploughing and sowing, thinking and willing, praying and getting a relief,—Tyndall stops at prayer, and pronounces his own scheme insufficient to admit of this last prevision.

And so of the answerers of Tyndall. They do harm certainly in the way that they reject his system. Law is not against prayer. Strict natural sequence does not forbid it. We are horrified at the thought that the nebular hypothesis should restrict our prayer. When, therefore, a preacher admits that where physics is fixed prayer has no province, I feel betrayed; because I know that miracle is equally fixed. If God could be changing nature, that would be equally settled. There is a beltistic universe. It must be built upon a single scheme. That scheme must be settled from eternity. To alter it must breed a worse. To pray against it would be utterly futile. And, therefore, the duty of prayer, like the duty of anything beside, is wove into the plan, and is of the very highest force; but can only be recompensed as itself a fixity in nature.

To speak squarely, therefore,—May a Darwinian pray? Undoubtedly. Why may a Darwinian pray? Because he is a theist. How is he a theist? Because he believes in a creation. How does he believe in a creation? He believes in an act that called a nebula into being that is to live by itself and produce all the realities of the universe. Is there a Providence to follow it? No. Is there a Providence at all? Yes. How is there a Providence at all? There is a Providence in the parent egg, such that it is to produce all results, and to act as though Providence did follow, and as though God did intervene to produce all that seems *ex tempore* in nature. May I pray, therefore? Certainly I may pray. Why may I pray? Because I will not be answered without. Why? Because my prayer and answer were arranged in the creation. It is arranging a great deal, I grant; but there is the audacity of the system. As a mere effect, prayer as arranged with its reply, and mercy as a gift to faith, are not things that should be rejected, if the universe of facts were bred in the womb of being.

For how differs the follower of miracle? He says, I pray, and God works a miracle. Or how the interference-theist? I pray, and God extemporizes a result. Be this ever so much the case, it was fixed eternally. And this, not by an arbitary plan, but by the very nature of Ethics. There is but one holiest possible world. To make it, there is but one holiest possible plan. What difference if that could be tied up in an egg? It would be but one difference, that of a God providing at a stroke, and that of a God following His work with no possible license beyond what has been originally decreed.

And take the wiliest reply. Suppose it be said, Evolution is physical. If I pray, that cannot alter Evolution, and all that can be thought is, that Evolution was arranged to meet that prayer from the first moment of time. But prayer can lead *now* to miracle, or, take the other theory, prayer can move *now* upon will. If things are not locked up in Darwinism, prayer can be operative at once; and the will of God can be actually moved at the time by my petitions. And yet, notice how little this relieves. Darwinism has one fixity; Ethics has another. It is true that prayer could ask for an immediate intervention of divine compassion. If I were the whole of the universe, I could conceive of some extempore results. But if the whole is beltistic,—and the plan is blent,—a girl speaking just so at a well (Gen. xxiv. 14, 18, 19), and a man hanging just then upon a cross, a sparrow not falling to the ground without my Father, then Darwinism is really less fixed than the Almighty; for Darwinism could be interrupted by miracle, but the Almighty never. It is a fancy, that prayer must have extemporized results; for the sequences of Ethics are just as fixed as the laws of matter.

II. Going over to the other kind of Revelation, I find myself infinitely more exposed.

Theism I can hardly *imagine* to be overturned; but a Deluge, or a birth from a first pair, or a Tower of Babel, or a resurrection of the body, I find much more liable to be overturned. I do not pretend that the Bible is not a book of Science. I know that it is. When it says, "In the beginning God created," it is as distinct a scientism as Boscovitch's atoms. It is misery to make such a defence. Nor would we hold with those who make the Bible to be merely popular. We should insist that it is precise. When it declares, that God "has made of one blood all nations," I claim that. And I make it literal. That is, the story of Adam and Eve is with me as special as Darwin's protoplasm. If I were a hot polemic, I would prefer that. For, believing as I do in a Scriptural triumph, I would make it as great as it can be; and not be found, when

Science begins to be confused, with half my battlements thrown down, and half my Scriptures gratuitously forsaken.

The Bible is either all or nothing.

Now that it is all, I satisfy myself in two particulars.

1. First, the *theoretical*.

Do you not notice that Darwin admits the greatest miracle?

THIS IS OUR ONE CORRECTIVE.

Jesus rising from the dead is a light achievement beside the original nebula.

This I firmly insist on.

Evolution may be conceived unending. Grant it. And let us have no varyings. Darwin speaks of more beginnings. Let us have one. And let us make the miracle the extremest possible. Let us suppose one mist, never again interfered with, to be the cause of all causes, and to be so endowed, from the first moment of its time.

Now I say, The man ready for that, is ready for Scripture. The man of protoplasm is the very man for Adam and Eve. I grant, the Garden is not the dictate of Science: I mean physical science; neither indeed could it be. Darwin himself admits all that. It is built on faith. But faith with us is itself a science. Give us Ethics, and its mates, and we are fenced with a higher science; and we return to Darwin, and say, We have miracle by your own confession; and now we claim all sorts of miracles. We are open to all the miracles in the Bible; only we admit that they violate nature: and that is precisely what you admit. We stand on the very definition of a miracle; and the Garden of Eden, and the Noachic Deluge, and the Plain of Shinar, and the Crossing of the Sea, and the

Incarnation of Christ, and the Resurrection of the Body, are lesser miracles than your original protoplasm.

2. But, says Darwin, there are *historic* difficulties; and here I admit is the critical field. Miracle *in genere* cuts its own way; but miracle in particular must agree with history. Miracle, as such, is like the burglar's jimmy: it may break the stoutest locks; but miracle, in particular, may break some little thread which with its tell-tale seal makes the burglar turn pale.

Now this we most plenarily confess. It is a contempt of this, that has worked such mischief in religion.

There are foot-prints on the dust of ages, that are more formidable facts than the most deep-rooted of the laws of nature. And let me say, distinctly; religion is on trial before these. It does harm to deny it. It is *mean* to deny it; because we have reaped the most splendid results by its history. And this I mean by *historic* proof. It has been the noblest of our outward evidences. And now, when Christianity has fought this battle, and for years and years and years gone in and come out victorious, I want her to go in again. To shirk, and say her books are parables, and wish her out of the broil, is all wicked. Science has been her finest ally. To be afraid of it, is to deny the Deity. And the foot-prints on the past must still come to give triumph to her among the concerns of man.

But now, after this prologue, to come to facts. The rocks have a certain chronology. That I confess. The world might be created six thousand years ago, and Darwin could not challenge it on the score of miracle. But then these rocks!

Now I admit all this. The world is older than six thousand years; and the argument that God might create all as it is, is not a *likely* one, and all empiricism is by *likeness*. I admit that worn teeth and dead ages, without particularizing the proofs, have been read correctly by the geologists of the planet. But so much the fairer the Christian venture. It has left all to the proofs. It has confessed itself perpetually at stake. It has been presented by the grand juries of a thousand years,—and yet it has not been cast. Speeches are now making which seem ominous of results; and yet History, which is the just appeal, has carried her as winning in the past, and with a bundle of Reports that say for her more than she at first imagined.

I will never stand against well settled Science.

But now look at one case. Darwin says, that man bears the marks of being developed. He must concede to miracle; but the miraculously created man he objects to, as telling another story. The miraculously created rock he objects to, and I share in his difficulty. The miraculously created man, then, he asks,—Why read his record in a different way?

Now, let us be careful: for just here we bring in what has perhaps never before been considered.

Suppose we were at Babel. The Bible asserts a miracle. Some men give it up as they do Eden. Suppose we enforce it. Suppose there were a birth of languages. What sort would they be? Undoubtedly a created sort. Suppose there were a division of peoples. How far would that go? Darwin would leave room for any miracle. But suppose he fitted-on his new argument. Suppose he talked of the foot-prints of the past. Suppose he looked at the Coptic, and said, This is a developed tongue. This points backward. Here are the very sibilants that must have sprung from a savage use. Here is the *hum* and the *hiss* and the *twist* and the *shatter*, and the seeds of speech, that show that it grew up from brutal utterances. Suppose he were to measure, and say, the Coptic was growing a million of years: would that be fair treatment? If God inspired languages, would they not be likely to be developed? And, intended for development while they last, might they not be started with a base of it in their first creation?

Now, travel with the question into Eden. Suppose God created trees on the fifth day, would you expect them to be developed trees? Must they be fibreless and ringless and bear no look of the past? Must Adam have no umbilicus, and would it be dishonest in God to give him any look of the past? If God divided the nations, might He not blacken the Copt? and give him the look of a separate species? Do you know much about it? If you honestly thought that it would hardly do that they should look developed, do you certainly know? And if Adam was created at a stroke, and with ample arrangements that he might develop a race, do you know how much he might look developed, and how much analogy with brutes might serve as a foundation for his history in the future?

Miracle is *a great corrective.* Where miracle can be posited, Science has to stand bowed. Miracle must not be wild. It must not hold up a fossil, and say, This tooth never chewed. It must not hammer a chalk cliff, and say, This cliff sprang at a word. It must respect its record as of the past. But to say of a single loaf, Christ did not create this, and to laugh at the pretence that He did, because forsooth here are the very bubbles of the yeast, is to trifle with the scope of miracle. What mortal can tell that the negro may not be a species from Babel? that language may not have looked derived? that Adam may not have been created at a stroke? and nevertheless be a base for our descent best if he appeared developed?

## CHAPTER XIII.

### EVOLUTION UNDER THE LIGHT OF ONTOLOGY.

EVOLUTION, escaping almost all cavil while it lives under the test of Revelation, comes into hard times at once when it comes among other Ontologies.

Here is its real difficulty.

How could God create protoplasm? I, for one, utterly scout it. I believe in Omnipotence; but Omnipotence has its limits; and here is one of them. Protoplasm would be God. To create a thing that could do all things, so that God might adjourn and go out of being, would be to create God; and this is the form in which the wheel turns round. Darwin admits creation; but others do not; and presently some wiser scheme moves round in the ring, and develops protoplasm into the Almighty.

Hence are to be distinguished other systems.

2. A second (Darwinism being the first) requires *concursus.* This scheme can be described by simply adding to the former the idea of God's continual support. We may maintain protoplasm. All the ideas of steady invincible Evolution: the development scheme: the survival of the fittest: all the effects in "selection" and the improvement of the species,—are just the same under this as under the other. In appearance the schemes are similar. This only supplies the fact that God flows into and upholds. Otherwise all is the same. Darwinism, in its detail, is similarly possible. And theism can have the same respect; that is, it can claim its miracles. It can open the

Bible, and claim any event upon the list, and make it the interruption of second cause, and the violation of physical law, precisely under this scheme as under the other. The only gain is, a higher probableness. For, protoplasm left to itself, and protoplasm sustained forever, will look exactly the same; the only difference being, a lesser miracle.

3. The poorest hypothesis of all is that which we shall mention as the third scheme. It is an itching to make prayer reasonable. It, therefore, posits a third interference. It not only imagines support; it not only declares for miracle; but it supposes a third thing, viz. an intermeddling of the Almighty by any random motive of His will. Its argument is, A physician can interfere: is God less free than a physician? Its reasoning is, A daughter is dying of disease. A physician can intervene: cannot the Almighty? There are imagined, therefore, three modes for the result, the Almighty's steady law, the Almighty's intervening care, and Almighty miracle. The three make up the system. Prayer, therefore, is like prayer to a friend. He can come in on the spot. Recently, there has been a great deal like this. But then how mad! A physician can come in. But why? Because he is in the chain of natural law. He is himself a part of the creation. To illustrate the system by a stone;—that it seeks the earth by law, but that a boy can interfere by will, is to forget that the boy is under the sweep of law. Of two things one. Either there is natural law, or there is not. If there is not, cut off the first part of the theory. If there is, cut off the third. For nature and miracle is all that can be conceived in an ontological system.

There may be *covert* miracle. A man starves, and

prays for bread, and crosses the hill, and a loaf lies upon the highway, and God may have created it. We do not know how frequent such things may be. I wish to say distinctly that the world may be full of them. But this only means that I do not understand the Almighty's administration. But this I know, God cannot be natural and unnatural. He cannot work by law and not. He cannot net-work the universe with rule, and lay down in the same measures a random system. He can break up the law by miracle. But this exhausts the possibility. Miracle can be covert, of course. But miracle of some sort is all that can alternate with a rule of nature.

4. A fourth system lays down the same chance for Evolution, and goes by the same rule of law, and brings in the same scope for miracle, but turns its back entirely upon an original protoplasm. It denies a nebula as anything but the power of God. So it follows with the universe. It pronounces atoms to be nothing: and deals with a dynamistic structure. And when simply challenged for its proof, it turns the tables. It makes its war simply on the ground of no proof,—that is, the law of parcimony. It challenges the five senses. It says, They see everything. In the not-self, at least, they tell all that is going on. Now it says, Notoriously you are conversant with power. Sense brings you that; and sense, it can be notoriously demonstrated, brings you nothing otherwise. Why do you assert a brutish atom? And so a system is built up that begins with no protoplasm, and goes on through the ages of eternity as a simple potence.

And yet it has the same appearances.

It may believe in Evolution, like any other theory.

It accepts settled laws; and counts them the effect

of one efficiency as making room symmetrically for the advent of another.

It pleads cause. Cause, dynamistically considered, is not simply the Great Cause, but differently, and in a secondary sense, power basing one exertion upon another. And, therefore, all theories,—of Christianity, for example, in everything that it may reveal; of miracle, breaking one thread, and substituting another; of prophecy, involving a decree; of Providence, shaping everything to a single scheme; and of Evolution itself in all its Darwinian extreme,—are just as possible dynamistically as with some other molecule.

5. Now change this theory a little, and we will adopt it personally. It arrogates too much. The atomic phantasy arrogates too much in positing the atom; but dynamism goes to the opposite extreme.

Let it say, We *know* nothing but power. There we will agree with it. Let it say, All positing of *substance* is a thing of fraud. That we hold. Let it explain, We mean *substance* in its more brutish sense. And then, settling its robes in this discreet attitude, which is simply of negation, let it say, NEVERTHELESS THERE MUST BE MORE THAN POWER; and we are with it at a bound.

Our objection to the brute atom is, that it pretends something; that it posits something visible; that it gives it an intelligent name, and works upon it as though it were a thing discerned. Whereas our last land in the voyage was, our idea of power. That is a shadowy mist; and to see anything further is a sheer deceiving. I only say, that, by a train of analogy, I am not at the end of my line. Analogy shakes her wand, and says, There is more yonder. She frowns if I say, I see it. She laughs, if I impute it to Intuitive

Belief. And she explains all, if I go back over the line of what is *like*, and see how she has pushed me along, and how, at the end of the light, she points out into the dark, and asserts the INVISIBLE.

We are dynamists, therefore, in a mere negative sense; appealing to parcimony; ridiculing the man who posits atoms; believing that efficiency is dark enough, but that a *brutum tertium* is utterly unknown; referring everything to the power of God; believing Evolution to exist, except upset by miracle; upholding prayer as involved in the original decree; believing that it is necessary, even though all travel on unchanged; believing that all does travel on unchanged, but only because the supplication was supplied; believing that we are answered in one case in ten million by miracle; and believing that we are answered then in a way differing nothing in its liberty, because the miracle itself is imbedded in a scheme that is unchanged.

See, therefore, how Ontological schemes lie in shadow, and how Ontological difficulties chiefly occur from Ontological cause. Ethical schemes can look blandly upon all of them; nay, Ethical law supplies their best light. A cause for all creation is best found in Ethics. And while Theology without Ethics would be a gloomy mass, with Ethics it escapes out of the Unknowable of Spencer, and posits a personal Jehovah. The universe becomes the best possible. A motive for it emerges at a stroke. The law of it supervenes perfectly. It assumes to itself but a single thread. And while unethically it would be a chaos of chance, Metaphysics, which is thought so dim, proves clearer than Physics, and is the part of Ontological schemes that survives the shock, when sense-calculations meet with overthrow.

Blessed be the influence, therefore, that stole *conscience* out of the vocabulary. Conscience meant consciousness. All through the Latin years, and early in our English history, conscience had no other meaning. It kept on that way all through the time of King James (see Ec. x. 20 *marg.* Heb. x. 2). But virtue was so much its most precious consciousness, that virtue stole all the name. And it is a fine lesson for our age, that, as men refined, they saw little wealth in consciousness but virtue, and ejected out of the original word all other forms of introspective vision.

THE END.

PRINTED BY LANGE, LITTLE & CO., NEW YORK.

BY THE SAME AUTHOR.

---

# FETICH IN THEOLOGY.

A Review of Dr. Hodge's Systematic Theology.

12mo. $1.75.

**For Opinions expressed by Prominent Professors see following pages.**

# LETTERS INTRODUCTORY

TO A

# SECOND EDITION.

---

I.

NEW YORK, Feb. 15, 1875.

REV. AND DEAR SIR,

In preparing a new edition of "*Fetich in Theology,*" a book that has provoked much comment both adverse and favorable, we are desirous of having the opinion, as to its essential views, of Professors in Theology of the same school of belief as that to which the author belongs. We desire to publish such opinions as an Introduction to the work itself. It is, perhaps, not aside from the ancient duty of the Professor to be a referee in matters of belief; and as you hold the Divinity chair in the most largely attended Seminary of your branch of the Presbyterian communion, we will be especially obliged if you will unite with others, also Calvinists, in sending us a proper judgment upon the points which this work involves.

Yours very truly,

DODD & MEAD.

To the REV. R. L. DABNEY, D.D.

UNION THEO. SEMINARY,* VA.,
Feb. 25, 1875.

To Messrs. DODD & MEAD,
Publishers, etc., New York.

DEAR SIRS,—You ask my candid opinion of the work of the Rev. John Miller, "Fetich in Theology, or, Doctrinalism Twin to Ritualism," published by you. If you are willing to accept an answer prompted by perfect sincerity and independence, I will reply that I had read this criticism on Dr. Chas. Hodge's Systematic Theology before you called my attention to it, with great interest and profit. Mr. Miller has, in my opinion, shown in it high ability, full scholarship, and fine acumen. His friends have, I think, cause to regret its title, on the ground that the supporters of Dr. Hodge will regard it as too biting, and even disrespectful to him; although all who know Mr. Miller are aware that he is incapable of either bitterness or discourtesy. His style is in several places so highly tropical, and in others so compressed, that I fear those passages will prove, to many hasty or imperfectly taught readers, not wholly intelligible. The professional student finds an astonishing amount of acute, just, and profound matter condensed in these brief chapters. There are also points of exception taken which explanations on the part of Dr. Hodge's advocates will probably remove. Yet others of Mr. Miller's exceptions I regard as well taken; and his criticism is timely and valuable. The Gospel system set forth in the Scriptures is obnoxious to the deepest prejudices of the natural heart. It has always been the object of violent or subtile perversions.

---

* Southern Presbyterian Church.

Hence, it is a subject of profound regret, when one whom so many regard as an authorized and able expounder as Dr. Hodge, so misrepresents the belief of the friends of the Gospel, as to exasperate unnecessarily any of the angles of God's truth, to provoke needless opposition, or to obscure the glory of its divine Author in any degree. When such mistakes are made by a hand so influential, protest is usually found as difficult as it is necessary. Hence, I highly honor the moral courage of Mr. Miller in this criticism. He could not but foresee, knowing the degree in which the writer criticised is "the fashion" among Presbyterians, and being aware of the spirit of subserviency, the moral cowardice, and the impatience of independent thought which characterize his day, that the professed friends of the truth, whose battle he is really fighting, would leave him to wage it single-handed, or even oppose him. So it was plain that he would receive public applause from those dissenters from the truth whom both he and Dr. Hodge have been all their lives opposing: as the event has verified. This applause is to Mr. Miller an inconvenience; because it affects to claim him as making common cause for error. It is true that the approbation coming from the advocates of the so-called "Liberal" theology, is a preposterous blunder; that Mr. Miller has nothing in common with these men—not even opposition to Dr. Hodge; for while they would injure him because they regard him as a formidable enemy to their erroneous system, Mr. Miller only seeks to correct him, in order to make him a more formidable enemy to it; that the system which Mr. Miller upholds is in more utter—because more intelligent, consistent, and scriptural—opposition to theirs. But none the less is this applause an inconvenience to the friends of the truth.

In the *Southern Presbyterian Review*, of April, 1873, I published a review of some parts of Dr. Hodge's work. I may indicate my own estimate of it by some quotations from this review (see pp. 168, 170).

"Among the other characteristics of this treatise, which present themselves to a cursive examination, may be noted the following:

1. "Dr. Hodge asserts that our knowledge of God is 'intuitive,' and then *argues for the proposition* that there is a God! This argument, ignoring the usual theistic method in a manner rather marked, relies chiefly upon the ethical *phenomena* of the soul."

2. "Those who have had the privilege of Dr. Hodge's conversation, are aware that the denunciation of the claims of philosophy to be a true science has been rather a favorite topic with him; and this opinion is not obscurely indicated in his Theology. Yet we know of no standard Reformed treatise which makes so much use of philosophy, or contains so large a proportion of philosophical speculation."

3. "The author, under many heads of divinity, displays the multifarious forms of error with more fullness than his own views of what is true."

4. "If we might judge by the author's citations in what direction his theological reading chiefly lay, we should conclude that German heresy, in its different forms, had received more of his attention than any other department, orthodox or heterodox. Next would come the works of the Continental Protestants—Lutheran and Reformed. The teachers and leaders of Scotch and Scotch Irish Presbyterianism are very scantily noticed; and, so far as we now remember, there is not a single reference to the theology of the Anglican Church, or its great masters,

to intimate that the author had ever heard of them. So, American theology appears chiefly in the names of its heresiarchs, and for purposes of refutation."

"This extract ...... gives us also a very characteristic specimen of Dr. Hodge's method as a debater. Under an appearance of simple, Saxon straightforwardness, he most adroitly modifies, and by modifying, disparages, the view he intends to assault: and he gains credit for his own, by associating it with unquestioned truth, and claiming for it, with a quiet dogmatism, the universal adhesion of the orthodox learned."

You will see from the above, that while Dr. Hodge's great learning and force are admitted, no very great value is placed by me upon his huge work. I should, like Mr. Miller, protest against the adoption of it as the representative, for our day, of the Westminster theology. The unfitness of the work for this purpose arises from the dogmatism of Dr. Hodge's temper, often deceiving himself, and often his readers. With an appearance of simple directness, and clear logical method, he is often inaccurate and confused; while the illations, seemingly so close, are in fact disjointed. My chief objection to being held responsible for this work as a showing for our Presbyterian theology, is that species of one-sided *hardness* which Dr. Hodge's logical ultraism gives it. Many of Mr. Miller's points are, I think, well taken against this tendency. In reply to most of them, it is true, Dr. Hodge's friends will probably be able to point to statements in other parts of the work, correcting or softening these erroneous colorings. We are glad to allow all the weight to these modifying statements to which they are entitled, and to acquit the work of all fatal intentional error. But the general impression remains, that this presentation of doctrine gives us, not the God of the Law and Gospel to worship, the Being of consummate moral beauty, glory, and goodness; but a God of hard force and bare sovereignty.* For instance:

Dr. Hodge begins by saying, that our belief in God is "innate:" and then explains it by saying, it is "intui-

* This practical estimate is singularly—because very artlessly and independently—confirmed by a letter, which something akin to chance has thrown within reach, just as these replies are coming in for publication. It is from a niece of the most eminent Divinity professor that Virginia ever gave to the Northern Church. It is to another lady, and without the most remote idea of any other perusal:—"I have read 'Fetich'—would you believe it?—not only with pleasure but with eagerness! (I have not finished it either, but that is because I am so busy.) I thought it would be rather heavy reading for one of my reach, and so left it long untouched on my book-case; but when I fairly waded in, I sat up late as one does over a novel. Perhaps it would not be such fascinating reading, except for the novelty and beauty and often queerness of the language, that tolls you along through whatever is too abstruse—for I don't love abstruseness. When I opened the book I said to myself, It don't matter one bit what Dr. Hodge and Mr. Miller write and wrangle about the nature of God; it only matters to love Him with all the heart, and mind, and soul, and strength; but I find it does matter indeed, for I shall have to thank 'Fetich' all my life, for making it possible for me to love a good, holy, beautiful God, without that hazy discomfort which has from my very childhood hindered my worship. I don't know where I got that unworthy idea of God; but after reading the first part of this book, and *re* and *re*-reading it, I found my eyes wet with tears of glad emotion. Lo! *this* was my God, whom I had known through such a hindering, distorting haze, and now saw for the first time in such loveliness and beauty that I needed no spur to worship Him. I do thank Mr. Miller from my heart, and only wonder that everybody had not told me before what he has done for Presbyterianism. I shall attack Mamma in my next letter that she did not urge me to read it sooner."

tive." Now, in the sense of the philosopher : it would not be innate if it were intuitive ; for our real intuitions are not innate ; but only the principles or laws of reason which give them to us afterwards are innate. And, second : our belief in God is not intuitive ; it is a *near*, a *clear*, a *just conclusion* from all our rational and moral intuitions. It is thus a truth which every right mind infallibly gets, upon coming to think.

In stating the great and priceless argument from our intuitions of conscience, Dr. Hodge seems to teach that our judgment of moral obligation only recognizes God as *supreme*. But does might make right, in God's case, any more than in a man's? My reason tells me, that I am immediately and infinitely bound to obey God, because His is a holy supremacy : because the will which controls me is infinitely excellent.

Is an act right solely because God requires it : or has He required it because it is right? The Bible teaches me the latter, with the Westminster Assembly, and the great Reformed divines, like Turrettin. Dr. Hodge seems to obscure this blessed truth, and to argue as though there were a hankering for the opposite answer, which resolves obligation into God's power, instead of His righteousness.

We go with Dr. Hodge in condemning Optimism, where it says that the greatest beneficence to creatures is God's ultimate end. But he seems to demand of us that we shall say with him, that God's own glory is His ultimate end, in a sense so hard as to resolve God's whole providence into a scheme of infinite selfishness. When we say : God's own infinite perfections of wisdom, love, and holiness will surely prompt in Him a providence which will prove beltistic in this sense : that it will, on the whole, doubtless secure in the most perfect way that whole set of ends which God sees to be (We blind creatures can see but in part what they should be), as a whole, most consistent with His holiness: it would seem that this scarcely contents Dr. Hodge.

When we come to the awful mystery of God's dealings with our race in its first father, Adam, Dr. Hodge is scarcely content to claim for God (what every reverent mind gladly concedes) a width of discretion in applying the immutable principles of justice agreeably to His transcendent wisdom, holiness, goodness, and sovereign proprietorship in us, as far above any application we creatures are entitled to make of the same principles, as the heavens above the earth. But he appears to crave to drive us to the wall until we acknowledge that, because God is supreme, He deals judicially with his creatures, upon no principles of distributive justice at all! And should even the reverent mind reply: "I see not how I could believe that of this lovely, holy God, were I to try:" Dr. Hodge would rejoin: God does that way: and so, you shall believe it or be damned, whether you can or not. There is, it appears to us, a sort of perverse and perilous zeal to exasperate the difficulties of a difficult problem of divine providence, into the hardest shape.

When we come to God's punitive justice—where other Calvinists say, that God's holiness prompts Him to punish —Dr. Hodge prefers the statement which represents God as punishing for the sake of punishing, in the same immediate sense in which He blesses for the sake of blessing. Here again, these solemn dispensations of severity, where purity, truth, and justice combine with goodness, to visit the deserved penalty on the guilty, in Dr. Hodge's hands freeze into the harshness of a power simply vindicatory.

When we meet the objection: "If the sinner is *unable* to repent, to love, to believe, how can it be just to require these of him?" the great Reformed divines taught us, with the Saviour, to answer: It is just, because his ungodly disposition is his inability. But Dr. Hodge requires us to say; No: his inability is something more than that. But if this inability is rooted somewhere else than in the spontaneity, and requires for its removal something else than renewal of heart, can we punish the sinner for his helplessness, without harshness? Dr. Hodge seems to insist on that harshness.

When we inquire into the tie between saving faith and repentance, the Scriptures answer that they are twin graces, both the offspring of regeneration, entering the soul to bless it simultaneously, and co-operating instrumentally, the one to purge, and the other to justify. We had believed that both graces touched the head and the heart: so that while repentance was inspired by a *knowledge* of God in Christ, faith led the man to believe with the *heart* unto salvation. This Gospel-philosophy Dr. Hodge reverses, making an intellectual faith somehow result in a heart-repentance as its consequent. Thus again, the very bond which instrumentally unites the sinner to his Saviour, is hardened into a logical process.

It is not surprising that Dr. Hodge, after outraging the necessary intuitions of the soul, should suppose himself constrained to depict that rationalism which is the antithesis of humble faith, as an *over use* of the reason. The Westminster theology had taught us to regard it as the *abuse* of the reason. Is it not unfortunate, that Dr. Hodge should seem to give the intelligent adversary of the Gospel this pretext for saying: "The price, at which

I am invited to adopt the Bible theology, is the abnegation of my essential manhood"?

In the former half of my Review, to which I have referred, I have already made the attempt to subject Dr. Hodge's theory as to the nature of inability, regeneration, repentance, and faith, to a radical examination. I think I have there shown, that his peculiar teachings on those points are not those of the Bible, nor of the great Reformed divines, nor of sound philosophy; and that, with all their hardness of aspect, they are yet, in fact, short of the real truth touching the sinner's ruin and recovery.

Very respectfully, etc.,

ROBERT L. DABNEY.

---

II.

REPLY (TO A LIKE COMMUNICATION) OF REV. JOSEPH T. COOPER, D.D., PROFESSOR OF SYSTEMATIC THEOLOGY IN THE SEMINARY OF THE UNITED PRESBYTERIAN CHURCH.

ALLEGHANY, March 23, 1875.

Messrs. DODD & MEAD.

DEAR SIRS,—I read some time ago "*Fetich in Theology*," in relation to the merits of which you ask an expression of my judgment. The style is very peculiar, and, in some of the sentences, there is a lack of perspicuity. It is, however, vigorous, terse, and well freighted with *thought*. With some of the positions of the author I cordially concur.

It would be an act of injustice to Dr. Hodge, whom I have been accustomed to venerate as an able defender of the faith, to give an opinion, in relation to the question whether he has been fairly represented by Mr. Miller. Before doing this I should feel bound to give the matter a more thorough examination than my engagements at present will permit.

I, however, cordially approve of the republication of the work; for it will lead to a more thorough examination of the Calvinistic system to which Mr. Miller professes an adherence. His object evidently is to present some of its features in an aspect less stern, and more in accord with our moral intuitions. If this can be done without compromising the truth, all its friends, and, I am well persuaded, none more so than Dr. Hodge, will greatly rejoice. At all events, the discussions contained in this book cannot fail to quicken the intellect, and, it is hoped, lead to a more discriminating view of the abstruse but important topics on which it treats.

Should a different title for the work be selected it would be more agreeable to my taste.

Yours respectfully,

J. T. Cooper.

---

III.

Reply of Rev. A. B. Van Zandt, D.D., Professor of Systematic Theology in the Seminary of the (Dutch) Reformed Church.

New Brunswick, N. J. April 2, 1875.

Messrs. Dodd & Mead.

Gents,—In reply to your note requesting an expression of opinion in regard to the essential views set forth in "*Fetich in Theology*" I can give you only my general impressions. And I give you these as bearing upon the purpose which you have intimated of issuing a new edition of the work.

The significance of this book is almost certain to be misunderstood. It is the author's misfortune, that his work is more likely to receive the applause of those with whose views he has no affinities, than of those with whom he is substantially in accord. The so-called "Liberal School" will probably claim a larger interest in it than can possibly be made good from its pages. Whilst, on the other hand, the Orthodox may feel scandalized by this very claim, and utterly misjudge its spirit and intent.

Moreover, the fact that the discussions of the author turn chiefly upon the positions taken, or supposed to be taken, by Dr. Hodge, may even cause the book to be regarded as an unfriendly attack upon that distinguished and venerated man, or upon that system of theology of which he is so prominent a representative.

But these are accidents, which do not affect the importance of the questions discussed, and ought not to prejudice the author's discussion of them. The book, whatever may be its faults, is evidently the product of an earnest, independent mind. It is the outcome of bold and vigorous thought, which has been occupied long with the questions upon which it treats. Its logic is sometimes compressed to the verge of obscurity, and there are some expressions which startle us, as being on the verge of irreverence. But a careful reader will be convinced that its reasonings are too cogent to be easily brushed aside, and that its aim and intent is the conservation of truth, in order to holiness.

Without indicating any points of agreement or difference with the author, I have no hesitation in saying that, as a contribution to the theological literature of the day, his book deserves the thoughtful perusal of all who care to examine the great questions upon which it treats, and the bearing of the different modes of their treatment upon the great controversies of the age.

There is undoubtedly "*a way of putting*" the old theology, which puts it at a great disadvantage. The fear of toning it down below the requirements of truth, may easily lead to the mistake of formulating it into an aspect of unnecessary harshness. How far Mr. Miller has convicted the distinguished theologian whom he criticises, of this mistake, or has himself shown a more excellent way, is a question which I have not assumed to discuss. But it is a question which may properly awaken a very deep interest in the book which you propose to reissue.

Respectfully yours,

A. B. VAN ZANDT.

www.ingramcontent.com/pod-product-compliance
Lightning Source LLC
LaVergne TN
LVHW021148110826
845150LV00005B/1159

* 9 7 8 1 4 2 5 5 4 6 7 4 8 *